VINTAGE

LATA

YATINDRA MISHRA is the author of five collections of poetry and some well-received books on Indian music, cinema and arts in the Hindi language such as *Girija, Devpriya, Sur Ki Baradari, Akhtari, Gulzaar Sa'ab: Hazaar Rahen Mud Ke Dekheen* and *Shahernama Faizabad* (ed.). The original Hindi version of this book, *Lata: Sur-Gatha*, won the 64th National Film Award and the MAMI Award for Best Writing on Cinema (2016–17).

IRA PANDE is a writer, columnist and an accomplished translator. Over the years, she has translated short stories, novellas, memoirs, autobiographies and literary portraits. She was awarded the Crossword and Sahitya Akademi award for her translation of Manohar Shyam Joshi's novella *T'ta Professor* in 2010. She has also translated Shivani's stories and memoir *Amader Shantiniketan*, as well as *Apradhini: Women without Men*, a collection of works about jailed women.

LATA

A Life in Music

English Translation of the National Award–Winning
Hindi Biography *Lata: Sur Gatha*

YATINDRA MISHRA

Translated by **IRA PANDE**

VINTAGE
An imprint of Penguin Random House

VINTAGE

Vintage is an imprint of the Penguin Random House group of companies
whose addresses can be found at global.penguinrandomhouse.com

Published by Penguin Random House India Pvt. Ltd
4th Floor, Capital Tower 1, MG Road,
Gurugram 122 002, Haryana, India

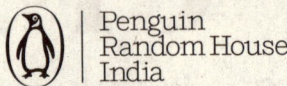

Penguin
Random House
India

First published in Viking by Penguin Random House India 2023
This edition published in Penguin Vintage 2025

ISBN 9780143472339

Typeset in Adobe Garamond Pro by Manipal Technologies Limited, Manipal
Printed at Replika Press Pvt. Ltd, India

www.penguin.co.in

MIX
Paper | Supporting
responsible forestry
FSC™ C016779

Contents

Preface

There is no Indian, I firmly believe, who has not fallen in love with Lata Mangeshkar's voice at least once at some stage of his or her life. The memorable songs she sang in the fifties and sixties sent the whole country swaying to her music. This is why I consider myself blessed that I was among those chosen few to whom Lata Didi gave her personal time and blessings. This book owes everything to her generous participation in its formation.

From about 2010, she and I shared countless conversations that became the core of the research that went into this book. I still remember the thrill I felt when we had our first conversation. But I also recall how terrified I was as I realized that here was a love-struck fan face-to-face with the queen of melody. These conversations went on till about the end of 2014 and I record with gratitude how patiently and lovingly she answered all my questions as I discovered the great journey of her personal and professional life, layer by fragrant layer.

Our conversations went beyond music to include such disparate subjects as the national movement, Partition, Gandhi ji, literature and culture, religion and spirituality, her lifestyle, political leaders she has known, friends and family and the vast world of arts she was connected to. This book is really, then, an attempt to understand her not just through her contribution to film music but to see Lata Mangeshkar through the eyes of a vast number of her associates and admirers who shared the world she had created. I can truthfully say that my interactions with her will forever remain one of the most significant parts of my life, although I cannot say how successfully I have been able to reproduce her prodigious legacy for my readers. Whenever she gave me her time, even if it was just a half-hour snatched from her busy calendar, she gave me and my questions her full attention. That was the person I have tried to portray in this work.

Our conversations spurred me to also study the various stages of transition Hindi films have gone through. I do not think any writer, historian or critic can ever do full justice to the vast repertoire of musical styles she has left of film music but one among so many musical forms she presented the world. These include devotional bhajans, *ghazals*, Marathi *abhangs, naat qawwalis*, slokas and mantras, folk songs, poems and patriotic songs. The vast musical universe that she created must surely be unparalleled anywhere in the world.

All I wish to tell my readers is that if one is to understand the full richness of her legacy, one has to also be sensitive to her innate modesty and the simplicity of her life as a dedication to a higher cause. Her life, as you will discover, is a long saga of struggle, pain and self-denial, yet she never allowed these to divert her attention from her one true calling—her complete devotion to her music. The saga of her personal life is defined best by the journey of her musical life. This is why I have chosen to call the book *Lata Mangeshkar: A Life in Music*.

I am grateful to several people who helped me in the making of this book and I will acknowledge them separately but here, along with my deep gratitude to Lata Didi, I wish to thank the entire Mangeshkar family whose assistance helped me immeasurably. My own parents, Jyotsana Mishra and Bimalendra Mohan Pratap Mishra come first in the long line of the members of my family to whom I owe a debt of gratitude for initiating and nurturing my love of music. My aunts, Jwalanti and Aparna Mishra, my sisters Manjari and Shubhangi who held my hand throughout the writing of this book were a source of strength. Others I wish to thank are my close associates Ashwani Shukla, Ravi Rai and Jaiprakash Sharma who were my literary advisers.

Finally, as I place this book into the hands of my readers, I pray that they will find it helpful in understanding my magnificent obsession with this divine personality.

Yatindra Mishra
October 2022

Translator's Note

This book has been so long in reaching its finale that at one stage I had given up hope that it would ever be published. Without going into the details behind its inordinate delay, I do wish to record how proud it made me to be asked to translate it from the original Hindi into English. Yatindra's faith in my abilities and my own admiration of Lata Mangeshkar were behind my determination to persevere with it. When I first read his book, Yatindra's impressive research and simple devotion touched me in so many ways that it is difficult to express in simple words. No wonder he was awarded the National Award for the Best Work on Cinema that year.

The original Hindi version of this book was published in 2016, when Lata jiwas still alive and so it was written in the present tense. I had finished the first draft of its translation into English well before she passed away so when it was sent to me recently for the final checks, it presented with my first problem. To change the tenses from present to past throughout the translation was not an option to be even considered, for even a single oversight could mar it. Again, since both Yatindra and I had dealt at length with the copy I had given him almost three years ago, I had almost forgotten why I had taken certain liberties with editing out those bits that seemed repetitive in Yatindra's two-part script. Finally, the English language itself gave me some questions to ponder over as it is bereft of those registers that make Hindi (and most Indian languages) musical in a way that is really difficult to capture in the clipped and clinical vocabulary of English.

Yatindra and I had several conversations over these problems and found to my delight that he and I had no disagreements over the basic style and content of my translation. I explained to him how the readers who will hear his voice in English may find it difficult to accept a word-for-word translation and how certain bits may sound clunky and over-sweet if done so. He had already captured the sweetness of Lata ji's voice and personality in the telling of his saga—any additional flourishes would only damage the purity of his devotion and research. He was more than generous in seeing my point and barring some requests to include a few episodes he considered vital to his narrative, left it to me to make any editorial and language decisions I felt were needed. His suggestions, made in his endearing old-world Awadhi style of speaking, touched me deeply and I want him to know this. I hope the reader will remember this when going through this text.

We both also agreed to speak of Lata ji in the present tense: for one, that was the mode in the original book and speaking of her as someone who is dead and gone killed something so vital in conveying her extraordinary hold over the millions of her admirers who consider her a *Gandharva-kanya* (someone who is divine and so indestructible). I think we all agree that as long as her voice is heard by her countless admirers, she will be among us. '*Meri awaaz hi pehchaan hai* . . .' (My voice is my identity) is a song that was played on a loop at her funeral, if you remember. I think she invested something so important in that line that she will continue to stay among us as a living legend for a very long time.

Ira Pande
October 2022

PART 1

THE EPISODES

I

Kalpavriksha kanye lavuniya Baba gela
Vaibhavane bahuruni ala yal ka ho baghayala?

(Baba, the tree you planted is in full bloom,
It fulfils our every desire.
Will you ever come to see it?)
A Marathi *bhava geet* by the poet P. Sawalaram

The historic song '*Aayega aanewala*' from *Mahal* (1949) and
the entry of Lata Mangeshkar into the world of Hindi film
music are somewhat similar. The song opens with these lines:

Khamosh hai zamana, chup chap hain sitare
Aram se hai duniya, bekal hain dil ke mare
Aise main koi aahat is tarah aa rahi hai
Jaise ki chal raha ho koyi man main hamare
Ya dil dharak raha hai ik aas ke sahare . . .

(The world lies hushed, and silent the stars
The earth is asleep, restless the lovers
Suddenly, there is a stir, as if someone is coming
And our heartbeats quicken with expectation)

3

Nearly seventy years after this song was sung, one is tempted to say that the lines describe Lata Mangeshkar's entry into our hearts. To her countless fans, the world was comatose before she awoke it with her clear, sweet voice.

When she was a child, her father had told her, 'Just as words make up a poem, its notes make a song meaningful. When you sing, both these must be equally alive.' Our mythology is replete with stories of divine beings that descended to earth to present bewitching music and dance. Her dear friend Naushad once quoted a few lines from the famous Urdu poet Momin to pay her a moving compliment:

> Us ghairat-e-naahid ki har taan hai deepak
> Shola sa lapak jaye hai aawaz to dekho
> (The notes that emerge from her exquisite voice
> Are like flaming sparks that leap out of a burning lamp)

So let us begin this great singer's journey that is defined by her unique voice. Her fans have written paeans of praise that place her above every other singer, but the best compliment perhaps is that of the legendary violinist Yehudi Menuhin who exclaimed after listening to her, 'How I wish my violin could sing like you!'

2

The first raga she learnt to sing was Puriya Dhanashree. Her father, the legendary singer Pandit Dinanath Mangeshkar, lovingly seated his daughter in his lap as he initiated her into the world of classical music. To this day, she considers the

Puriya Dhanashree she learnt from him among her favourite ragas, along with Kaushik Dhwani, Patmanjari, Divya Hindol and Hamsadhwani. The choice of this raga was unusual, to say the least, for generally the ragas chosen to initiate a student into Hindustani classical music are Bhairavi, Bhoopali or Yaman. Puriya Dhanashree is an evening raga tinged with a note of sadness, and brings to mind the mood evoked by the play of light and shade, golden sunsets and approaching nightfall.

The raga he chose to initiate his little daughter into music was unusual to say the least. Perhaps not even her father, and certainly not the little child he held in his lap, had any inkling of the importance of the occasion. Nor did they know that one day this child would light up the world of music with her incredible talent and voice. For she was blessed with the gift of coaxing joy and sorrow from the notes with equal ease.

3

Dinanath Mangeshkar owned a drama company known as Balwant Sangeet Mandali, which once staged a musical play titled, *Saubhadra*. Based on the legend of Arjuna and Subhadra, Dinanath played Arjuna in this production and little Lata, his 9-year-old daughter, was given the role of the sage Narada.

Before sending off her to the opening performance, her mother—Shuddhimati—lovingly dressed her daughter's hair with a flower. Lata was made to wear a yellow *pitambar* (silk dhoti) and was handed a *tanpuri* (baby tanpura) that the sage Narada was said to have always carried. 'I know people will cry "Once more!" the way they ask you for an encore,' Lata told her father confidently before she went on the stage to sing

'*Pavana vamana ya mana*,' while her father watched proudly from the wings. And, as she had predicted, the audience burst into applause when they heard this prodigy, crying over and over again, 'Once more!'

That applause and those cries for encores mark the beginning of Lata Mangeshkar's extraordinary musical journey. Her joy at her success and the fact that her father was witness to it were all she had hoped for. As for her father, he was convinced that his little girl had the makings of a great performer and decided then that he must groom her for a career in his drama company. As a reward for her successful debut, he commissioned a short playlet, *Gurukul*, based on the friendship of Krishna and Sudama and their childhood pranks. Lata played Krishna while her little sister, Meena, was given the part of Sudama.

Not surprisingly, even today Lata Mangeshkar has a special place in her heart for the applause and blessings she received for her performances in *Saubhadra* and *Gurukul*. It is a different matter that the qualities that charmed her listeners then have since won her innumerable fans and admirers. For her, what makes those early plays memorable is that her father was present to witness her success. Even those who never heard the songs that she sang all those years ago agree that, once heard, her clear and sweet voice is unforgettable.

4

It must have been 1940 or so, Lata didi recalls, when Dinanath came to Delhi to record a song for All India Radio (AIR). By now, Lata had started accompanying her father on his musical engagements and he often gave her a small role in his plays so that she could sing something he had taught her on stage. She recalls emotionally that when she first accompanied him on that radio recording, he sang raga Khambawati, and the words were 'Aali ri main jagi sari raina'. The next number was a Marathi *natya sangeet* composition, set in Yaman: 'Radha dhar milind jai-jai, Madhu milind jai-jai, Rama ramana hari govind'. This was to be the only time she would accompany her father for a performance on radio because just a year later, Pandit Dinannath passed away on 24 April 1942, in tragic circumstances.

All that is left for his daughter to remember was how tightly she held his hand on that trip as he sang *Khambawati* and that Marathi composition, which probably lay in some forgotten corner of the AIR archives. Just remembering the details of that episode fills her with pain.

5

The label on every HMV (His Master's Voice) gramophone record as well as the company's catalogue proudly carried the names of the era's renowned singers. However, the ordinary viewer was often puzzled by the artwork on the HMV label that had a dog listening intently to a gramophone. The image was created by the British artist Francis Barraud for HMV and had a touching personal story behind it: The gramophone belonged to Francis's brother Mark, whose loyal dog, called Nipper, crept closer to the gramophone when he heard the voice of his dead master, Mark. In time, this label became the hallmark of excellence in recording and the voice of virtually every great singer or musician of that time became available to listeners through HMV's records. The announcement in the catalogues and publicity material ran something like: 'Listen to Devika Rani (or Miss Dulari or Leela Chitnis) on this dog-stamp machine (*kutta chhap* machine) . . .'

In those days, record companies did not print the name of an artiste on their labels unless she had become a famous filmstar. Outside films, the singers of light classical music (often dancing girls who traced their ancestry to Mughal times), were deliberately denied the privilege of a signature on the label. Other famous recording companies, such as New Theatres Records, Megaphone, Twin, Columbia, Odeon Records Germany, et al., only printed the names of renowned singers whose records would guarantee sales, although there were some exceptions. For instance, the records of Begum Akhtar—famous for her *thumris*, *dadras* and ghazals—were released in the market as those of 'Akhtari bai Faizabadi, film star' since she had acted in a few films.

It is astounding to learn that even Lata Mangeshkar was not accorded the honour of a name in her early records. Her first big success as a playback singer came with *Mahal* (1949), where she sang under the music direction of Khemchand Prakash. Even then, the label of the record called her Kamini (the name of Madhubala, the film's lead actress). It is difficult to believe today that 'Aayega aanewala'—counted among her most famous playback numbers—was not acknowledged as Lata Mangeshkar's voice when it was first recorded. However, in tracing Lata Mangeshkar's long and difficult journey from anonymity to incredible fame, we cannot forget that several less fortunate singers died without ever being able to claim what was rightfully their work.

6

Lata ji recounts her early days as if her musical journey began just the other day. We start with the recording of '*Aayega aanewala*' (c 1948) and she tells me how, in the absence of proper recording studios, recording was very different from what it is today. In order to find a suitable space, they had to hunt a quiet corner—behind a tree, or the interior of a roomy car—a place where outside sounds would not seep in.

'The shooting for a film called *Lahore* was on at Bombay Talkies and both Jaddanbai and her daughter Nargis were present,' she tells me. 'When I started recording the song inside an empty studio, I saw Jaddanbai listening very intently. Later, she called me over and said, "Come here, beta. What is your name?" "Lata Mangeshkar," I replied politely. "You are a Marathan, aren't you?" she observed. I nodded. "Mashallah!" she exclaimed, "How perfectly you pronounced '*baghair*' in '*Deepak baghair kaise parvane jal rahe hain*'! I was thrilled to hear that 'baghair'", she went on. "Not everyone has such a clean pronunciation, my child. I can tell you will go very far in life."'

Didi recounts how delighted she was with this compliment coming from someone as senior and famous as Jaddanbai but it gave her reason to become nervous as well. 'I thought, *baap re*, such famous people hear my voice and observe it so minutely,' she says disarmingly. She also adds that when she was standing in front of Jaddanbai, she could not get herself to add that she was Dinanath Mangeshkar's daughter, although she knew that her father and Jaddanbai were close acquaintances. She just stood there, tongue-tied by shyness and modesty. Throughout her life, these two qualities were to become both her strength and her weakness.

When 'Aayega aanewala' was released, it became such a hit that it swept Lata along with the sales to unimaginable levels of fame and popularity. 'My only regret,' she remembers sadly, 'is that the song's music composer, Khemchand Prakash, did not live to see all this.' One gets the feeling that her joy would have been far greater if she had been able to share its success with the person who created it for her. Just as she never forgot his contribution, Lata also never forgot the advice Jaddanbai gave her then. 'To understand the spirit of a song, pause and reflect on each word to get to its depth, meaning, nuance, effect and sub-text,' Jaddanbai had told the young singer. It was a lesson Lata followed religiously and, apart from the daily *riyaz* (practice) to develop her voice, she read a few stanzas from the Bhagwad Gita and Urdu poetry to understand the words that make up a lyric. Doubtless, this is what gave her music such a wide range and such luminosity.

7

Her songs conjure up so many faces that are shaped by her voice. How she manages to create the features of a personality with the notes she sings is an achievement that few can equal. As we heard her through the gramophone records, it was a Nargis, a Madhubala or a Waheeda Rehman that swam before one's eyes. Her silvery voice remained faceless yet spread such a web of magic that the singer and the song merged effortlessly into the face we wanted to see in our mind's eye.

8

Pandit Dinanath took a decision that was to later become the defining quality of his family's religious tradition. He chose a new name for his family to give it a unique identity. As a Brahmin from the Goa region, he belonged to a traditional clan of Brahmins chosen to read the Rudri (a special prayer for Shiva) at the morning *abhishek* (ornamentation) of the deity. Such Brahmins were usually given the generic clan name of Abhisheki. They were also Bhatt Brahmins, which means that they had the right to perform all the traditional rituals associated with the worship of Shiva.

Dinanath's father was called Ganesh Bhatt Abhisheki and his mother was Yesubai Rane. Ganesh Bhatt belonged to the Abhisheki clan of Konkan Brahmins while Yesubai was a Marathi. However, Dinanath wished to create a unique name for his family that would announce its exceptional musical talent and love of the arts. His ancestral village was called Mangeshi, and the presiding deity of the local temple was Mangeshi, one of the several names of Shiva. 'Mangeshkar', the name Dinanath adopted signified that his family would henceforth always be protected by the hand (*kar*) of Lord Mangeshi.

Ever since, the members of this family have dedicated themselves to the service of music and apart from Dinannath and Lata Mangeshkar, Asha, Usha, Meena and Hridaynath have all been successful artistes in this world of music. Perhaps the blessings of Lord Mangeshi do indeed bless the exceptional musical abilities of the Mangeshkar family after all.

9

In 1943, 14-year old Lata arrived in Bombay to sing at a dance festival, accompanied by her aunt, Gulab Godbole. She stayed with her uncle, Kamalanath Mangeshkar and devoted all her time to practising her music, determined to take her father's musical legacy forward. It is believed her uncle was not too pleased about this little girl shouldering the burden of her father's reputation and felt that if she failed to live up to her father's name, she would bring shame and dishonour to his name. Other relatives, among them Padmini Kolhapure's grandfather, Krishnarao Kolhapure, felt the same way. Krishnarao Kolhapure was himself a musician of repute and associated with the royal court of Baroda where he was called to play the veena. He also played the sitar and had worked in his father's drama company.

Naturally, their criticism upset Lata and she broke down in front of her aunt Gulab one day. Her aunt gave her some advice that encouraged her to carry on: 'Just think of your father,' she told her niece, 'and everything will fall into place.' That afternoon, an exhausted Lata dozed off and what followed was an omen, she feels. Her father appeared to her in a dream, singing a famous song 'Shura me vandile' from his play, *Manapman*.

Lata sang a *natya sangeet* composition at that conference, although she cannot recall its words. She then sang a composition of her father from his play *Randundubi*—'*Divya swatantrey ravi, atma tejo bal*'—which she remembered her father singing brilliantly. Dinanath's special touch was that the composition set in raga Malkauns would veer towards Bhairavi and then return to Malkauns once again. Obviously, this prodigy sang it exactly as she had heard her father sing it, because Lalita Pawar, a famous actress of the time, called her after the performance to say that she was so impressed with what she had heard that she would give Lata an award of 25 rupees. I ask Didi whether she ever received that money, and she laughs it off by saying that Lalita Pawar immediately took off her gold earrings and handed them to Lata. Her fame spread to Kolhapur after this and people began to say that Master Vinayak, who owned a film company that Lata worked in, should appoint her as a singer because this girl was obviously made to sing.

10

In the beginning, long before she became a known playback singer, Lata Mangeshkar and her family lived in Nana Chowk. The family included the mother (Mai), sisters Asha, Meena and Usha and brother Hridaynath as well as their cousin Indira Joshi and her three children. Between 1945 and 1952, this is where they lived, in two small rooms next to a dharmshala that housed a Shiva temple. The family managed to screen off a part of the common gallery and that became their sitting room. Shankar Seth Mandir, Nana Chowk, was their first 'proper' home, she tells me.

Among those who stayed on the upper floor was someone called Papa Bulbule, who was a cameraman in Master Vinayak's outfit. When Master Vinayak passed away in 1947, Papa Bulbule took Lata with him to introduce her to Central Studio to meet the musician Harishchandra Bali. Bali heard her and immediately promised to use her in a song he had composed for the film, *Love Is Blind*. Lata was paid 300 rupees (a good sum in those days) and that is how she was able to rent the two rooms in Nana Chowk. Until then, her family used to live with others from Master Vinayak's company (Praful Pictures) in a narrow lane in Khetwari, a little-known part of Girgaum. Remembering the hardships the family suffered in the years after her father's sudden death moves her even after all these years.

In front of the temple at Nana Chowk was a large platform, where the residents and others sat under the shade of a tree. Sometimes, shehnai players and the temple priests also came there to take a break. In the afternoons, when most people were resting, this is where Lata would practise her music by raising her voice to drown out the surrounding noises. Her sweet voice would often bring people out of their siesta to listen to the bhajans and riyaz. One day, her bhajans would become so popular that there was hardly a temple in the country that did not resound with her voice as the radio, tapes, records and cassettes took her voice far and wide.

From Nana Chowk, the family moved to Walkeshwar where they lived till 1960. Finally, Lata Mangeshkar was able to move to her own flat in Prabhu Kunj, at Peddar Road where her neighbours included Kalyan ji–Anandji and Madan Mohan. Prabhu Kunj has been her home ever since she moved there almost half a century ago.

11

Often when one listens to Indian classical music, one is transported to a certain space deep inside the listener that evokes the primeval and the unchanging. The power of music to take one to another level of consciousness is well-documented and exists outside classical music as well. People find themselves dancing or going into a trance-like state because the mood evoked is something that is so compelling in its appeal.

Music emerges from the deepest recesses of our collective unconscious and this is as true of classical, raga-based compositions as it is of our lilting folk melodies. It is because they touch some deep, unknown depth in us that a stray song, or a snatch of music can suddenly transport one to another plane of being. So it is perhaps music alone that becomes a link between the eternal, unchanging nature of human life and the immediate moment.

All this makes one wonder whether music has some other-worldly attributes that exert a strong effect on listeners. This becomes significant in the case of what is known as *sugam* sangeet, or music that is not bound by the rigid grammar of our classical *gharanas* and ragas or the seasonal cycle of folk music. The Hindi writer Nirmal Verma has expressed this eloquently when he reportedly declared: 'It is not that we become free of our tensions when we listen to music, but that we embark on a road that takes us to a stress-free and peaceful state of being. As we proceed, we find all the chains that bound us loosening the coils that cause us pain and unhappiness. This state, which can be described as a restoration of balance or of a release of tension, is like the rope that quivers for a while after its coils and knots have been loosened.'

12

Around 1879–80, Balwant Pandurang Kirloskar, also known as Anna Saheb Kirloskar, formed the Kirloskar Natak Mandali, which is reputed to have introduced Marathi plays and Natya Sangeet to virtually every Marathi home and made them enormously popular. Apart from Dinanth Mangeshkar, other eminent artistes associated with this drama company included such famous names as Balgandharva, Master Krishnarao, Pandit Bhaskar Bua Bakhale, Bapu Saheb Pendharkar, Govind Ballal Deval, Govind Rao Tambe and Ganpatrao Bodas. After Anna Saheb passed away, Shripad Krishna Kolhatkar kept the company running with the earnings from his plays.

Lata Mangeshkar says that when her father arrived in Maharashtra from Goa to join the Kirloskar Natak Company, he was just 14 years old. By this time, Pune, Sangli, Miraj, Kolhapur and Bombay had become important centres for stage performances often studded with Marathi Natya Sangeet. Kirloskar Natak Company first staged Krishnaji Prabhakar Khadilkar's *Manapman* in 1911 with Balgandharva in the lead role. In 1918, Dinanath left the Kirloskar Company along with his friends Chintaman Rao Kolhatkar and Krishnarao Kolhapure to form the Balwant Sangeet Mandali. It is significant that when Dinanath staged *Manapman*, considered his best presentation, he was doing it with actors who had staged it earlier for another company. However, although this popular play had a distinguished past with many famous singers and performers, when Dinanath decided to stage it, he made some significant changes. The task of composing its music was given to the talented harmonium player and musician, Pandit Govindrao Tambe, who later composed music for many V. Shantaram films, such as *Ayodhya ka Raja* (1932) *Jalti Nishani* (1932), *Sairandhri* (1933) and *Maya Machindra* (1975). Govindrao composed several songs and tunes but the most popular song, which had never been set to music or sung in earlier productions of this play, came to Pandit Dinanath. He composed the music for this song ('*Shura mi vandile*') himself and went on to make history with it.

Apart from *Manapman* and *Saubhadra*, the Balwant Sangeet Mandali also commissioned some new works which made it very popular all over the region. Among such plays were Vir Vamanrao Joshi's *Randundubhi*, Veer Savarkar's *Sanyast Khadga*, Ram Ganesh Gadkari's *Bhav Bandhan* and *Rajsanyas*. After the success of these plays, particularly *Randundubhi* and *Sanyast Khadga*, Dinanath Mangeshkar was hailed as the best artiste of his time.

Lata Mangeshkar proudly remembers how the legendary Balgandharva had declared that if Dinanath Mangeshkar would agree to join his drama company, he would strew the path with rose petals and spray the red carpet with attar to welcome him. Dinanath, he had declared, could melt a listener's heart with his voice. She recalls that the friendship of these two stalwarts gave a new direction to the development of this form of entertainment in Maharashtra and brought glory to the Marathi language. *Ugra-mangal*, *Tratika*, *Deshkantak* and *Ramrajya Viyog* were some of the other popular plays the company staged. So from his debut in Kirloskar Natak Company productions, Pandit Dinanath rose to the pinnacle of his career within a few years. His death at the young age of 42 cut short a brilliant career but even in the short life he was fated to have, he achieved what many are unable to reach after decades. He left behind memories of a great talent and so many unfinished dream projects that he is still mourned by those who value his contribution.

13

For the last half-century, Lata Mangeshkar has ruled over the music scene of the film industry so completely that it is difficult to even imagine where the film music industry would be since 1947 if she had not been there. It is a happy coincidence that her entry point into playback singing took place at a moment that was a rare moment of convergence. A perceptible cultural shift and a strong sense of pride in creating a new nation brought in its wake a surge of creativity that filled those early years of independence with extraordinary energy and joy. Naturally, the films of that time are inspirational and idealistic: this is the path that Lata Mangeshkar entered enthusiastically.

In 1948, when Lata and Mukesh sang a duet ('*Ab darne ki baat nahin, angrezi chhora chala gaya, voh gora-gora chala gaya*') created by Master Ghulam Haider for the film *Majboor*, they touched the heart of every Indian. The same Ghulam Haider recorded his last song for a Bombay film (*Padmini*, 1948) with Lata ('*Bedarad tere dard ko seene se laga ke*') before he left that same night for Pakistan.

Lata Mangeshkar has witnessed so many landmark events that she has become a sort of chronicler of the music film world. In tracing that historic journey, let us start with 1947. K.L. Saigal had just passed away and Noorjahan, known as Mallika-e-tarannum (the empress of song), had migrated to Pakistan. The departure of these two giants from the music world had placed the industry in a very tenuous position. Serendipity had its own role to play in what happened after this point. Virtually all the great music composers of that time—Ghulam Haider, Khemchand Prakash, Anil Biswas, Husnlal–Bhagatram, Naushad and Shankar-Jaikishan—had already seen in Lata Mangeshkar the promise of a great future. Similarly, the release of five landmark films in 1949—*Mahal, Bari bahen, Ladli, Andaz* and *Barsaat*—would change Lata's life forever.

The huge success of these films swept along Lata to the point where she reigned virtually unchallenged over the music world for the next 50 years. It must be emphasized that it was not just the success of these films that made this possible. Her fresh and joyous voice, blessed by a divine talent and refined by her training in classical music, led many to believe that no film could succeed if it did not have her voice behind it. So when she trilled, '*Hawa main urta jaye, mera lal dupatta malmal ka*' (*Barsaat*), it was as if she was waving triumphantly from a place very high up in the sky.

14

Several small stories and anecdotes from her past have the potential of a saga of their own. For instance, her first public performance with her father took place in Sholapur at Nutan Theatre. After a short composition in Raga Khambawati and two natya sangeet numbers from *Manapman* ('*Shura mi vandile*') and *Brahmakumari* ('*Suhasya tujhe manasi mohi*'), the exhausted little child put her head down in her father's lap and slept while he sang classical ragas all night.

Her father first named her Hridaya but later changed it to Lata. They say that he decided to change his daughter's name because he was very impressed with the character of Latika, a female role he played in 1919 in the Marathi play *Bhav-bandhan*. Lata's father adored this child and teased her by calling himself *Tata-baba* like she did. Lata played the games that children play but her favourite pastime was to stage home productions of her father's plays with her siblings, cousins and neighbours and her cousin, Pandharinath Kolhapure (Padmini Kolhapure's uncle), who would be cast as the villain. It is also said that once, when she had cheated a neighbouring shopkeeper by passing on some fake coins, she was sent back to apologize and return the purchase. She says that that was the day she decided never to cheat or lie.

She was born in Indore on 28 September 1929. The house belonged to her aunt, who lived in a part of the town known as *Bagh Vakeel ka Para*. The doctor who brought her into this world was a lady called Dr Motabai. Little did she realize then what a special baby she had just helped to bring into the world and that she herself would be remembered as the doctor who delivered Lata Mangeshkar! Later, Lata would travel all over Maharashtra with her father's Balwant Sangeet Mandali, imbibing the culture of the region from what she saw in towns such as Pune, Kolhapur, Satara, Goa, Miraj and Sangli.

As a girl, she had a strong desire to dedicate herself to social service and had several long discussions on politics and revolution with Savarkar, a close family friend. He persuaded her to follow her father's footsteps instead and harness her extraordinary talent to spread social awareness through her voice. Observing her life's journey, one can see how prescient Savarkar was when he advised her to follow the path of music instead of politics and revolution. Her voice, which is like listening to silver bells tinkling in the breeze, has brought sweetness and joy into countless lives. Moreover, the high benchmark she has set for others to follow is not a mean achievement. Her life, with its history of hard work, dignity, simplicity and honesty, is itself worthy of respect.

15

Of the innumerable classical compositions she learnt from her father, Dinanath, the ones Lata can still recall are Raga Malkauns, Hindol, Jaijaiwanti and Puriya Dhanashree. She remembers clearly the Jaijaiwanti he taught her (*Tan jahaz, man sagar ratnakar aprampar*) and how he had instructed her to take a *taan*. She hums the Hindol composition he taught her '*Kanchan baran hindol*' for me on the phone. The well-known Malkauns composition ('*Pir na jani*') is another raga she remembers her father teaching her, as well as his lessons in Khambawati ('*Aali ri, main jagi sari raina*'). As for Raga Puriya Dhanashree, the first raga he chose for her initiation in classical music that hovers between the dwindling light of late evening and early night. To her, it is the raga that lights the evening lamp in her prayer room and she tells me how she sings its '*Sadarang nit uthkar det duain*' as a prayer.

All this is not easy for her to recall and even as she talks of the various ragas and their persona, you feel that she has regressed to a time when she was a child in her father's lap. Her hand caresses his book of musical notations and the tanpura he used at his practice sessions. For me it was an astonishing discovery that our question and answer sessions became a dialogue between me and the Mangeshkar father and daughter. Whenever she sings something for me, I felt he was standing in front of me. She confesses that whenever she is confronted with a problem, he appears to her in her dreams . . .

Often, as she recalls incidents from her past, I feel I am in the audience of a small town in Maharashtra and a play starring Dinanath is about to begin. This may be because whenever we speak of her past, she dives into a dream world where parents never really die.

16

'If I had done my riyaz as I should have and paid my classical music more attention, perhaps I would have been a better artiste,' Lata Mangeshkar tells me with a great deal of regret for a path she was unable to take in her musical journey. She says her father had once declared that one can hear *Gandhar* (the note 'ga' in Hindustani classical music) each time Lata opens her mouth because it lives inside her. So it is strange to hear her say that even after such extraordinary success, she still has some lingering regrets.

'I wish I could sing like Ustad Bade Ghulam Ali Khan,' she told me once. I find it ironic that she should say this because the Ustad himself had once said enviously of her, 'Damn, this girl (kambakht) never goes off-key!'

There is another interesting story about the two of them. Once, while on a visit to Bombay to perform at Girgaum's Laxmibagh, Ustad Bade Ghulam Ali Khan had planned to sing Raga Yaman. While rehearsing it one morning, the notes from Lata's rendering of this raga ('*Ja re badra bairi ja*' from the film *Bahana*) came floating from a radio nearby. His attention was immediately drawn to her voice and he was so impressed with what he had heard that he told a student, 'Ever since I have heard that girl's Yaman, I have forgotten my own! Her Yaman has so taken hold of my mind and heart that even though I want to, I can't sing Yaman tonight.' It is believed that he sang another raga that evening.

It is difficult to find such mutual admiration between two great artistes anywhere, leave alone one who only sang classical ragas and one who hardly ever did. Nevertheless, one yearned to sing like him and the other bowed to her superior rendering of a raga he was renowned for.

It is interesting that she paid tribute to this great doyen of the Patiala gharana in her own way. There are several examples when she has sung variations of his thumris in her film songs: for instance, his thumri in Bhairavai ('*Jamuna ke teer*') becomes '*Kaise jaoon jamuna ke teer*' in Lata's rendering for *Devta*, while his '*Tori tirchi najariya ke baan*' in Pahari sounds remarkably similar to Lata's '*Na maro najariya ke baan, akeli ayi paniya bharan*' (*Pehli Jhalak*). The immortal '*Yaad piya ki aaye, ye dukh saha na jaaye*' in Kaushik Dhwani by the Ustad is beautifully replicated by Lata as '*Balma anari man bhaye, ka karoon samajh na aye*' (*Bahurani*). All three compositions were created by C. Ramachandra for Lata.

17

It is often said that Rukmini Devi Arundale, Balasaraswati and Indrani Rehman were responsible for popularizing art forms that were previously only available in temples, private homes and courts. Lata Mangeshkar went a step further: by making available music on air and giving it legitimacy in critical circles, she stands above her predecessors in the world of popular music. It was she who forced record companies to print the name of a singer on their labels and catalogues.

Another reason for her success was a new scale that music composers were offered by her voice. Added to this was the fact that female characters were gradually acquiring an importance that early film scripts were unable to provide. From the long-suffering, stoic woman in most mythological and patriotic films, arose a new woman who could say, '*Aurat ne janam diya mardon ko*' (*Sadhana*); '*Saiyyan jhooton ka bara sartaj nikla*' (*Do Aankhen Barah Haat*) and '*Tere sab gham milain mujhko*' (*Hamdard*).

By the sixties, the heroine emerged as a strong, central presence. Her voice was also used to create special numbers that set the scene for a certain liberal space for women characters. This is probably why most of the songs she has sung in the late fifties and early sixties are still regarded among her best. *Parkh, Baiju Bawra, Chhaya, Bandini, Madhumati, Awara* to *Ganga Jamuna, Saraswatichandra, Arti, Teesri Kasam* and *Mother India*, to name just a few, follow a curve that is compellingly moving towards a strong female presence.

18

In 1942, Vinayak Damodar Karnataki (better known as Master Vinayak), coaxed by Shripad Joshi, employed 13-year old Lata in his Navyug Chitrapat Film Company. This was initially a three-month contract and Lata was hired to perform small roles in his film productions for a salary of 300 rupees. Earlier that year, in April, her father had suddenly died leaving his eldest child, Lata, to shoulder the burden of providing for the family. She had no alternative but to accept the offer from Master Vinayak, better known later as actress Nanda's father.

This is how Lata Mangeshkar made her foray into the world of cinema.

Her first role was a small part in his film *Pehla Mangalgaur*, where she played the younger sister of the well-known actress, Snehprabha Pradhan. However, following a tiff with the studio owners, Master Vinayak abandoned the film, which was later completed by R.S. Jannarkar.

At the end of her contract with Navyug Film Company in December that year, Lata prepared to move with her family to Kolhapur as part of Master Vinayak's Praful Pictures. She would be paid 60 rupees a month, which was raised to 200 rupees by 1947. For these five years and later in Bombay, this was what she did to earn a living.

In 1945, Master Vinayak shut down his film company in Kolhapur and came to Bombay. He continued to make films and Lata performed small roles in some of them. Among the films she acted are *Maze Baal* (1943), *Gajabhau* (1944), *Badi Maa* (1945), *Jeevan Yatra* (1946), *Subhadra* (1946) and *Mandir* (1948). Of these, *Bari Ma* is memorable because this is when she got an opportunity to perform along with the legendary Noorjahan in a film. In fact, if you hunt hard enough, you may be able to locate an old Columbia Record with the song she sang in it—'*Mata Tere Charnon Main*'—which was picturized on her as well. By this time, Noorjahan's triumphant rule over film music was coming to an end and her famous swan song, '*Diya Jalakar Aap Bujhaya*' is rendered for this film. Lata considers this her favourite Noorjahan song to this day.

The first song Lata sang was for the Marathi film *Gajabhau* in 1943, a strangely prophetic number that declared: '*Hindustan ke logo ab to mujhe pehchano*'. This was not her first playback song in Hindi, which was '*Pa lagoon kar jori re, Shyam mose*

na khelo hori re' for the film *Aap Ki Sewa Mein* (1946) for
Datta Davjekar. What is significant about this number is
that gradually, this little 13-year-old daughter of Dinanath
Mangeshkar was successful in picking up where her father's
untimely death had snapped the link with Master Vinayak's
film company.

19

Gurudev Rabindranath Tagore wondered how wonderful it
would be if one could write poetry using the colours extracted
from the juice of fragrant flowers. In a similar way, I wonder
whether any song that comes out of Lata Mangeshkar's throat
acquires a special emotional intensity. She manages to capture
the essence of an emotion, something that Tagore had wistfully
talked of.

20

Pandit Ravi Shankar composed a song for the film *Anuradha*
(1960) that has a haunting quality and stays with the listener for
a long time. '*Kaise din beete, kaise beetin ratiyan, piya jaane na*'. I
have not met a single person so far who has not felt the same way
about Lata's magical rendering of it, especially her coaxing of the
mood of longing in the phrase '*Kaise beetin ratiyan*'.

It is generally believed that when accompanying a singer as
part of an orchestra, a musical instrument attempts to echo the
singer's voice. In this song, one can clearly feel that the singer's
voice with all its sweetness and finesse echoes the liquid, gliding

notes of a sitar. I am sure that when he was rehearsing it with Lata ji, Pandit Ravi Shankar must have played it on his sitar for her. This is also corroborated by Shubha Mudgal, a well-known singer and musicologist. 'I am sure,' she nodded as I shared this discovery with her, 'that you are right. Pandit ji must have composed all the songs for this film on his sitar and as the song expands, you can follow the strains of a sitar emerge from Lata ji's throat. Look at how she has rendered "*Jane Kaise Sapnon Mein Kho Gayin Ankhiyan*" in another song from the same film,' and she hummed the melody for me to make her point clearer.

I was thrilled to learn that this was also noticed by those who follow music closely. I would request readers to listen to the song again to notice how beautifully Lata ji has enunciated the '*haye*' in this song. It is a sigh suffused with so many emotions: fear, pity and a deep sadness and when she takes the song to its crescendo, the impossible emotional pitch is matched by her own voice in what can only be described as faultless brilliance.

Everyone knows that a song in any film is the combined effort of the lyricist, the music composer and the singer. There are hundreds of film songs that stand out for one or the other quality but this song from *Anuradha* is a perfect blend of a maestro's sitar and a nightingale's voice, and rarely heard. Lata ji likes to quote a couplet by Sahir Ludhianvi to illustrate what I am trying to say:

Jo taar se nikli hai, woh dhun sabne suni hai.
To saaz pe guzri hai woh kis dil ko pata hai.

(Everyone has heard the music from the strings of an instrument. But who can say what the instrument suffered to produce that music.)

Her effortless inclusion into her voice of the musical instruments she has sung along with is an accomplishment that cannot be ignored. Each song she sang for Pandit Ravi Shankar in *Anuradha* displays this clearly that one must add a few more examples to make the reader aware of this aspect of her music. '*O Sajna, Barkha Bahar Ayi*' (*Parakh*); '*Meri Ankhon se Koi Neend Liye Jata Hai*' (*Puja ke Phool*); '*Hum Tere Pyar Main Sara Alalm Kho Baithe*' (*Dil Ek Mandir*) and '*Main to Pee ke Nagariya Jane Lagi*' (*Ek Kali Muskayi*) and '*Aaj Socha to Ansoon Bhar Aye*' (*Haste* Zakhm) are but a few illustrations, where she has matched each minute nuance of the stringed instrument with her own perfect rendering. However, the sitar is not the only instrument that she was able to bring across in her voice: the sarod flute, shehnai, sarangi and veena have all at some point or another sung along with her found a worthy competitor in her voice.

'*Main Piya Teri, Tu Mane Ya Na Mane*' (*Basant Bahar*; flute); '*Suno Choti Si Gudiya Ki Lambi Kahani*' (*Seema*, sarod) and '*Dil Ka Khilona Hai Toot Gaya*' (*Goonj Uthi Shehnai*; shehnai) are a few more where she has sung alongside maestros such as Ustad Ali Akbar Khan, Bismillah Khan and Pannalal Ghosh.

21

The famous actress-singer, Suraiyya, was at the peak of her popularity when Lata entered this industry. The second half of the fifties saw them both produce one hit song after another, whether they sang for Naushad or Husnlal–Bhagatram.

Together, they sang just four songs and one can see how both brought their own brand of magic into them. This is a tribute as much to their individual talent as it is to those music composers who created these songs. They are so perfectly matched that it becomes difficult to say who is more accomplished. My personal favourite is a song from *Sanam* (1951), '*Bedard shikari, are bedard shikari . . .sun baat hamari . . .*'. They both excel in their individual parts and one can sense a comfort between them that comes from deep mutual respect. However, it is easy to forget that whereas Suraiyya was an acclaimed voice by this time, Lata ji had entered it merely three or four years ago. It seems that what took Suraiyya years to accomplish was attained by this young entrant in just a few. Like Amirbai Karnataki, Zohrabai Ambalawali, Shamshad Begum and Rajkumari, the magic of Suraiyya's voice, too, had begun to fade by the time Lata Mangeshkar emerged as the new star on the horizon.

Lata ji was able to effortlessly take over from where film music had reached under her predecessors. Under the baton of Master Ghulam Haider, Husnlal–Bhagatram, Anil Biswas, C. Ramachandra and Naushad, she soared to a new height. I feel that in order to understand this, every Lata fan must listen to the following songs: '*O Pardesi Musafir, Kise Karta Hai Ishare*' (*Balam*, 1949, Husnlal–Bhagatram, Qamar Jalalabadi); '*O Door Des Se Aaja Re*' (*Shokhiyan*, 1951, Jamal Sen, Kedar Sharma); '*Mere Chaand, Mere Lal, Tum Jiyo Hazaron Saal*' (*Diwana*, 1952, Naushad, Shakeel Badayuni). There is a depth of emotion that Lata Mangeshkar is able to introduce that was eventually to become her signature. It was also what made her stand out against all the preceding singers and forge a place of her own.

22

During a conversation with well-known sitar player, Mahmood Mirza Sahib, who now lives in London, I realize what we also owe to Lata ji. 'Many people came to appreciate classical Indian music after they had heard Lata,' he told me. 'If she had sung a composition based on a classical raga, they would try and find out more about a Yaman, Bahar or Hameer . . . Their appetite whetted, they started to come to concerts of classical music and often stayed on. At a time when film music had entered every middle-class Indian home, and when film music was all that people heard, her igniting an interest in classical music was a great contribution, I feel.'

This observation drew my attention to the deep impact of film music on middle-class India. It also made me realize how many great classical musicians had played, sung or scored music for our films in the early years. Lata Mangeshkar herself acknowledges the contribution of K.L. Saigal in *Tansen* (1943), *Devdas* (1935) and *Bhakt Surdas* (1942) when he sang some unforgettable songs set to classical ragas. Her voice, trained in classical music, made it possible for our great composers to create some memorable songs set in classical ragas or studded with complex *taans*. Lata was able to effortlessly handle all the complexities that such a composition required of a singer. This opened an entirely new world of possibilities.

Anil Biswas was the first to experiment with this new genre. Similarly, Naushad, C. Ramachandra, Sajjad Husain, S.D. Burman and Madan Mohan believed that had it not been for Lata's expert handling of all their complex demands, they may never had tried blending classical music into popular songs. She understood perfectly the mood that they were trying to evoke and managed to pack into a three-minute recording the richness of each raga-based song she sang. As the trend grew, young girls in many middle-class homes were sent to learn classical music from teachers so that they could acquire a better understanding of Indian music.

Lata Mangeshkar's special talent was mined by so many composers over the years that classical music became a base for many filmy songs. From 'Chanda Re Ja Re Ja Re' (Ziddi, 1948, set in Raga- Chhayanat), 'Garjat Barsat Bhijat Ayilo' (Malhar, 1951, Raga-Gaur-Malhar), 'Baandh Preeti Phool dore' (Malti-Madhav-1951, Raga Jaijaiwanti), 'Marna Teri Gali Mein' (Shabab-1954, Raga- Pahadi), 'Hamare Dil Se Na Jana' (Udankhatola-1955, Raga- Bihag), 'Suno Chhoti Si Gudiya Ki Lambi kahani' (Seema-1955, Raga- Bhairavi), 'Piya Te Kahaan Gayo Nehra Lagaye' (Toofan Aur Deeya- 1956, Raga Asavari), 'Ja Re Badra Bairi Ja' (Bahana-1960, Raga-Yaman) to 'Mohe Panghat Pe Nandlal Chher Gayo Re' (Mughal-e-Azam, 1960, Raga Gara), 'Jao-Jao Nand ke Lala' (Rangoli, 1962, in Raga Bageshri), there are scores of songs that derive their sweetness from a classical raga. In many cases, they inspired listeners to seek out the more elaborate renderings to savour the raga. This is how film songs, recorded within a tight 3-minute duration, introduced complex classical ragas, such as Yaman, Hameer or Bahar, to so many Indians that they became better known even among those who had no special interest in Indian classical music.

23

Pyar ke jahan ki nirali sarkar hai
Muhabbat ke thane main yeh dil thanedar hai

Yeh dil havaldar hai . . . yeh dil chowkidar hai
Anokhi kachehri hai yeh . . . anokha kanoon hai
Muhabbat ki arzi ka naya majmoon hai
Aankhon ka dak-khana hai nazron ka taar hai
Muhabbat ke thane mein . . .
Pyaar ke school mein ek hi class hai
Laakhon ummidwaar koi-koi pass hai
Mushkil sabak hai yeh Par majedaar hai
Mohabbat ke thaane mein...
Pyar kiya jisne woh pyaar hi mein kho gaya
Itna samajh lo ki bekar ho gaya
Uske liye toh Har din itwaar hai
Mohabbat ke thaane mein . . .

This delightful duet is sung by Lata ji and Shamshad Begum in *Patanga* (1949) for C. Ramachandra, who has set Rajendra Krishan's playful lyrics into a lovely medley of sounds and melodies. Of all the lovely duets that Shamshad Begum and Lata ji have sung together, I rate this as their best performance. We all know how skilled C. Ramachandra was in creating unforgettable film songs and after R.C. Boral and Pankaj Mullick, he alone brought western orchestration to such heights when adapting it into Indian songs. His rhythm patterns, blending of local folk tunes with western musical instruments, the clever use of preludes and interludes – all these make his music instantly appealing and easy to recall. Even after all these years, the music he created appears startlingly contemporary.

A remarkable quality of this duet is the ease with which the two singers share the playfulness of the lyrics between them, tossing the lines from one to the other in complete harmony. Nowhere is one aware that Lata Mangeshkar was a recent entrant into this world or that she was singing with someone who had a long list of musical conquests behind her. And although some of Shamshad Begum's best songs were composed by Naushad, she is at her best here. The song also reminds us of the many duets that Lata ji has sung with other illustrious predecessors in this industry: whether *'Chup-Chup Khade Ho Zaroor Koi Baat Hai'* (with Premlata in *Bari Behen*, 1949) or *'Gore Gore, O Banke Chhore'* (with Amirbai Karnataki in *Samadhi*, 1950) or *'Jab Dil Ko sataave Gam To Chhed Sakhi Sargam'* (with Saraswati Rane in *Sargam*, 1950).

The contrast between the sweetness of Lata ji's pure soprano notes and Shamshad Begum's slightly rasping, deeper voice with its grainy texture create a magic that was to be repeated in *Baiju Bawra*, 1952 (*Door Koi Gaaye Dhun Ye Sunaye*), *Mughal-e-Azam*, 1960 (*Teri Mehfil Mein Kismat Azmakar Hum Bhi Dekhenge*), *Aan*, 1952 (*Khelo Rang Hamare Sang*), *Deedar*, 1951, (*Bachpan Ke Din Bhula Na Dena*), *Andaaz*, 1949 (*Dar Na Muhabbat Kar Le*) and *Baradari*, 1955 (*Chhodo-Chhodo Ji Baiyyan Mori* and countless other duets the two sang over the years.

Today, after listening to these gems, we can understand why Shamshad Begum had carved such a special niche for herself in the music industry. At a time when she had to compete with several great singers, her lusty Punjabi voice electrified Indian film songs. During the forties and fifties, she occupied a place that Lata ji was to inherit and make her own till the end of the century and beyond. Yet, even as Lata ji rose higher and higher, she and Shamshad Begum created several duets together that have stood the test of time.

During 1950–55, Lata Mangeshkar established herself firmly as the voice of Indian cinema as she delivered one

musical hit after another. It seemed as if every music director
wanted only Lata to sing in every film being made. Naushad
was perhaps the only music director who understood the
special quality of Shamshad Begum's voice and whether a film
had Noorjahan or Lata Mangeshkar, he always kept a special
niche for Shamshad Begum in every important assignment he
handled. In *Baiju Bawra* (1952), the opening lines of '*Door Koi
Gaye, Dhun Yeh Sunaye*' were given to Shamshad Begum before
Lata Mangeshkar's voice introduced Meena Kumari into the
scene. Listening to this song, it becomes clear why Shamshad
Begum realized that the competition for the premier place in
the world of film music was over and that Lata Mangeshkar
was the voice of the future. Her best contribution henceforth
would be a duet with Lata Mangeshkar and that is what
happened after the film's spectacular success. It is also true that
Lata Mangeshkar's best songs were recorded for Naushad but
what had become apparent to Naushad was also visible to the
other music directors: that there was no one who could rival
Lata Mangeshkar now.

24

A quality that fascinates me about Lata Mangeshkar's music
is that she has always sung for other people. The music
was someone else's and the face that mimed those words
on screen was not hers either. This is so different from
classical music, where a singer retreats into a private world
and sings for individual pleasure. This is as true of an Ustad
Bade Ghulam Ali Khan and a Bhimsen Joshi as it is of an
M.S. Subbulakshmi. There are also examples of singer-stars,

such as K.L. Saigal, Noorjahan and Suraiyya, who sang for themselves. On the other hand, when Lata sings for Nargis, Madhubala, Nutan, Waheeda Rehman or any other actress, she projects her voice outwards, to suit the oeuvre of the film star she sings for.

There is perhaps no other playback singer who has been able to successfully match her voice to so many different film personalities. In fact, when you listen to her songs on a record or CD, you can immediately conjure up the face Lata ji has sung it for: whether Nargis or Meena Kumari. This must surely have been a tremendous challenge for it could not have been easy to efface herself from a song sung with such feeling.

25

There are three songs composed by Anil Biswas in the fifties that deserve some attention as we try to trace the evolution of film music. All three were sung by Lata Mangeshkar because Anil Biswas had sensed that in her voice, he had found a quality that had long eluded him. Mind you, he had already composed some outstanding music for Amirbai Karnataki, Suraiyya, Parul Ghosh, Zohrabai Amabalawali, Nalini Jaiwant, Chandbala, Surinder Kaur, Leela Chitnis, Rajkumari, Shamshad Begum and almost all the big names of those times. Yet it was only after he found Lata Mangeshkar that his music soared to new heights. He first used her voice in three films made in 1948 (*Gajre*, *Anokha Pyar* and *Laadli*) and after he had tried her out in these films, he felt emboldened to compose more complex tunes. Some of Lata's most memorable songs were the result of this experiment.

The three Anil Biswas compositions are from *Gajre* (1948), *Tarana* and *Aaram* (1951). If one listens to them, one becomes aware of the play between the subtle and dramatic elements that Biswas had tried to insert by varying the rhythm and pace of his songs. To take just one example in '*Kab Aaoge Balma, Baras-Baras Badli Bikhar Gayi*' (*Gajre*), the changing rhythm of the raindrops is so exquisitely woven into the texture of the song that one can feel how a gentle shower becomes a heavy downpour in the course of a single cloudburst. And all this is achieved in just three minutes!

In each of the three songs I have mentioned, Lata ji seems to be weaving a trance-like situation. The credit for this goes in a large measure to Anil Biswas's compositions for when you listen to the other songs that he created in these three films, one becomes aware of the musical style that would become associated with his compositions. This is perhaps why many of us still bemoan that we no longer get the same kind of thrill from film music that one got from the compositions of Anil Biswas, Sajjad Husain or Ghulam Haider. The truth is that these great composers worked hard to coax Lata Mangeshkar's voice (itself a unique gift) to the point of perfection.

The song from *Gajre* mentioned above is a case in point. The complexity of the composition has been presented so beautifully by Biswas that it set a trend for future music directors to follow when raising the quality of film music. The plaintiveness of '*Kab Aaoge Balma?* (When will you come, beloved?') leads to that joyous shower of rain that I have referred to earlier. It was Biswas's genius that he was able to achieve this without the melodrama that a lesser composer may have chosen. This gradual expanding of the spectrum of feelings expressed in a film's music was possible only because he understood how to modulate musical notes to suit the lyrics.

Also listen to the rise and fall of the lines 'Mil-Mil Ke Bichhur Gaye Nain' (Aaram) that follow so naturally from the opening lines where the lyrics describe the first encounter of two lovers. Biswas has made Lata ji pack into a mere two and a half minutes the full range of feelings that the poet has described. Naturally, with such masters behind her, it is easy to understand how Lata ji developed her musical depth. The lessons of playback singing that she learnt from Biswas, C. Ramachandra, Naushad, Master Ghulam Haider and Sajjad Husain were written by master grammarians.

No wonder Lata ji told me once that she wished the young singers of today had been able to learn under the great composers that she was fortunate to have worked with.

In a biography of Anil Biswas by Sharad Dutt we learn of another lesson Biswas gave her. According to Dutt, Biswas did not always like the strong Marathi touch her music displayed. His own compositions, he felt, were like a Bengali rasgulla – rounded and soaked in sweet syrup. So he started making her practise some classical compositions he had learnt from his mother, which were very different in style from what Lata ji had learnt from her father and other gurus. He once gave her some lines to rehearse in the style that his mother's guru had taught her to sing. When Lata ji sang these for her guru, he was amazed at the result that emerged from merging the two styles.

'I learnt so much from Anil Biswas,' Lata ji recalls. 'It was he who taught me how to take a breath without disturbing the beat and pitch of a song.' It is a lesson she learnt so well that it is often difficult to say where she has drawn breath as she sings.

26

One day, in 1948, when she was recording a song for Anil Biswas 'Kab aaoge balma, baras-baras badli bhi bikhar gayi' (Gajre), Anil Biswas was so thrilled with his composition and her rendering that he told her, 'I want Raj Kapoor to come to my studio and listen to this song.' In those days, the office of R.K. Films was located in Mahalaxmi.

Many days later, a good-looking youth came to Lata's Nana Chowk home and told her very politely, 'You have to sing a few songs for Raj Kapoor saab, so please take some time off to come to R.K. Films.' Lata had seen Prithviraj Kapoor, Raj Kapoor's famous father and a towering stage personality, who looked like a Greek god. Lata told her sister Meena later that someone had come with a message from Raj Kapoor and was a most polite and handsome man himself. Perhaps everyone who works in R.K. Films is handsome, she laughed as she narrated this to Meena. A couple of days later, she went to the Mahalaxmi office, she was stunned when the young man she had mistaken for a spot boy carrying a message for her from Raj Kapoor was actually Jaikishan, of the famous Shankar–Jaikishan team. Later, she was also introduced to Shankar.

That encounter led to a famous friendship that eventually blossomed between Jaikishan and Lata Mangeshkar. In fact, this great bond was to include all the other members of Raj Kapoor's core team that included Hasrat Jaipuri, Shailendra and Mukesh. Naturally, Raj Kapoor and Nargis were the lynchpins that held the whole team together. This grand alliance would soon light up the film industry like the fairy lights strung along

Bombay's Marine Drive. A few days later, she recorded her first song for R.K. Films' *Barsaat*: '*Jiya Beqarar Hai, Aayi Bahar Hai . . .*', which is as fresh today as it was when she sang it almost 67 years ago.

> *Jiya beqarar hai, Chhayi bahaar hai*
> *Aaja more Baalma, Tera Intezaar hai . . .*

27

One day, as we were discussing a song by Arzoo Lakhnawi ('*Hansi-Hansi Na Rahi, Khushi-Khushi Na Rahi*') from a film (*Sipahiya*) made in 1949 by C. Ramchandra, she began relating episodes about him as if they had taken place just the other day.

I find this a rather endearing habit in her: we would be talking of Hasrat Jaipuri and she would remember something about Majrooh. She has such a fund of memories inside her that she herself has forgotten some. Yet it seems that they suddenly get nudged out of a state of hibernation when she recalls a similar incident, and the floodgates of memory open. God alone knows how many important events she has witnessed and how many layers of those days are still locked inside her.

This is what she is like: for her all her songs are fresh in her memory and what she sang for *Mahal* is almost as alive for her as what she sang decades later for *Rang de Basanti*. This is why no one not even a little-known poet like Arzoo Lakhanawi— can go unrecorded in her life.

28

Few people know that Lata Mangeshkar has scored music for Marathi films using a pseudonym. There is an interesting history behind this secret. Towards the end of the sixties, a Marathi producer-director called Bhalaji Pendharkar was making a film on Shivaji titled *Mohityanchi Manjula*. All the music directors he contacted were busy and unable to give him the dates that suited him, putting him in considerable tension. Lata Mangeshkar, aware of this problem he was facing and also because he was a family friend, suggested that she could help him out. However, Pendharkar realized that if his film flopped, it may affect her reputation and since she was already a household name by then, he declined this generous offer. This is when she told him that she was willing to take on the assignment under a pseudonym and the name he selected was 'Jatashankar'. However, Lata ji was not too pleased with his choice and instead took the name of 'Anandghan', from the saint Ramdas Swami's immortal poem of the same name (which can be translated as the clouds of ecstasy). Later, she was to score the music for a few other Marathi films using the same pseudonym. These films were: *Ram-Ram Pahvanam* (1950); *Mohityanchi Manjula* (1962); *Maratha Tituka Melvava* (1964); *Sadhi Manasam* (1965) and *Tambadi Mati* (1969).

Asha, Usha and Hridaynath have all sung the songs she composed for *Mohityanchi Manjula* and it became a sort of home production. She wanted to take her brother Hridaynath as her assistant but since he did not have the time, she took on Datta Davjekar and swore him to secrecy.

Funnily enough, this fact could not remain secret for too long because in 1966, the Maharashtra government chose to award a film where she had scored the music (*Sadhi Manesam*). The other film being awarded was *Mohityanchi Manjula*. Since she was involved with both, she could hardly keep the matter secret. However, she discontinued scoring music after *Tambdi Maati*.

29

V. Shantaram's iconic film, *Jhanak Jhanak Payal Baje* (1955), is a treasure trove of beautiful music set to classical ragas. Anyone who has seen the film has been deeply impressed with the brilliant pairing of thumris and dadras with the film's classical kathak dance numbers. There is one sequence in the film that I wish to draw the reader's attention to: the scene that encapsulates a year's dance training given by a guru to his two disciples. Vasant Desai was able to capture the entire year through the clever use of the ragamala, a classical music device that strings various ragas in the order of the seasons they depict. One is left stunned by the brilliance of the composition but equally impressive is the manner in which Manna De and Lata ji have rendered this difficult task, along with the kathak *bols* of Pandit Gopikrishna. It is one of the most important experiments in film music, I think.

It begins with Manna De's chanting of the Sanskrit sloka, '*Gurur Brahma, Gurur Vishnu, Gururdevo Maheshwarah*' in Raga Yaman, followed by an enchanting Raga Basant, '*Rut basant ayi ghan-ban upvan, drum milind prafullit sugandh mand pavan aavat milind madhukar madhup gunjat rut basant*'. This melts soulfully into Manna De's Miyan malhar '*Ayi Ghata Umad-Ghumad Shyam Baran*', sung to the beat of a Pakhawaj.

At this point Lata's sweet voice enters with a Shuddh sarang '*Patjhar Ayi, Chhayi Dard Udasi . . .*', with the sad strains of a sarod deepening this mood.

This mood is dispelled when she bursts into a Tilak Kamod, '*Ab ke sajan ghar aa ja, o more saiyan man ka phool khila ja*', with the joyous peal of ghunghroos and a surbahar adding lustre. Desai's orchestration using virtually every kind of instrument and percussion are brilliant to say the least but it is equally important to note that of all the voices available to him, his choice of Manna De and Lata Mangeshkar becomes completely clear because no one else could have brought his vision to life so competently.

Desai blended two classical devices, the ragamala (a garland of ragas) and the baramasa (the cycle of seasons), to perfection to bring alive the passage of a year in just one song. Few film songs have achieved such a glorious result.

30

As we go deeper into discovering the influences and persons who played a significant role in shaping Lata Mangeshkar's musical world, our conversation veers towards C. Ramachandra. The two inspired each other in interesting ways, for, while Lata introduced him to the emotional depths of the Marathi bhava-geet tradition, he mined this special quality of her voice to create some truly memorable tunes for her. In fact, it was often said in those early days that he worked harder to create the songs he wanted her to sing. This is why his name is one of the foremost that comes to mind as we discuss the early years and the foundation that was laid when Lata ji started her film career.

It is an undeniable fact that C. Ramachandra was a genius in composing the genre known as '*virah geet*' (songs of parting and longing). These songs are steeped in a pathos and sadness that twist one's heartstrings. For instance, '*Mujhse Mat Pooch Mere Ishk Main Kya Rakha Hai*' (*Anarkali*, 1953); '*Tum Kya Jano Tumhari Yaad Main Hum Kitna Roye*' (*Shinshinati Bublaboo*, 1952) to '*Darad Jagake Thes Laga Ke Chale Gaye*' (*Sipahiya*, 1958) and the unforgettable, '*Kat-te Hain Dukh Main Din, Pahlu Badal-Badal Ke*' (*Parchhayin*, 1952). How Ramachandra managed to keep the sweetness of her voice inviolate through the pain and underlying sadness without making the song mawkish or maudlin is sheer genius.

To come now to Lata's rendering of these songs, it can be said that just as she had mastered the art of bringing the full flavour of a classical raga into a brief three-minute record, she extracted the deepest emotions of the song perfectly. C. Ramachandra's knowledge and appreciation of the genre of Marathi bhava-geet, folk music and classical ragas was matched by Lata's own understanding of these genres. This is how the two created their own special brand of music.

So, whether it was songs of pain, classical numbers or dance beats, the two together brought magic to each genre. You can hear a classical thumri in '*Na Maro Najariya Ke Baan*' (*Pehli Jhalak*, 1954), a joyous folk song '*Kanha Bajaye Bansuri aur Gwale Bajayein Manjeere*' (*Nastik*, 1954) or '*Radha Na Bole Na Bole Na Bole Re*' (*Azad*, 1955). YouTube will provide listeners with scores of such soulful numbers by tapping their names.

Chedd gayo mohe sapne mein shyam
Ho nindiyaa khuli to main akeli thi ram

Chor salona aaya sapne me chori-chori
Dheere Dheere aa ke haye pakdi kalaiyaan mori
Dar-dar pucha maine chor ka naam
Nindiyaan khuli to main akeli thi ram . . .

Interestingly, despite the fact that they were composed decades ago, these songs catch the attention of even those contemporary listeners who rock to different beats. Music such as this can truly be called timeless and universal.

31

I once asked her, 'Didi, what is the scale you sing in?'

'Yatindra ji,' she laughed, 'even Burman dada, Madan Bhaiyya and Naushad saab never asked me this question! However, now that you ask I'll say that in the early days I used to practise my scales using the first black key. Where film music is concerned, I usually preferred the fourth white key. In the western scales, this would be "F", the third white would be "E" and the black two would be "D" sharp. Most of my songs in the upper scales (such as, "*Aji, Roothkar Ab Kahan Jaiyega*" film *Arzoo* by Shankar-Jaikishan) are in black two.'

Readers may not be aware that most duets between a male and female singer are set in a higher scale so that they can sing together. Generally, no matter how sharp a female voice, it can sound screechy in the upper registers while matching a male voice. This never troubled Lata ji because of the extraordinary range of her voice: she can soar effortlessly to any pitch and often leaves the male voice far behind her in duets. She can happily traverse three octaves in a single three-minute song without her voice showing any sign of strain. It is difficult to say whether this is a divine gift or the result of her rigorous training and discipline.

This analysis is done keeping a harmonium or piano in mind because these were the most popular instruments used while composing and accompanying a singer in the film industry. When one adds to this incredible ability her mastery over the fine *taans* and *murkis* demanded of her while rendering classical numbers, one is left wondering why she regrets that she did not practise enough to become a full-blown classical musician. One can think of few classical singers who could match Lata ji's scale and mastery over notes.

32

She rates Shailendra among her favourite lyricists, although in a career spanning decades and hundreds of films, she has known a large number of outstanding poets and writers. However, in the galaxy of poets who wrote in Hindi, Shailendra, Pandit Narendra Sharma, Neeraj and Rajendra Krishna are the ones whose works Lata ji has most enjoyed when singing.

While talking about Shailendra, we discuss how not just the fine quality of his work but also how the emotions he expressed occasionally disturbed her deeply. She names 'Aaja Re, Pardesi, Main To Kabse Khari Is Paar' from *Madhumati* to tell me how he managed to plant such deep meaning into seemingly simple lines. 'Just reflect on "*Main nadiya phir bhi main pyasi, bhed yeh gehra baat zara-si . . .*" from the same song,' she tells me, 'and you will understand why I consider him one of the finest poets of his time. This is why I enjoyed singing what he wrote because he drew me into the deepest recesses of life. I found this strangely soothing and satisfying.'

I wonder how many singers reflect so deeply on the lyrics they are given to sing. I have also noticed that when we discuss an individual song, she invariably likes to dwell on the poet and the poetry of the lines. She is also appreciative of the vocabulary of poets, for instance, her admiration for Pandit Narendra Sharma is largely due to the pure Hindi that he chose when writing lyrics. How many, she wondered aloud once, had his command over the Hindi language? This came from her as we were discussing his morning song, '*Tum Asha Vishwas Hamare Rama* ('*Gagan Sadan Tejomaya*' *Umbartha: Marathi*)' and the significance of the words of '*Satyam, Shivam, Sundaram*'.

She applies the same measure as she assesses the Urdu poets of those times: Behzad Lakhnavi, Arzoo Lakhnavi, Jan Nissar Akhtar. Her favourite contemporary Urdu poet is Gulzar and she derives deep pleasure from each lyric he has written for her songs: whether '*Surmai Sham Is Tarah Aye*' (*Lekin*) or '*Tujh-Se Naraz Nahin Zindagi, Hairan Hoon Mai*' (*Masoom*). Suddenly she is reminded of Jan Nissar Akhtar's '*Ab Voh Ratain Kahan, Ab Voh Batein Khana*' from *Yasmin* (1955), with C. Ramachandra's music.

She has so many memories to share that if you mention Naushad saab, she will also remember something by Shakeel Badauni that is related to those memories. Shailendra and Hasrat Jaipuri were her special friends and the three of them gave some memorable songs to R.K. Films. Apart from these, there are some poets who are not connected with cinema but whose works have been a delight to sing, such as Raghuvir Sahay and Padma Sachdev. Her first concern is to understand the words of a lyrical composition and often, she has internalized these words so deeply that they have become a part of her emotional universe.

33

sapanaa ban saajan aaye
ham dekh dekh musakaaye
ye nainaa bhar aaye, sharamaaye
sapanaa ban saajan aaye

bichh gaye baadal bankar sagar
indradhanushh pe hamne jaakar
jhuule Kuub jhulaaye
ye nainaa bhar aaye, sharamaaye
sapanaa ban saajan aaye

neel gagan ke sundar taare
chun liye phuul samajh ati nyaare
jholii mein bhar laaye
ye nainaa bhar aaye, sharamaaye
sapanaa ban saajan aaye

mast pavan thii, ham the akele
hil-milkar barakhaa sang khele
phuule nahin samaaye
ham phuule nahin samaaye
ye nainaa bhar aaye, sharamaaye
sapanaa ban saajan aaye

In *Shokhiyan* (1951), Jamal Sen created an exquisite number ('*Sapna Ban Sajan Aye*') that not many know or remember. The lovely lyrics of the song were written by Kedar Sharma for a song to be picturized on the co-star but the heroine of the film was the famous Suraiyya. Jamal Sen has composed the song in

Raga Yaman and of all the raga-based songs that Lata ji has sung for a host of composers, this stands out in my mind as her best. Jamal Sen seems to have outstripped all those famous music composers who are remembered today as the industry's finest.

Jamal Sen belonged to a family that traced its lineage to an ancestor, Kesari Sen, who was Tansen's student. His father, Jiwan Sen, was the court musician at several royal durbars. Jiwan Sen used to compose music for the Parsi Theatre and perhaps, after being exposed to this wide range of experiences, his talent rested on a solid foundation. Jamal Sen was also an accomplished tabla, dholak and pakhawaj player. He had also worked with Master Ghulam Husain in Lahore and played the dholak and table for the film *Khazanchi*, famous for its music.

All this is visible in the song I have referred to above. The delightfully musical prelude accompanied by the soft beats of a pakhawaj is followed by the tinkling of *manjiras* (brass bells) creating an effect that has the listener instantly enrapt. And then Lata ji weaves her magic with some exquisite taans—which, I feel, are among her finest—that seem to describe the beauty of the heroine. The recurrent lines ('*Yeh nain bhar aye, sharmaye*') are rendered so softly and tenderly that they reverberate in one's head for a long time.

With this one song, Jamal Sen has created a space for himself in the long list of Lata-gems. It is for this reason that he needs to be remembered because while we often talk of Lata ji's Naushad or C. Ramachandra compositions, we must also salute those single numbers she sang for lesser-known composers for they are as important in understanding the range of her voice. There are countless other composers whom one must also remember here: Bhola Shreshta (*Bhola Shankar*, 1951); P. Govindram (*Jalpari*, 1952); Shardul Kwatra

(*Pilpili Sahib*, 1954); Amarnath (*Garam Kot*, 1955); Shivram (*Shrawan Kumar*, 1960); Avinash Vyas (*Kailashpati*, 1962); Dilip Dholakia (*Private Secretary*, 1962); Ramlal (*Sehra*, 1963); Vedpal Verma (*Bhootnath*, 1963); V. Balsara (*Vidyapati*, 1964); Ram Kadam (*Pinjra*, 1973); Shambu Sen (*Mrigtrishna*, 1975) and Govind-Naresh (*Meera–Shyam*, 1976).

34

There are some songs where one feels that quite apart from the narrative of the film and the quality of music, they are the field on which Lata Mangeshkar tests her voice, a place where she allows her vocal chords to freely soar, quiver or emote. Just as the frescoes of deities in a temple are embellished by painters with creepers and flowers around them, she embellishes her songs with certain touches that make them even more beautiful. Let me leave the reader with a few songs in this category that come to mind: '*Jogiya Se Preet Kiye, Dukh Hoye*' (*Garam Kot*); '*Tum Kya Jaano Tumhari Yaad Main Hum Kitna Roye*' ((*Shin Shinaki Boobla Boo*); '*Jo Main Janti Bisrat Hain Saiyan*' (*Shabab*); '*Taqdeer Ki Gardish Kya Kam Thi*' (*Sitara*); *Na Milta Gham To Barbaadi Ke Afsane Kahan Jaate*' (*Amar*); '*Tum Na Jaane Kis Jahan Main Kho Gaye*' (*Saza*); '*Tarap-Tarap Ke Kati Umr Ashiyane Main*' (*Do phool*); '*Mayi Ri, Main Ka Se Kahoon Pir Apne Jiya Ki*' (*Dastak*) . . . The list is endless.

35

It is often said that Shankar–Jaikishan used Raga Bhairavi in almost every great tune they composed for films. In fact,

they used to call it 'sada suhagan', or one that never loses
its lustre. Their partners were the lyricists Shailendra and
Hasrat Jaipuri and singers like Lata ji, Mohd Rafi, Mukesh
and Manna De. Dattaram was their favoured percussionist,
who left a 'Dattaram theka' (beat) for others to follow in
film music. So behind the magic of Shankar–Jaikishan was a
whole team of like-minded artistes. Lata ji herself admits that
she was really made to work hard by them in her early years
but also concedes that their appreciation of music, rhythm,
poetry and emotional depths were lessons that always stood
her in good stead.

It was precisely their attention to the details of music
composition that gave them the ability to extract the best
from all the singers and instrumentalists they worked with.
Just a cursory glance through some of the songs that Lata ji
sang for them will make this clear: 'Yeh Sham Ki Tanhaiyan'
(*Aah*, 1953), 'Sham Gayi, Raat Aayi Ki Balam Aa Ja' (*Shree
420*, 1955), 'Main Piya Teri Tu Maane Ya Na Maane' (*Basant
Bahar*, 1956), 'Us Paar Saajan, Is Paar Dhaare', 'Rasik Balma
Haye, Dil Kyun Lagaya Tose' (*Chori Chori*, 1956), 'Mere Sapne
Main Aana Re Sajna' (*Rajhat*, 1956), 'O More Sanware Salone
Piya' (*Kanhaiya*, 1959), 'Jiya Ho Jiya Ho Jiya Kuch Bol Do' (*Jab
Pyar Kisi Se Hota Hai*, 1961), 'Ehsaan Tera Hoga Mujh Par'
(*Jungli*, 1961), 'Tera Mera Pyaar Amar' (*Asli Nakli*, 1962), 'Ye
Hariyali Aur Ye Rasta' (*Hariyali Aur Rasta*, 1962), 'Hum Tere
Pyar Mein Sara Aalam Kho Baithe Hain' (*Dil Ek Mandir*, 1963),
'Unki Pehli Nazar Kya Asar Kar Gay' (*April Fool*, 1964), Main
kamsin Hoon, Nadaan Hoon, Naajuk Hoon' (*Aayi Milan Ki
Bela*, 1964), 'Aa Ja Aayi Bahaar Dil Hai Beqaraar' (*Rajkumar*,
1964) *up to* 'Aji Rooth Kar Ab Kahan Jaiyega' (*Aarzoo*, 1965),
'Mujhe Tum Mil Gaye Humdum' (*Love in Tokyo*, 1966), 'Aa,

Aa Bhi Ja Raat Dhalne Lagi' (*Teesri Kasam*, 1966) . . .the list is endless and dizzying.

It is worth pointing out that the duo worked extra hard to extract something special from her in each song they composed for her. Conversely, it was as if she herself was eager to give something more to their compositions and took each difficult song as a challenge and justified their faith in her. Just think of '*Meri Jaan Meri Jaan Pyar Kisi Se Ho Hi Gaya Hai*' (*Yahudi*, 1958), '*Jaao-Jaao Nand Ke Lala Tum Jhuthe*' (*Rangoli*, 1962), '*Neel Gagan Ki Chhaav Mein Din Rain Gale Se Milte Hain*' (*Aamrapali*, 1966), '*O Basanti, Pawan Paagal, Na Ja Re Na Ja*' (*Jis Desh Main Ganga Behti Hai*, 1960), '*Iss Duniya Mein Jeena Ho To Sun Lo Meri Baat*' (*Gumnaam*, 1965), '*Tera Jana Dil Ke Armaano Ja Lut Jana*' (*Anaadi*, 1959), '*Tera Teer Oo Bepeer Dil Ke Aar Paar Hai*' (*Shararat*, 1959), '*Baagad Bam-Bam, Bam-Bam Baaje Damroo*' (*Kathputli*, 1957), '*Oo Mere Shaahe Khubaan, Oo Meri Jaane Janana*' (*Love In Tokyo*, 1966), '*Sabhi Kuch Hai Tujhmein Magar Ye Kami Hai*' (*Pyaar Muhabbat*, 1966), '*Oo Mora Nadaan Baalma, Na Jaane Dil Ki Baat*' (*Ujala*, 1959) *or* '*Sajan Sang Kahe Neha Lagaye*' (*Main Nashe Main Hoon*, 1959), *or the lilting* '*Murli Bairan Bhayi, Ho Kanhaiya Tori Murli*' (*Nayi Dilli*, 1956) as a few examples of this unique relationship to understand what I am trying to get at.

Each one of these has something that they were convinced only Lata could give their song, whether it was a touch of Arabian music, a classical raga or the incredibly high pitch. In the fifties and sixties, there was just no one who could give voice to such a wide variety of styles and demands. This is why one has to concede that Lata ji's success in these two decades under the S-J banner installed her as the undisputed queen of melody for the rest of the century. From *Barsaat* (1949) to *Sangam* (1964), she produced one hit song after another for this talented duo and made them the most sought-after composers of their time.

sham gayi raat aayi ki balam aa ja
taro ki barat aayi ki balam aa ja
oo balam aa ja, ab to sanam aa ja
raat din ke milan ki ghadi me
thandi-thandi sawan ki jhadi me
do dilo ne jo bandhe the bandhan
unme khoyi khadi main, khadi main
yaad mulakat aayi ki balam aa ja . . .

The evening is merging into nightfall
Ushering in a star-lit sky.
Come to me now, beloved, as they merge into one.
At this magical time when cool Spring showers refresh lost souls,
Come to remember the ties that bind our hearts together.
I stand lost in my memories and yearn to be with you . . .

36

As her listeners listened to the popular songs she sang for the film world, they were quietly introduced to some of the greatest classical musicians of that time. In, *Jhanak-Jhanak Payal Baje'*, the famed table player of Banaras, Samta Prasad (popularly called 'Gudai maharaj') played the tabla and the dafli. Similarly, Pandit Hariprasad Chaurasia, Pandit Shivkumar Sharma, Ustad Bismillah Khan, Ustad Ahmad Jan Thirakwa and Ustad

Allarakha Sahib have all accompanied her at some point or another. She kept her ear cocked for any fresh talent she could spot and recommended the person to her music composers. Several players of the violin, mandolin, guitar, clarinet, piano, trumpet, cello, vibraphone, accordion and viola owe their breaks into film orchestras to her. Naturally, they stand behind her like loyal troops flanking a beloved general and give their best whenever they have accompanied her.

Just as she blended her voice perfectly with the orchestra behind her, she was able to transmit the earthiness of a rustic folk tune as competently as a complicated classical raga for two different composers with ease.

Naushad once penned a poem in praise of her, where he dubs her 'the voice of Hindustan':

Rahon main tere naghme, mehfil main sada teri,
Karti hai sabhi duniya, taarif Lata teri;
Dewane teri fun ke insaan to phir insaan hain,
Hud yeh hai ke sunta hai awaz Khuda teri;
Tujhe naghmon ki jan ahle-nazar yoon hi nahin kehte,
Tere geeton ko dil ka humsafar yoon hi nahin kehte;
Suni sabne muhabbat ki zaban awaz main teri,
Dharakta hai dil-e-Hindostan awaz main teri.

(Your voice is heard in every street and music assembly. The world praises your music and your voice. Forget mere mortals, for it is said that even He listens to you enraptured. Not for nothing are you called the Queen of melody and the heartbeat of our lives. Each one of us has heard your songs of love, and every heart in India throbs with your songs.)

37

One of the great verses of Mirabai, a famous bhakti poet of medieval times, goes like this:

Maaee mhaaro supanaa maa paraneya re dinanaath
Chhappan kotaan janaa padhaaraya dulho shree brijanaath
Supana ma toran bandhyaree supanaa maa gahaya haath
Supanaa maa mhaare paran gaya paaya achal suhaag
Meera ro giridhar milyaree, purav janam ro bhaag . . .

(Mai, I was married in a dream to Dinanth. Sri Brijnath was present there among sixty-five thousand other suitors. I put my hand in his in that dream, Ma, and married him. I consider this sacred ceremony my surrender to His protection and love forever.)

Whenever the music of Lata Mangeshkar is assessed, her uncanny resemblance to that devout singer, Mirabai, is frequently invoked. Several classical musicians—among them Subbulakshmi and Kumar Gandharva—have tried to bring forth the metaphysical nature of Mira's love for Krishna, yet it is Lata Mangeshkar who was able to actually enter the spirit of the verses she sang and become a Mirabai herself. Her effortless blending of earthly desires and metaphysical love become significant if we understand her devotion to her Muse.

In the haunting bhajan above, Mirabai dreams that she has married her divine lover. Keeping intact the immaculate and pure love depicted in Mirabai's verse, Lata ji is able to transport the listener to the country that Mirabai longs to go to with her dream lover '*vahi des*'. This, in fact, is the title of the special disc of Mira bhajans (*Chala vahi des*) that she chose with the help of scholars such as Pandit Narendra Sharma. To date, she regards it, along with millions of her fans, as her finest collection. The music, complicated and intense, was scored by her brother Hridaynath whom she considers one of the most exacting and learned composers.

In creating this collection, it was the constant effort of the Mangeshkar siblings to give a contemporary appeal to these ageless bhajans without disturbing their innate spirituality. Having perfected the art of entering another mind when she sang playback numbers for accomplished actresses such as Meena Kumari, Nargis and Waheeda Rehman, no one other than Lata ji truly understood the levels that she had to pierce to reach that synchronicity required of her when presenting the emotions of this great poet-Queen after centuries with such fidelity.

> *sakhi ri laaj bairan bhyi*
> *shri laal gopal ke sang kahe naahi gayi*
> *chalan chahat gokul hi te rath sajayo nayi*
> *rath chadhaye gopaal layi gayo haath mijat rahi . . .*

38

Lata Mangeshkar and S.D. Burman gave us some songs that are difficult to describe and capture in words. Both these people had a talent for blending melody with sweetness and their combination became a byword in creative brilliance. Not all these were film songs but each flowered slowly under the expert direction of a maestro and the delivery of a genius.

Folk music has been a popular tradition among our music composers and some of the songs they created in the fifties and sixties are early examples of this genre. From those of the fifties and sixties, such as '*Oo Le Ke Jiya Piya Kahan Jaoge*' (*Madbhare Nain*, 1955), '*Jani Tum To Dole Daga dayi Ke*' (*Dr. Vidhya*, 1962), '*Ye Tanhayi Haye Re Haye*' (*Tere Ghar Ke Saamne*, 1963), '*Tere Khayalo Mein Tere hi Khwabon Mein*' (*Meri Soorat Teri Aankhein*, 1963) '*Kaise Kahoon Tose Jiya Ki Main Batiyan*' (*Kaise Kahoon*, 1964), '*Husn Ki Bahaarein Liye Aaye The Sanam*' (*Benzeer*, 1964), '*Kitni Akeli Kitni Tanha Si Lagi*', '*Khayi Hai Re Hamne Kasam Sang Rehne Ki*' (*Talaash*, 1969), to the seventies with songs such as '*Mera Antar Ek Mandir Hai Tera*', '*Jaise Radha Ne Mala Japi Shyam Ki*' (*Tere Mere Sapne*, 1971), '*Sandhya Jo Aaye Man Udd Jaye*' (*Phagun*, 1973) and '*Ye Jab Se Huyi Jiya Ki Chori*' (*Uss Paar*, 1974), we can trace a definite progression. So, it was not just Anil Biswas, C. Ramachandra and Madan Mohan who extracted the sweetness of Lata's voice as Burman dada's role is also not inconsiderable in her musical career.

Her soft enunciation of words, her effortless liquid notes – all these were brilliantly harnessed by S.D. Burman. Like the other composers mentioned above, he recognized that Lata was able to match his composition perfectly with her voice. Her delicate rendering of the sophisticated tunes Burman dada set was offset by her picking out the tender notes with unmatched purity. This latter quality, which was Dada's signature gift to film music, was also mined by Anil Biswas, Ramachandra, Roshan and Madan Mohan in other numbers. Her fans can find such gems on YouTube, to hear for themselves how faithfully Lata manages to bring out the individuality of each composer while still stamping the song with her own genius.

Just listen to a gem, '*Kitni Akeli Kitni Tanha Lagi Unse Mil Ke Main Aaj*', and you will understand how the words, music and voice are all yoked together in perfect harmony.

39

Viswas Nerurkar once declared that Madan Mohan's famous style was acknowledged after he composed some unusual songs for Adalat in 1958. This is when his genius in composing ghazals was accepted as his unique signature. For a long time after the success of these songs, every film director wanted to include at least one ghazal in his film. Another critic, Raju Bharatan says that it was when Madan Mohan encountered Talat Mehmood in Lucknow, when both of them worked in its AIR station, that he began to see the great possibilities of this genre. Thus far, the ghazal had been the preserve of the 'Lahore' musicians: Ghulam Haider, Pandit Amarnath, Husnlal–Bhagatram et al. It was Madan Mohan who, for the first time, released the ghazal from this 'Punjabi' stranglehold and gave it a depth and gravity that was most pleasing and artistically superior.

One must keep in mind both these observations while assessing the role Madan Mohan played in Lata Mangeshkar's musical journey. Equally, one cannot overlook the enormous influence of Begum Akhtar's ghazal-singing on Madan Mohan. He was a minute observer of the Begum's style and it was rumoured that he composed his ghazal only after Begum Akhtar had heard it and incorporated any changes she suggested. This exceptional friendship between the two most talented devotees of the ghazal naturally produced the best examples that we have of this genre in Hindi films. He may have isolated himself from mainstream film music because of his obsessive preoccupation with the ghazal but anyone who hears Madan Mohan's music will agree that it was a magnificent obsession.

Madan Mohan's work can be divided into two neat segments: his ghazals and the rest. It can be said that had he not been supported by Talat Mehmood and Lata Mangeshkar he may never have reached the heights he did but this is just an idle academic speculation. Apart from his deep feeling for Urdu poetry was his genius in handling musical interludes, pauses and orchestras, the secret behind his success was his deep knowledge of ragas and the Urdu language. *'Hamare Baad ab Mehfil Mein Afsane Bayaan Honge'* (*Baagi*, 1953), *'Badi Barbadiyaan Lekar Meri Duniya Mein Pyar Aaya'* (*Dhun*, 1953), *'Chal Diya Dil Mera Tod Ke Yun Akela Mujhe Chhodke'* (*Fifty-Fifty*, 1956), *'Na Haso Hum Pe Zamane Ke Hain Tukraaye Huye'* (*Gateway Of India*, 1957), *''Hum Pyar Mein Jalne Walon Ko, Chain Kahan'* (*Jailer*, 1958), *'Yun Hasraton Ke Daagh Muhabbat Main Dho Liye'* and *'Unko Yeh Shikayat Hai Ki Hum Kuchh Nahin Kehte'* (*Adalat*, 1958), *'Hai Isi Mein Oyaar Ki Aabroo Vo Zafaa Karein Mai Wafa Karu'*, *'Aapki Nazron Ne Samjha Pyar Ke Kabil Mujhe'* (*Anpadh*, 1962), *'Wo Jo Milte The Kabhi Humse Deewano Ki Tarah'* (*Akeli Mat Jayioo*, 1963), *'Agar Mujhse Muhabbat Hai Mujhe Sab Apne Gam De Do'* (*Aapki Parchhaiyaan*, 1964), *'Nagma-O-Sher Ki Saugaat Kise Pesh Karu'* (*Gazal*, 1964), *Wo Chup Rahein To Mere Dil Ke Daag Jalte Jain'* (*Jahaanaara*, 1964), *'Na Aasma Na Sitaare Fareb Dete Hain'* (*Neela Aakash*, 1965), *'Na Tum Bewafa Ho Na Hum Bewafa Hain'* (*Ek Kali Muskayi*, 1968),

'*Hum Hain Mataa-E-Kuchaa-O Bazaar Ki Tarah*' (*Dastak*, 1970), '*Rasm-E-Ulfat Ko Nibhayein To Nibhayein Kaise*' (*Dil Ki Rahen*, 1973), '*Aaj Socha To Aansoo Bhar Aaye*' (*Haste Zakham*, 1973), '*Hai Tere Sath Meri Wafa Main Nahi To Kya*' (*Hindustaan Ki Kasam*, 1973) and '*Ruke-Ruke Se Kadam Ruk Ke Baar-Baar Chale*' (*Mausam*, 1973)—these are but a few of the unforgettable ghazals the two have created together.

In a certain sense, every music composer has had a special fondness for a particular kind of voice: Shamshad Begum for Naushad, Mukesh for Shankar-Jaikishan, Asha Bhonsle for O.P. Nayyar and Kishore Kumar for R.D. Burman. Just a cursory glance through the ghazals she has sung for Madan Mohan will convince a listener that for Madan Mohan that singer was Lata Mangeshkar.

However, this fondness extended far beyond the ghazal. Just a quick recap of her other songs for Madan Mohan—'*Saanwari Surat Man Bhayi Re Piya*' (*Ada*, 1951), '*Chain Nahi Aaye Kahaan Dil Jaaye Sajanwa Ho*' (*Samundar*, 1957), '*Mori Payal Geet Sunaaye*' (*Baap-Bete*, 1959), '*Hindolna Jhulan Aayi Balma*' (*Senapati*, 1961), '*Meri Veena Tum Bin Roye*' (*Dekh Kabeera Roya*, 1957), '*Jiya Le Gayo Jee Mora Sawariya*' (*Anpadh*, 1962), '*Badli Se Nikla Chand*' (*Sanjog*, 1961), *Khanak Gayo Hai Bairi Kangana*' (*Rishte Naate*, 1965), '*Lag Ja Gale Ki Phir Ye Haseen Raat Ho Na Ho*' (*Who Kaun Thi*, 1964), '*Teri Aankhon Ke Siva Duniya Mein Rakha Kya Hai*' (*Chirag*, 1969) '*Khelo Na Mere Dil Se O Mere Saajna*' (*Haqeeqat*, 1965) '*Mere Naina Bahayein Neer*' (*Bawarchi*, 1972), '*Betaab Dil Ki Tamanna Yahi Hai*' (*Haste Zakham*, 1973)—will illustrate that it was the quality of wistfulness and longing that he mined out of her in each composition.

40

Few people understand the arduous process that lies behind each film song before it is released. For instance, a poet's lyrics are set to a suitable metre for a song by someone else; someone then composes a tune and someone else sings it. Again, there are simply scores of people who play the accompanying music in the background and their choice and orchestration is given to an 'arranger' while the direction of the orchestra is handled by yet another person. Then there is the technical part which is the responsibility of the sound recordist and technicians. Behind one song, therefore, is a galaxy of ghost presences that we can neither see nor sufficiently appreciate.

It is in this sense that Indian film music is a unique phenomenon. Moreover, even while composing, a composer may choose to set it within a classical raga or a folk tune, specific to a particular region with its own tradition. Then there is the influence of western music—sometimes lifted whole, sometimes as a musical device—that gives rise to a whole new range of problems and adjustments. Those familiar with classical music will understand that ragas are never bound by fixed notations: a raga sung by one singer may be different the next time he presents the same raga on another occasion. Film music, on the other hand, once recorded, is fixed even if it is inspired by a raga.

Take, for example, Lata Mangeshkar's beautifully rendered Bhoopali in 'Jyoti Kalash Chhalke' (Bhabhi Ki Churiyan). No matter how often you hear it, it will sound the same whereas a Bhoopali sung by a classical musician will change each time it is rendered. This is where even the classical numbers among film songs differ radically from their more orthodox practitioners.

Listen to Bhoopali by Ustad Alladiya Khan: it is so different from the same raga sung by Pandit Krishnarao Shankar Pandit and both are very different from Lata ji's *Jyoti Kalash Chhalke*. Lata ji has sung the same raga in *Chori-Chori* (1956) as a joyous number (*'Punchhi Banoo Urti Phiroon Mast Gagan Main'*) and in *Rudaali* (1993) (*'Dil Hoom-Hoom Kare'*). This quality is what provides Indian film music with such a wide range of possibilities.

41

Shailendra wrote an immortal song of longing and love, *'Aja Re Pardesi, Main To Kabse Khari Is Paar'* for *Madhumati* in 1958, which Salil Chaudhuri set to divine music for the film. What makes the song historic is the fact that this was the first time that a Filmfare Award was given to a singer: and that person was Lata Mangeshkar. Many fans say that the song marks the apogee of film music and Salil Chaudhuri's brilliant orchestration of the piano, violin, mandolin, flute and many other musical instruments as well as his deft weaving of musical interludes, make it a standalone composition.

Salil Chaudhuri has said somewhere when he started composing this number he made the seventh chord the base note and was unable to get the effect he wanted. Lata Mangeshkar then made a suggestion, although she is scrupulous about keeping her suggestions to herself and does not like to interfere with a music director's instructions. She asked Salil da to try using the fifth note (*pancham*) for she felt that it would provide the liquid note he was looking for. Lata ji and Salil Chaudhuri shared a mutual respect for each other that comes alive if one listens to the mellifluous songs that came out of this partnership: '*Oo Sajna Barkha Bahar Aayi*', '*Barkha Bahaar Aayi*' (*Parakh*, 1960), '*Neend Pari Lori Gaaye*' (*Chardiwari*, 1961), '*Ja Re Ja Re Ud Ja Re Punchhi*' (*Maya*, 1961), '*Machalti arzoo Khadi Baahein Pasare*' (*Usne kaha tha*, 1960), '*Jaagiye Gopal lal Banshi*' (*Jawahar*, 1960), '*Manzil Teri Khoj mein*' (*Pinjare Ke Panchhi*), '*Teri Yaad Na Dil Se Ja Saki*' (*Chaand Aur Soorat*, 1965), '*Sathi Re Tujh Bin Jiya Udaas Re*' (*Poonam Ki Raat*, 1965), '*Pyaas Liye Manwa Hamara Ye Tarse*' (*Mere Bhaiya*, 1972), '*Na Jane Kyu Hota Hai Ye Zindgi Ke Sath*' (*Chhoti Si Baat*, 1975), '*Rajnigandha Phool Tumhare*' (*Rajnigandha*, 1974), '*Roj Akeli Aaye Roj Akeli Jaaye*' (*Mere Apne*, 1971), and '*Raaton Ke Saaye Ghane*' (*Annadata*, 1972) to name just a few.

42

The amusing fact about her is that when you ask her to list what she likes and dislikes, the 'like' list gets longer and longer while the 'dislike' one stays ridiculously small. Whether listing her favourite songs, possessions or whatever, she takes you round on a tour of the country and gets carried away by her memories. She loves *jalebis* (but they must be crisp and dipped in a saffron-infused syrup); *gulab jamuns* from Indore, Goan fish curry, prawns—all these are her favourite foods. It is an interesting discovery for me that she is an efficient homemaker as well. She makes delicious *sooji ka halwa* and her chicken curry is famous among her close friends. She loves *samosas*, not stuffed with the usual potato or peas but keema-filled ones.

In the early days, she tells me, she often went to 'Gaylord's' in Marine Drive for lunch, which was also Jaikishan's favourite restaurant. The two of them went there to unwind after a long or tiring recording session at R.K. Films. She loves really hot and spicy food, especially the Kolhapur style dishes. She also relishes *pani-puris* and tart mango pickle and limes. Among sweets, *shahi tukra* is her preferred dessert and her thali often includes a *jowar-roti*. She likes Mexican, Chinese and French food but is not particularly fond of Italian cuisine. The great revelation to me is that she hates vegetables and only eats them because her doctor has prescribed them as a necessary part of her diet! So she suffers them.

I like seeing this side of her and I feel that if you stop seeing her only as an iconic singer you will find her no different from a beloved aunt-like figure. 'You tell me, Yatindra ji,' she says, 'I am an ordinary person like any other woman. I can't only be a singer all the time, just as I can't sing all the time. If I have a headache, I like a good oil massage . . .and often when I am bored I long to go out and roam the streets of Bombay like an ordinary person.'

We have had many such intimate conversations in the course of the ten years when I visited her regularly to research this book. On condition of respecting her privacy, she has shared some aspects of her deep friendship with Rajsingh Dungarpur and her close friend in Canada. Nowadays she is looked after her loving family of siblings and nieces and nephews. She regards her secretary, Mahesh Rathore, almost like a brother.

Despite this circle of love and the enormous love and adulation of her fans, she is often lonely. Ironically, her voice that has brought peace and succour to so many hearts is itself wrapped in the loneliness of someone who has remained single for some reason or another. When she is feeling low, she advises me to leave my research aside by gently telling me, 'I am not feeling so good today.' I know then that I have nothing to offer her by way of a consolation.

43

Naushad once created a song for Mehboob Khan which goes, '*Duniya main hum aye hain to jeena hi padega, jeevan hai agar zahar to peena hi padega*'. (If we have taken birth in this world, then we have no option but to live and if life serves us poison, we have no option but to drink it). This song from *Mother India* (1957) became a symbol of the indomitable will of the protagonist Nargis, the archetypal Indian mother who battles every setback to survive. The song (which also has Lata ji's sister Meena's voice) is an example of how adept Naushad was at sensing the mood underneath a situation and harmonizing his music to the mood of the situation on screen. Similarly, Naushad's number '*Na Milta Gham To Barbadi Ke Afsane Kahan Jaate*' (*Amar*), is another example of how beautifully music can plumb the depths of a poetic thought.

Naushad created some unforgettable songs with Lata and Mohd Rafi. From *Andaz* (1949), *Aan* (1952), *Amar* (1954) to *Mother India* (1957), the combination of Mehboob Khan, Naushad and these two singers brought the screen alive with thrilling songs. Behind the melodic aspect lay the larger political and social background that came to haunt audiences with their message. Creating socially relevant films was an important part of Mehboob Khan's creative style and he found a sympathetic partner in Naushad. This is why in film after film, he preferred to trust Naushad rather than, say, Salil Chaudhuri or Anil

Biswas (two other talented musicians of the time) with his musical scores.

The music of *Andaz* ('*Uthaye Ja Unke Sitam*'), *Amar* ('*Khamosh Hai Khevanhaar Mera*'), *Aan* ('*Tujhe Kho Diya Humne Pane Ke Baad*') was but a prelude to the grand symphony of *Mother India*. '*Nagari-Nagari, Dware-Dware, Dhundhoon Re Sanwariya*' is so germane to the story of the film that it seems impossible we would have fully understood the pain of Nargis's fruitless search for her missing husband without its presence. It is a tribute to Naushad's genius that he made no compromise with the musical aspect of his songs when weaving in the message of social awareness. On the other hand, he uses certain folk tunes that have embedded in them centuries of memories of human emotions. In this, Lata's mellifluous and sweet voice rose to the occasion each time as she translated each emotion and feeling he wished to highlight with her splendid rendering. To make this point clearer, it is useful to speculate whether a Shamshad Begum or a Suraiyya could have brought the same degree of pathos and emotional intensity as Lata has invested in the songs of *Mother India*.

In discussing Lata ji's contribution to the music of Naushad it is also relevant to point out that just as she brought out with great sensitivity the pathos of the above songs, she matches the joy and abandon of those folk tunes that he composed for her elsewhere. In *Aan* ('*Aaj Mere Man Main Sakhi Bansuri Bajaye Koi*'); *Amar* ('*Ummidon Ko Sakhi Pi Ki Nagariya Kaise Le Jaaon*') *and Mother India* ('*Matwala Jiya Dole Piya, Jhume Ghata Chhaye Re Badal*') are some examples that illustrate this aspect of their musical relationship. In fact, some of the most mellifluous songs created by this pair are those where Naushad borrowed generously from the rich tradition of his native Awadh's kajri, dadra, thumri and other semi-classical musical forms. A few examples are: 'More Saiyan Ji Utarenge Paar, Nadiya Dheera Baho' (Udankhatola); 'Jogan Ban Jaaongi Saiyan Tore Karan' (Shabab); 'Tumhare Sang Main Bhi Chaloongi Piya Jaise Patang Sang Dor' (Sohni-Mahiwal); 'Mohe Panghat Pe Nandlal Chher Gayo Re' (Mughal-e-Azam); 'Tere Pyar Main Dildaar Jo Hai Mera Haal-E-Zaar' (Mere Mehboob) and 'Dhundo-Dhundo Re Sajna, Dhundo Re Sajna Mere Kaan Ka Bala' (Ganga-Jamuna).

We have not yet discussed the famous ghazal of Awadh, a genre of exquisite grace and sophistication, because the credit for that belongs to Madan Mohan rather than Naushad but it is important to point out that it was said of Naushad that he never made one singer the central pole of his musical axis. He managed to find place for a whole range of voices from Shamshad Begum, Talat Mehmood, Uma Devi to Suraiyya and Lata Mangeshkar. However, the only two voices he chose for almost all his duets belonged to Mohd Rafi and Lata Mangeshkar. This says a lot for his perception and their talent.

In conclusion, all that I can say is that in recalling the partnership of Lata ji and Naushad I have revisited almost all the songs that I consider the finest in the realm of Indian film music. Whether a devotional bhajan, folk song, dance number, qawwali, *naat* (dirge), or *virah-geet* (songs of parting and longing), there are few musicians who could coax the same degree of feeling from Lata ji's voice.

44

If one wishes to savour the best of Lata Mangeshkar's devotional songs, then one must hear her renderings of Marathi abhang verses—such as those composed by Jnaneswar, Tukaram, Bhaskar Ramchandra Tambe, P. Sawalaram. Among these, there are some, for instance, Tukaram's '*Kamodini Kaay Jaane*'; '*Agaa Karunaakar*'; '*Sundar Te Dhyan*' (music by Sriniwas Khale); Sant Jnaneswar's '*Mogra Phulala*'; '*Runjhunu Runjhunu Re Bhamara*' and '*Are-Are Jnana*' (music by Hridaynath Mangeshkar) and P. Sawalaram's '*Ganga–Jamuna Dolyaat Ubhaya Ka*' (music by Vasant Prabhu). In each of these, she appears to have transcended to another plane that is far, far away from this earth.

To make this clearer, let me quote Harish Bhimani who describes this experience beautifully:

'*Runjhunu Runjhunu Re Bhamara, Sandi Tu Avgunu Re Bhramara*' these are lines written by the beloved Marathi bhakti poet Jnaneswar, where he implores the bee to give up its eternal love-song. The music provided for this number by Hridaynath was unbelievably sweet and brought to mind the sound of the clear, sparkling water that gurgles out of the Gangotri glacier to become the mighty Ganga. So soothing and sweet was it that one wanted to hear it forever. The meaning of the words was not always clear because of our limited knowledge of the Marathi language but that was no barrier to savouring its innate spirit that is, in a sense, beyond the words of the verses. The term "unparalleled" would not be out of place to describe the experience.'

A deep sense of serenity and purity are essential attributes of the best devotional music, and compositions such as '*Mogra Phulala*' and '*Kamodini Kaay Jaye*' are best expressed in the tradition of Marathi bhava-sangeet that manages to capture and transmit a quality of other-worldliness and majestic divinity. It is interesting to learn that composers Hridaynath Mangeshkar,

Vasant Prabhu and Sriniwas would sit with Lata ji as they'd compose the tunes for these devotional songs. The result is that words meld into the spiritual core of the songs and bring its essence to the listener. As the poet Sitakant Mahapatra describes evocatively, even after Krishna left Vrindavan for Dwarka, the cows would head home at *godhuli* because they could still hear the silent notes of Krishna's magical flute beckoning them. And just as the Sufi singers surrender themselves so completely to the music they sing, Lata ji becomes the singer and the song.

When singing the abhangs of Jnaneswar, Lata Mangeshkar loses herself in the embellishment of the glory of Vitthal. She worships Him with her voice.

In an unforgettable abhang, she sings '*Kamodini kaay jane . . .*' to ask why the lotus does not realize that it was born to be offered to the glory of the Lord. It is not a mere coincidence that we can see the similarity this has with Lata ji's devotional songs and why she was able to evoke that special dimension of bhakti that moves us still. It is as if she knew that the highest point of her talent was always meant to be the worship of the divine.

45

If you wish to hear Lata ji at her sweetest and most tender, then you need to listen to the songs she sang for Roshan. He was the one composer who preferred to use the classical raga as the base on which to raise the structure of a song. Since she herself enjoyed this quality, it inspired her to give his compositions some of her best renderings.

Roshan was famous for his rigorous training in classical Hindustani music. He was a student of Lucknow's Marris College of Music and then sat the feet of the legendary Baba Alauddin Khan of Maihar. Later, he came into contact with Ustad Bundu Khan and Manohar Barve and polished his knowledge further. From Ustad Alauddin Khan he picked up certain ways in which he could use classical music in film songs and because he had learnt to play the sarangi there, he realized how close its strains were to the human voice. This had a profound effect on the way he used the human voice in his compositions.

This is probably also why he had no peers in composing ghazals and sad songs. Among those he composed for Lata ji, *Malhar* (1951), *Naubahar* and *Rag-rang* (1952), *Taksaal* (1956), *Aji Bas Shukriya* (1958), *Madhu* (1959), *Arti* and *Zindagi aur Hum* (1962), *Tajmahal* (1963), *Chitralekha* (1964), *Mamata* (1966), *Devar* (1966) *Bahu Begum* (1967), *Noor Jehan* (1967) and *Anokhi Raat* (1968) are unforgettable for their music.

Here, I would like to dwell on a little-known song he composed for *Tajmahal* because it is so startlingly true of the present times, where India and Pakistan are concerned. The poet Sahir Ludhianvi may have penned these lines for a film that is set in Mughal India but it also seems to question the world of today, riven with rivalries, conflict and violence. '*Khuda-e-bartar teri zameen par zameen ki khatir yeh jang kyoon*' the opening lines question why brothers fight over the land that belongs to all of God's children. If you can follow its Urdu and its powerful message to all of humanity then you will also realize why Roshan alone had the intellectual and musical sophistication to set it to music. Another song in the same film ('*Jurm-e-Ulfat Pe Hamain Log Saza Dete Hain*') is also worth savouring for its keen insight.

It is this quality of being able to coax out and linger over the meaning of the lyrics that Roshan is best remembered for.

Listen to his songs in *Mamata* ('*Rehte The Kabhi Hum Jinke Dil Main*'), *Bahu Begum* ('*Duniya Kare Sawal To Hum Kya Jawab Dain*'), *Chitralekha* ('*Sansar Se Bhage Phirte Ho, Bhagwan Ko Kya Tum Paoge*') and you cannot but be moved by the majestic gravity of their music and lyrics. Roshan had the talent to use classical music to enhance the meaning of a contemporary idea.

> *Khuda-e-bartar teri zameen par Zameen ke khatir yeh jang kyun hai?*
> *Har ek fath-o-jafar ke daaman pe Khoon-e-insaan ka rang kyun hai?*
> *Zameen bhi teri hai hum bhi tere, Yeh milkiyat ka sawaal kya hai?*
> *Yeh katl-o-khoon ka rivaaj kyun hai? Yeh rasm-e-jang-o-jadal kya hai?*
> *Jinhe talab hai jahan bhar ki, Unhi ka dil itna tang kyun hai?*
> *Gareeb maao shareef behno Ko amn-o-ijjat ki zindagi de,*
> *Jinhe ata ki hai tune taakat, Unhe hidayat ki roshni de,*
> *Saron mein kibr-o-guroor kyun hai? Dilon ke sheeshe pe jang kyun hai?*
> *Kaza ke raste pe jaane walon Ko bach ke aane ki raah dena,*
> *Dilon ke gulshan ujjad na jayein, Mohabbaton ko panaah dena,*
> *Jahan mein jashn-e-wafa ke badle, Yeh jashn-e-teer-o-tafang kyun hai?*
> *Khuda-e-bartar teri zameen par zameen ke khatir yeh jang kyun hai ?*

Apart from this, what is also visible in Roshan's music is his love for the practitioners of the Bengal school of music, such as Anil Biswas. This along with his love of the tradition of kirtan-singing and folk tunes gave him a vast reservoir of musical traditions to draw upon. His genius lay in the fact that he could gauge perfectly when the rigour of a classical raga or the playfulness and emotional quality of a folk tune or devotional song should be used. He used Lata ji's voice as he experimented with his favourite musical instruments: the sarangi, dilruba and harmonium.

46

When listening to her I am often reminded of an arrow that pierces one's heart because her voice has a sharp precision that can only be compared with an arrow. And when Lata ji shoots that arrow to hit one's heart, it is as if the emotions locked inside it come spilling out in waves.

Uday Bhawalkar, the talented young vocalist, explained to me what it is about her voice that is so mesmerising. 'A perfect note (*sur*) is the essence of any music and to understand and practise it I listened over and over again to Lata ji's voice to understand how she manages to hit the right note each time, without fail. What emerges from her is a pure, true and *satwik* (other-worldly) sound and one I have not heard in any other singer's voice. What she is able to invest in a three-minute record is the most perfectly balanced and pure music anyone has ever heard. It is undeniable that there are countless vocalists in the classical world of Hindustani music who have taken music to dizzying heights but as a singer I can tell you that the quality that can kill one with sweetness is something I have found only in Lata ji's voice.'

This is high praise from someone who is an acknowledged practitioner of one of the most difficult musical genres (Dhrupad) and a solid endorsement of her greatness as a

singer. Neither is it a condescending certificate from a classical
musician to someone who has always sung for films: it is a
tribute from one singer to another regardless of the fact that
their musical traditions follow different streams. He does not
hesitate to call himself her devoted fan, just as Ustad Bismillah
Khan did before him. In fact Ustad Bismillah Khan once
declared in my presence, 'I can wager that if Saraswati ever
lived she must have been like Lata Mangeshkar. I tell you,
barkhudar, she must have had the same sweetness we hear in
Lata's voice today. Neither could Saraswati have been sweeter
than Lata nor is Lata less sweet than Saraswati must have been.'

After such a compliment, what else is left to add?

47

The time has come now to remember certain numbers that are
different from the popular duets sung by Lata Mangehskar and
Mohd Rafi. Among them are some that never made it to the top of
the hit-lists of radio programmes but they linger on our memory
for their composition, melody or lyrics and deserve mention. Just
as we often miss some small shells, conches and pearls that slide
away unnoticed into the sea, these songs have some extraordinary
facets. If we can create a hit-list of just their duets, these would
have to be included. Here are some examples from that list:

'*O Mahi O, Dupatta Mera De De*' (*Meena Bazar*, 1950,
music by Husnlal Bhagatram)

'*Khamosh Kyun Ho Taro, Ummidon Ke Sahare*' (*Alif-Laila*,
1957, music by Shyam Sundar)

'*Main Tumhi Se Poochti Hoon, Mujhe Tumse Pyar Kyun
Hai*' (*Black Coat*, 1959, music by N. Dutta)

'*Bheegi-Bheegi Palkain Utha Meri Jaan Gham Na Kar*' (*Do Gunde*, 1959, music by Ghulam Muhammad)

'*Piya Kaise Miloon Tujhse Mere Paanv Pari Zanjeer*' (*Saranga*, 1963, music by Sardar Malik)

'*Baar-Baar Tujhe Kya Samjhaye Payal Ki Jhankar*' (*Arti*, 1962 music by Roshan)

'*Tere Bin Sune Nayan Hamare*' (*Meri Surat Teri Aankhain*, 1963, music by S.D. Burman)

'*Bhul jaae sare gam, dub jaae pyar mein*' (*Nausherwan-E-Adil*, 1957, music by C. Ramchandra*).

'*Piya kaise milu tujhse mere paav padi zanjeer*' (*Saaranga*, 1960, music by sardar Malik*).

'*Chale hai kahaan sarakaar Hamein beqaraar kar ke*' (*Nache Nagin Baje Been*, 1960, music by Chitragupta*)

'*Ek baat hai kehne ki Aankhon se kehne do*' (*Samson*, 1964, music by Chitragupta*)

'*Ho nazuk-nazuk badan mora*' (*Aulad*, 1968, music by Chitragupta*)

As one listens to these duets, one is struck at how perfectly they match their voices and modulate their singing to glide smoothly together. It also reminds us that often the finest songs are those that did not become very popular but reach one's heart and stay on.

48

Lata ji's '*Rasik Balma*' from *Chori-Chori* (1956) is still considered by several Lata fans as her best song. Written by Hasrat Jaipuri, it is set in a blend of Shudh Kalyan

and Bhoopali. The opening bars are a plaintive wail of a
sarangi that set the mood for the rest of the composition.
Shankar–Jaikishan used the sitar and sarangi brilliantly in the
background to establish that they had few equals in arranging
the background scores of film songs. Like most of the
popular songs composed by S–J, this song, too, was basically
Jaikishan's composition. However, it would be unfair to give
the entire credit to Jaikishan because without Lata ji's voice
and Hasrat Jaipuri's lyrics, he could not have spun the magic
that is part of the song's eternal appeal.

There is an interesting anecdote about 'Rasik Balma': when
Mehboob Khan was convalescing in Los Angeles after a massive
heart attack, he would regularly call Lata ji to hear her sing this
song. Perhaps the haunting beauty of the number brought him
relief. In any case, there can be no greater proof of the healing
power of music, I think.

Although there are few songs that can be equated with 'Rasik
Balma', Shankar–Jaikishan have created many songs where
they almost challenged Lata ji to sing at a pitch few would
dare to attempt. In time, this almost became a signature of the
songs they composed for her voice. 'Yeh Sham Ki Tanhaiyan,
Aise Main Tera Gham' (Aah); 'Aaj Kal Main Dhal Gaya' (Beti-
Beta); 'Sajan Se Kahe Neha Lagaye' (Main Nashe Main Hoon);
'Ruk Ja Raat Thahar Ja Re Chanda' (Dil Ek Mandir); 'Aji Rooth
Kar Ab Kahan Jayega' (Arzoo) . . . the list is endless.

49

Her perfect enunciation of Hindi, Urdu, Marathi, Sanskrit has
been widely appreciated but here I wish to highlight Lata ji's

handling of those sounds that have no meaning yet how she recreates the sound they instantly bring to mind. For example, how she manages to 'sing' the tinkling of an anklet, the buzzing of a bee and so on. Think of '*Jhan jhan jhan jhan payal baje, kaise jaaon pi se milan ko*'; '*Hanse tim-tim-tim, taron ke deep*'; '*Ghanan ghan ghananananan barkha ki rut ayi*' or '*Hai jhilmil-jhilmil yeh sham ke saye . . .*'.

As an example, savour these lines from a song from *Meri Bhabhi* (1969):

Pavan jhakora sang mere gaye
Ki gungun gungun gungun gungun hawa chale
Ude man bhanwara gagan mein jaye
Ki gungun gungun gungun gungun hawa chale

Majrooh Sultanpuri, that great lyricist and poet, used sound to convey the wafting breeze that comes across so naturally that it makes a strange kind of sense-meaning. To understand this, we will have to absorb the deep meaning of *dhwani* in Indian music, a word that defies its simple English translation as sound. Dhwani refers to the primordial sounds that are part-onomotopoeia and part melody but wonderfully expressive of certain sounds that can only be conveyed though vibration. Lata Mangeshkar's musical repertoire offers us scores of examples: *Jhan jhan jhan jhan payal baje, kaise jaaon pi se milan ko* (*Buzdil*; S.D. Burman; 1951); *Chhun chhun chhun baje payal mori, aa ja chori-chori* (*Hum Log*; Roshan; 1951); *Tiru lilla, tiru lilla, tiru lilla la, gaye lata, gaye lata* (*Daaman*; K Dutta; 1951); *Hansein tim tim tim, chhote chhote tare* (*Sanskar*; Roshan; 1952); *Tandana tandana tandana, mushkil hai pyaar chhupana* (*Mayurpankh*; Shankar-Jaikishan; 1954), *Tara rara rum mere dil main sanam* (*Hooe-e-Arab*; Ghulam

Mohammad; 1955); *Ghanan ghan ghananana barkha ki rut aayi* (*Ekadashi*; Avinash Vyas; 1955); *Rimjhim jhim-jhim badarwa barse* (*Taangawali*; Salil Chaudhary; 1955), *Baghad bum-bum bum-bum baje damroo* (*Kathputli*; Shankar Jaikishan; 1957) *Haye jhilmil-jhilmil ye sham ke saaye* (*Laal Batti*; Salil Chaudhary; 1957), *Chala dildaar vai-vai, le ke mera pyaar vai-vai* (*Duniya na maane*; Madan Mohan; 1959). *Even a light-hearted Mera naam Rita Christina, yayi yayi yayi yayi yaa* (*April Fool*; Shankar-Jaikishan; 1964) will give you an idea of what I wish to highlight.

Apart from bringing a sound alive, these 'hook words' are also used as a device to keep the rhythm in place. If it were not so, these words would appear little more than comical interludes.

50

The mujra is a vital part of the Indian dance and music tradition and appears in some form or the other in several films of the fifties, sixties and seventies. It gave an opportunity to a film director to inject some glamour while highlighting the dancing abilities of an actress. Traditionally, the mujra was performed at the homes of royal families or the feudal lords of Uttar Pradesh to celebrate an important occasion, such as a wedding or birth of an heir. The tradition reached its apogee in the last decades of the nineteenth century and continued in a decimated form till about 1935 or so. One comes across accounts of these performances in the old Imperial Gazettes of the region and in books and novels of that time.

In Hindi films, it was extensively featured from the forties onwards and the costumes were inspired by the style of the

Awadhi nawabi courts. However, from the fairly taut structure of the kathak dance form and the thumri and dadra when presented in a court, the film mujra developed its own style and genre. Thus the mujra, almost always performed by dancing girls and prostitutes in courtly times, was mainly associated with their dissolute lifestyle and reputation.

Perhaps this is a reason why Lata Mangeshkar never felt comfortable with mujra songs and often declined to sing them. This was despite the fact that several such compositions were mostly based on the folk traditions of North India. In the early years of her career, under the direction of such reputed music directors as Anil Biswas, S.D. Burman, Madan Mohan, Shankar–Jaikishan, Naushad, and Ghulam Mohammad, Lata ji has sung such numbers. However, she was always careful to ensure that the lyrics were never vulgar or cheap. In *Devdas* (1955), *Char Dil Char Rahein* (1959), *Sadhana* (1958), *Adalat* (1958), *Mughal-e-Azam* (1960), *Chote Nawab* (1961), *Mamta* (1966), *Benazir* (1964), *Mujhe Jeene Do* (1963), *Sautela Bhai* (1962), *Dulhan ki ek Raat* (1966), *Gunaho ka Devta* (1967), *and Pakeezaah* (1971), we have heard some memorable mujra numbers sung by her, including that perennial favourite: '*Ab aage teri marzi*', '*Intezaar aur abhi… aur abhi*', '*Yahan to har cheez bikti hai kaho ji tum kya kya kharidoge*', '*Unko ye shikayat hai*', '*Mohe panghat pe Nandlal chher gayo re*' '*Chura ke dil ban rahe hain bhole*', '*Jaa main tose naahin bolu*', '*Kabhi aye haqeekat-e-muntasir*', '*Rahte the kabhi jinke dil mein*', '*Chaahe to mora jiya layi le sawariyaa*', '*Baharon ki mehfil Suhani rahegi*', '*Raat bhi hai kuch bheegi-bheegi*', '*Ram kare kahin naina na uljhe*', '*Chalte chalte yun hi koi mil gaya tha*' and Pakeezah's '*Thare rahiyo oo banke yaar*'.

Readers will agree that, rendered by her, these immortal
songs bring to mind the great thumri singers of Banaras and
Awadh, such as Rasoolan Bai, Siddheshwari Devi and Bari
Motibai to endow a gravity and elegance into the composition.

Later, as the mujra became merely a means of cheap
entertainment and titillation, the purity and innocence of the
original style was almost completely erased.

51

She has always declared that she dislikes Holi because she hates
being sprayed with colour and that she always wears white saris,
with coloured borders. However, I notice that her toenails are
painted in bright red.

Oddly, despite her aversion to colour, her voice refuses to
conform to this austerity and the sounds that burst out of her
throat would put a rainbow to shame.

52

Raj Kapoor was deeply involved in the music compositions of
his films. Not only was he knowledgeable, he would not give
his approval until he was satisfied that it matched his exacting
standards. His core team included Shailendra and Hasrat
Jaipuri (lyricists), Shankar–Jaikishan (music directors) and
Lata–Mukesh (singers). He did not like ready-made stuff, that
is, songs that a composer put together with popular devices
picked from a musical kitbag. He dismissed such music as
'popatiya' (parrot-like) and was truly happy with those songs

that S–J had composed at a very high pitch for Lata Mangehskar and Mukesh. He was also very partial to Bhairavi-based compositions, although S–J have used Shivranjini, Bhairav, Kedar, Shudh Kalyan and Bhoopali as well for R.K. Films.

Lata ji has several anecdotes from those times: her soaring voice in 'O Basanti Pawan Pagal' from *Jis Desh Main Ganga Behti Hai* was in R.K.'s eyes a standalone song and the rest ('*Mera Naam Raju Gharana Anaam*'; '*Kya Hua Ye Mujhe Kya Hua*' or '*Begaani Shaadi Main Abdulla Deewana*') were dismissed as '*popatiya*' songs. One can understand why. Lata ji also reveals that one of the reasons why she admired Raj Kapoor's commitment to his work was that he made it a point to be present at every stage of a song's composition: from lyrics, to song rehearsal, to recording. More than anyone else, he realized the critical place given to songs and music in Hindi cinema, a fact incomprehensible to most western film critics. In a Hindi film, music is almost as important—if not more—than the story and acting in it. Recall the significant placement of songs such as *Hawa mein udta jaye mera lal dupatta mulmul ka* (*Barsat*, 1949); *Jaago Mohan Pyare* (*Jagte Raho*, 1956); *Awara hoon ya gardish mein hoon aasman ka tara hoon* (*Awara*, 1951); *Ramayya vastavaiya* (*Shree 420*, 1955); *Raja ki ayegi baarat* (*Aah*, 1953) or *Jeena yahan, marna yahan iske siwa jaaana kahan* (*Mera Naam Joker*, 1970), her observation of Raj Kapoor's musical genius becomes clear.

It is because Raj Kapoor fully appreciated this fact that his films were always a cut above the other films of his time. Sit through any film he made—even the most banal—and its music will never disappoint you even if the story and acting may. One can also see why he considered some songs classy and dismissed some as '*popatiya*'. One day, I would love to ask

Lata ji to place all the contemporary songs she would dismiss as
'*popatiya*' but I know she will never agree to my request.

53

An astonishing fact about Lata ji's voice is that it has never
lost its freshness and youthful sweetness through all the six-odd
decades of her career. Think of her warbling, '*Kashmir ki kali
hoon main, mujhse na rutho babuji*' for a young Saira Bano in
Junglee (1961) and you can almost hear a young girl flirting.
Then, 12 years later, she sings '*Bahon mein chale aao*' for Jaya
Bhaduri in *Anamika* and her voice is as fresh and lovely as ever.
One can quote hundreds of examples to elaborate this point
about her seemingly ageless voice but keep in mind that it is
almost impossible to date her songs by tracking the changes
in the timbre of her voice. Her songs from the sixties—for
Asha Parekh '*Sayonara, Sayonara*' (*Love in Tokyo*); for *Sadhna*
'*Nainowali Ne Hai Mera Dil Loota*' (*Mera Saya*), for *Nootan*
'*Kayi din se jee hai bekal*' (*Dulhan ek raat ki*) and for *Indrani
Mukherjee* '*Baharo, Mera Jeewan Bhi Sanwaro*' (*Akhiri Khat*)—
have a piercing sweetness which is audible even after 25 years
in the songs she sang in the nineties in films such as '*Jamuna ke
tat par jab natkhat banshi waale ki*' (*Saudagar*), '*Chudi maza na
degi, kangan maza na dega*' (*Sanam Bewafa*), '*Kabhi tu chhaliya
lagta hai, kabhi deewana lagta hai*' (*Pattar Ke Phool*) and '*Meri
bindiya teri nindiya na chura le to kehna*' (*Lamhe*). And do
remember that she was past 60 when she sang these!

It is enough to make one wonder how she does it. *Patthar Ke
Phool* introduced us to the seductive Raveena Tandon and we
are almost unaware that her 'voice' was Lata Mangeshkar, who

has sung some remarkable duets with S.P. Balasubramaniam. *'Sajna Tere Bina Kya Jeena'*; *'Tumko Jo Dekhte Hi Pyaar Hua'* and *'Dil Diwana Bin Sajna Ke Mane Na'* remind one of those unforgettable beauties from the past who warbled in Lata ji's voice. Dimple Kapadia and Rishi Kapoor in *Bobby*, Rati Agnihotri and Kamalahasan in *Ek Duje Ke Liye*, Vijeta Pandit and Kumar Gaurav in *Love Story*, Bhagyashree and Salman Khan in *Maine Pyaar Kiya*, Madhuri Dixit and Salman Khan in *Hum Aapke Hain Kaun*, and Aishwarys Rai and Shahrukh Khan in *Mohabbatein*, were all fresh young screen partners Lata Mangeshkar's voice helped to create.

So, from Nutan, Meena Kumari to Raveena Tandon in *Patthar Ke Phool*, Madhuri Dixit in *Hum Aapke Hain Kaun* (1994) and Aishwarya Rai in *Mohabattein* (2000), Lata ji's voice has remained unchanging and ever fresh. I can think of no other singer who can equal this record.

54

In 1961, Lata ji sang a devotional number in *Hum Dono* that has become almost the anthem of those times. *'Allah Tero Naam'* rises above a personal prayer to become a benediction for a young nation grappling with multiple problems. Those Indians who were too young to have attended one of Gandhi ji's famous prayer meetings found in the lyrics and sweetness of this song a whiff of purity that evoked all the emotions that patriotic music is capable of.

The words, penned by Sahir Ludhianvi, are a marvellous mixture of Hindi and Urdu and his clever use of the phrase *'Ishwar Allah tero naam, sabko sanmati de Bhagwan'* instantly recall Gandhi ji's favourite hymn: *'Raghupati Raghav Raja Ram, sabko sanmati de Bhagwan'*. Critics have hailed it as the most important statement of the country's secular aspirations and a modern national anthem of sorts.

The lyrics need to be remembered to understand its emotional content:

Allah tero naam, Ishwar tero naam
Sabko sanmati de Bhagwan
Maangon ka sindoor na chhoote
Maa-behno ki aas na toote
Deh bina na hatke na praan
Oo sare jag ke rakhwale
Nirbal ko bal dene wale
Balwano ko de de gyan

Let us now look at the rhythm and music behind these words. The beat used (Deepchandi *taal*) is a slow, ponderously paced rhythm that gives the singer time to pause between musical phrases. Thus, it is a perfect choice for a song that encompasses such a vast ambience of emotions and feelings. Similarly, its basic raga (Gaur sarang) gives Lata ji the apt range of notes within which to place her sweet appeal.

India's original Nightingale (so hailed by Gandhi ji) was M.S. Subbulakshmi, who was incidentally the person who brought alive *'Raghupati Raghav'* at Bapu's prayer meeting. The inheritor of this mantle was surely Lata Mangeshkar. Several stories are circulated about the song and its composer, Jaidev, with whom Lata ji was supposed to have had a serious tiff. According to some sources, it was S.D. Burman who intervened to resolve it, according to others it was Jaidev's friend Sahir Ludhianvi who played that role and so on. Lata ji herself had related to me the circumstances that led to her accepting Jaidev's invitation to sing this song.

Remarkably, for a song so serene in its musical composition and delivery, it seems to have had a fairly noisy background of tiffs and tantrums. However, to listeners unaware of this—or even those who know—all this pales into insignificance under the beauty of the lyrics, music and Lata ji's voice.

55

Among her greatest accomplishments is Lata ji's unmatched talent in singing songs of pain and longing. At one time or another, all of us have drawn solace and sympathy in the voice that seems to plumb the deepest layers of human emotions. Surprisingly, some of these are devotional songs penned by Mirabai, a character in history that Lata ji worships. Her brother Hridaynath has experimented with a completely new way of interpreting Mira bhajans and Lata ji sings them with the same ease and unhurried grace that she has given to other Mirabai compositions sung for others.

'Jo Tum Todo Piya' (Jhanak Jhanak Payal Baje); 'Jogiya Se Preet Kiye Dukh Hoye' (Garam Coat); 'Piya Te Kahan Gayo Nehra Lagaye', 'Girdhari Mhane Chakar Rakho Ji' (Toofan Aur Deeya), 'He ri main to prem deewani' (Naubahar, 1952), 'Mere to Girdhar gopal doosro na koyi' (Rajrani Meera, 1956) and 'Jo tum todo piya' (Silsila, 1981) are a few examples. It is as if she has internalized the pain and longing behind Mirabai's verses so completely that they have become a part of her own pain. Love and longing, courage and sacrifice, joy and sorrow—all these are exquisitely rendered by a person who seems to have experienced each emotion herself before voicing it in a song.

56

Pandit Kumar Gandharva is acknowledged among our classical music singers as one who could plumb the deepest layers of folk music to enrich his style of singing devotional songs. It is also known that he was among those who considered Lata ji as one who understood the innate relationship between classical and folk elements. Among all the playback singers he had heard, he chose her alone for this understanding.

However, there was more to his appreciation of Lata ji's musicality than this fact alone. He claimed that the principal reason for Lata ji's immense popularity among the masses was her musical sense. 'An important part of her music is the purity of her voice quality,' he said. 'Noorjahan was a great singer, no doubt, but there was a hint of intoxication in that voice. Lata's voice, on the other hand, betrays no such distraction: it is pure and pristine in its appeal. It seems to me that the austerity and cleanliness of her personal life has a lot to do with this and I regret that many composers did not make better use of it. I would have put her voice to a greater test.'

Another distinct and unique quality is her clear enunciation and her way of melting two sounds into each other, he felt. 'This is a rare quality and Lata makes it seem so easy and effortless that you almost miss it.'

These two qualities that Pandit Kumar Gandharva saw in her are indeed what so many classical musicians are unable to present even in long recitals. That she is able to do so in the limited framework of three minutes speaks volumes for her and for this great doyen's perceptive analysis. Just as some of life's greatest truths can be said in a pithy aphorism, Lata Mangeshkar is able to present the full flavour of a musically perfect piece in a fraction of the time it may take a classical musician to spin over a three-hour recital.

Critics often wonder whether Lata could have been able to sustain her gift of musical precision if she had to give a recital stretching over three hours, rather than a song done in three minutes. To that, my question is: could those great classical artistes who take three hours to unveil the majesty of a raga have been able to capture its essence in three minutes?

This makes her as important a musician, Kumar Gandharva feels, as a learned classical artiste. What can one add to this verdict from one of the greatest scholar-musician this country has ever heard?

57

Madan Mohan often used ragas that are seldom heard in north India, such as Bhinna Shadaj, Charukeshi, Hamsadhwani and Shivaranjini. Not surprisingly, he would choose Lata Mangeshkar to sing these compositions.

It is interesting to recall what music critic Aniruddh Banerji has to say about Madan Mohan's musical style. 'When she sang for Madan Mohan,' he claims, 'Lata Mangeshkar uses *shruti*, a quality that is more prevalent in Carnatic rather than in Hindustani music.' No doubt, Lata ji with her sensitive ear realized that for the kind of ragas that Madan Mohan chose, this style would be more appropriate.

It is this tacit understanding between them that make his compositions quite different from those of the other composers she has sung for. To understand this more comprehensively, listen to 'Khanak Gayo Hai Bairi Kangana' (based on Raga Khamaj for *Rishte Naate*); 'Naino Main Badra Chhaye' (based on Raga Bhimpalasi for *Mera Saya*); 'Ja Re Badra Bairi Ja' (based on Raga Yaman for *Bahana*, 1960); Raga Ahir Bhairav for *Meri Veena Tum Bin Roye* (*Dekh Kabeera Roya*, 1957), 'Bainya Na Dharo' (based on raga Charukeshi for *Dastak*, 1970), 'Maine rang li aaj chunariya' (based on raga Peelu for *Dulhan ki ek Raat*, 1966); 'Tu jahaa jahaa chalega' (based on raga *Nand* for *Mera Saya*, 1966); 'Meri veena tum bin roye' (based on raga Aheer Bhairav for *Dekh Kabeera Roya*, 1957); and 'Aaj mile man ke meet' (based on raga Bhairavi for *Nawab Siraj ud-Daulah*, 1967).

58

R.D. Burman once spent a long time in Calcutta learning the sarod from Ustad Ali Akbar Khan. It is a different matter that the real reason for this long stay was because he was enamoured of the musical sessions when Pandit Ravi Shankar and Ustad Ali Akbar Khan practised their *jugalbandhis* (duet performances). He was fond of telling friends how the foundation of his musical compositions could be traced to these electrifying sessions. He also learnt how to play the tabla from Pandit Samata Prasad, Gudai Maharaj to understand the finer aspects of beat and rhythm.

In addition was his great interest in western musical styles. This came to him from the little clubs and homes of the posh and westernized people who lived in South Calcutta, among whom were members of the Dev-Burman royal clan. In those days, a famous record shop called Melody, was situated in Rashbehari Avenue. Pancham (his popular nickname) was introduced to western music here and later, one of his main team members—Kersey Lord—educated him about the finer aspects of jazz, Latin American and European, as well as Cuba's Big band style and Middle Eastern music. All these were to leave a lasting impression on R.D. Burman and he freely used these various styles in his compositions for Bombay films to bring a breath of fresh air into the tired and repetitive repertoire of Hindi film music.

His admirers were legion but even here, the compositions he created for Lata were distinctly different as were the duets he made her sing for him. He was able to mine the tenderness of her voice in 'Ghar Aja Ghir Aaye Badra Sanwariya', 'Chura ked il ban rahe hai bhole' (Chote Nawab, 1961); O mere pyar aaja (Bhoot Bangla, 1965); 'Kajre Badarwa re, Marzi teri hai kya zalima' (Pati-Patni, 1966) Aaja Piya tose pyar karoon (Baharon Ke Sapne, 1967); 'Aap chaahein mujhko aarzo hai kisko' (Pyaar ka Mausam, 1969), 'Kisliye maine pyaar kiya' (The Train, 1970), 'Dilbar dil se pyaare' (Kaarwaan, 1971), 'Bada Natkhat Hai Re Krishna Kanhaiya' (Amar Prem, 1971), 'Bangle ke peeche . . Kantaa laga' (Samaadhi, 1972), 'Do nainon mein aansoo bhare hain' (Khusboo, 1975) 'Mere naina sawan bhadon (Mehbooba, 1976), 'Aajkal paanv zameen par nahi padte mere' (Ghar, 1978), 'Saawan ke jhule pade' (Jurmana, 1979), 'Rimjhim gire saawan' (Manzil, 1979), 'Bhor bhaye panchhi dhun ye sunaye' (Aanchal, 1980) to 'Tujhse Naraz Nahin Zindagi' (Masoom, 1982), 'Seelee hawa chhoo gayi' (Libaas, 1991) and 'Jaane Kya Baat Hai' (Sunny, 1991).

The soft tenderness of these solos was offset by the boisterous duets that he composed for her: '*Ni Sultana Re, Pyar Ka Mausam Aya*' (with Mohd Rafi, *Pyar Ka Mausam*), '*Chunari Sambhal Gori*' (with Manna De, *Baharon Ke Sapne*), '*Vada Karo Nahin Chhodogi Tum Saath Mera*' (with Kishore Kumar, *Aa Gale Lag Ja*) '*Panna Ki Tamanna Hai Ki Heera Use Mil Jaye*' (with Kishore Kumar, *Heera-Panna*) and so many others.

Despite his penchant for experimenting with bold and new tunes, it is interesting that he only trusted Lata ji with his most sober and serious songs. Perhaps this is why she considers him among the most important composer to enter the Bombay film music scene after the end of the Shankar–Jaikishan era.

59

S.D. Burman's '*Piya Tose Naina Lage Re*' (*Guide*, 1965) is universally accepted as one of the best songs ever composed in Indian film music. The song is eight minutes long (itself an unusual experiment) and its use of interludes and melodies between the vocal parts of the song are equally worthy of attention. These owe their presence to the fact that since 1955, R.D. Burman had started to assist his father and had introduced new ideas about orchestration, foreign beats and instruments that gave S.D. Burman's music a new life. As a marriage of two traditions, this song is quite unique.

Basically set in rupak taal, its music uses various combinations of the ragas—Chayanat, Vrindavani sarang, Gaur malhar and Maanj khamaj. In the interludes, R.D. Burman has used the saxophone along with the flute, santoor and pakhawaj with the violin to bring incredible energy into the rigid raga structure.

Above all, it is the marvellous synergy between the melodic structures of the song and its picturization, which leaps from one dramatic dance number to another.

The same goes for the manner in which the changing moods of the situation and dancer have been captured by Vijay Anand, the film's director. The celebration of Holi and Diwali are interspersed with the passage of time by weaving in day and night, beautifully rendered by Shailendra's sensitive and romantic lyrics. It is hard to understand how a committed Comrade could also melt one's heart with such tender love poetry. It is easy to understand why Lata ji considers this as one of the best songs she has ever sung. Recall the manner in which this from the section on Diwali: *Aa sajan payal pukare jhanak jhan-jhan jhanak jhan-jhan and later, Jane kyun baj utthe Kangana chhanak chhan-chhan chhanak chhan-chhan.* Or the segment in the Holi song of the same composition: *Tan badan mora kaanpe thar-thar, dhinak dhin-dhin dhinak dhin-dhin* and the finale with the thrilling notes in *Chamakna us raat ko jab milenge tan-man, milenge tan-man.* These are woven like the flowers in a garland adorning the dancer's swinging plait.

All these make this song one of the most magnificent compositions made by S.D. Burman for Lata. Of course, the director, the choreographer (Master Hiralal) and the heroine (Waheeda Rehman) have all contributed in different ways to the legend of this song but it is the combination of Burman and Lata that knits it all together. Their mutual respect for each other's talent is visible in several other songs that S.D. Burman and Lata ji have created together: 'Ab Aage Teri Marzi' (*Devdas*, 1955); 'Ghayal Hiraniya Main Ban-Ban Doloon' (*Muneemji*, 1955); 'Raat ka samaa jhoome chandrama' (*Ziddi*, 1964) 'Pawan Deewani, Na Mane Udaye Mora Ghunghata' (*Dr

Vidya, 1962); '*Hoton Mein Aise Baat Main Daba Ke Chali Aayi*' (*Jewel Thief*, 1967) and '*Megha Chhaye Aadhi Raat, Bairan Ban Gayi Nindiyaa*' (*Sharmilee*, 1971).

60

Of all the different kinds of songs she has sung over the years, Lata ji's lullabies are in a class of their own. For a woman who neither married nor ever savoured the love and pain of motherhood, Lata ji's lullabies capture the sweetness of maternal love in ways that are amazing. Personally, I attribute this to the fact that after her father's death she became the surrogate parent for her large family of siblings. In the course of several meetings with her over the years, her boundless love for her family manages to sneak into our conversation in one way or another. Perhaps it is this quality that seeps into her voice as she sings the lullaby for a composer. Salil Chaudhuri (in *Do Beegha Zameen*, *Char-Diwari* and *Awaz*) has created some unforgettable lullabies for her but it is the one she sang in *Mother India* that haunts her. She tells me how when she sang '*O Mere Lal Aaja, Tujhko Gale Laga Loon*' for Nargis who cries out plaintively for her errant son to return to her, she was so moved that it was difficult to keep her voice from breaking down during the recording. As she narrated this to me, I felt she was suddenly transported to that cruel day in 1942, when her father left her to care for the family and passed away.

Her own loving nurturing of her younger siblings have bestowed her with the emotional depths that she brings to these tender lullabies. Just as our great dancers were able to become the characters they perform on the stage, Lata ji is able to bring the special love of a mother for a sleeping child despite never having been one in her own life. One of most popular songs was 'B*ara natkhat hai re Krishna Kanhaiya, ka kare Jasoda maiyya* (*Amar Prem*, 1971) where she conveys the half-angry, half-amused Yashoda talking of her lovable scamp, Kanhaiya.

A haunting tenderness is what makes Lata ji's lullabies unforgettable. If you can, do listen to the one she has sung for music director Ravi in *Chirag Kahan Roshni Kahan* (1959). The words ('*Tim-tim karte tare kehte hain saare, so ja tohe sapnon mein nindiya pukare*'), spill over with the loving glances of a mother (Meena Kumari in this case) as she softly pats her child to sleep. The words, composed by Ravi himself, are unmatched for the sheer joy and peace contained in the composition. There is a complementary 'sad' version of the same song and Lata ji excels in both.

Tim-tim karate taare ye kahate hain saare
So ja tohe sapanon men nindiya pukaare
Sapanon ke desh ka chndaa maama raaja
Bula raha hai baja-baja ke saat suron ka baaja
Chori-chori khidki se karen ye ishaare
So ja tohe sapanon men nindiya pukaare

Rang-birangi pariyaan tujhe jhule mein jhulaaengi
Billi, tota, maina ki kahaani bhi sunaaengi
Achchhe-achchhe tujhe khilaune dengi pyaare-pyaare
So ja tohe sapanon men nindiya pukaare

Baadalon ki paalaki men munne ko bithhaa ke
Chnda maama saara jag laaega ghuma ke
Laut ke aye shaan se mera raaja mere dwaare

So ja tohe sapanon men nindiya pukaare
Tim-tim karate taare ye kahate hain saare

Sad version-

Tim-tim karate taare ye kahate hain saare
So ja tohe sapanon men nindiya pukaare
Jahaa bhi rahe tu raja rahe khushaal
Aur kya duaayen tujhe du main mere lal
Jug-jug jiyo mere nainon ke ujiyaare
Duniya ne kiya mujhe aisa majboor
Karna hi pada mujhe akhiyoon se door
Kuch bhi zamana kahe main hi teri maa re
Tim-tim karate taare ye kahate hain saare
So ja tohe sapanon men nindiya pukaare

Listen to the message of the twinkling stars
Close your eyes and enter the world of dreams,
Chanda mama, the king of this land, is waiting to greet you
With song and dance. He peeps from the window
To say, come quickly to my magical world.

Beautiful fairies of enchanting hues will take you to a swing
They'll tell you stories of cats and parrots and mynahs
They will load with many toys too
So hurry up and shut your eyes.

He will make you sit on a throne of clouds
And take you on a journey round the world
Before dropping you back into my arms.
So hurry up and sleep

Sad version-

> Listen to the message of the twinkling stars
> Sleep now and enter the world of dreams
> May you be happy wherever you go
> What more can I wish for you, my child?
> May you live a thousand years!
> The world has forced me to send you far, far away.
> Yet always remember that I am your mother
> No matter what others may say

My personal favourites, however, are 'Dheere Se Aa Ja Ri Ankhiyon Mein' (Albela, 1952, for C. Ramachandra); 'Hanse Tim-Tim-Tim Chhote-Chhote Tare' (Sanskar, 1952, for Roshan) and 'Jhunjhuna- Jhunjhuna Jhume Gagan Jhume Pawan' (Awaz, 1960, for Salil Chaudhuri), among others. A related genre is the songs she has sung for child artistes, where she almost becomes a child as she croons the words. She tells me that she imagines the situation and wills her voice to follow the lead of her emotions. I am reminded of her lugging her baby sister Meena to school in Sangli to the Muralidhar Pathsahala one day, many years ago. If you listen to a beautiful number she sang for Roshan in Rishte-Naate (1965), you will understand what I am trying to explain: 'Aa ri nidiya ki pari, Meri gudiya ko sula, Chand ke palne main tu, Meri maina ko sula . . .'.

61

Lata Mangeshkar likes to play with musical notes. It is as if she treats her voice as a boat and lets it glide on the river of music,

carefully watching and controlling its progress. Her calm
and unhurried voice negotiates all the eddies and swirls she
encounters to successfully complete her journey. Her capacity
to bring a certain freshness into each composition reminds of
how rural women cover the ember of the fire in the kitchen
chulha to ignite a fresh flame the next day. It seems to me that
she keeps a bit of herself and her inner music inside her to be
able to light a fire for the next day's offerings. The spectrum
of notes and emotions that she contains inside her are truly
mind-boggling.

62

Apne aap raaton me Chilmane sarkti hain
Chaunkte hain darwaje Sidhiya dhadakti hain
Ek ajnabi aahat aa rahi hain Kam-kam si
Jaise dil ke pardon par Gir rahi ho shabnam si
Bin kisi ki yad aaye Dil ke taat hilte hain
Bin kisi ke khankaye Chudiya khanakti hain
Koi pahle din jaise Ghar kisi ke jaata ho
Jaise khud musafir ko Rasta bulata ho
Paav jane kis janib Be-uthaaye uthte hain
Aur chham chhama chham-chham Payale chhankti hain
Jane kun balon me Ungliya pirota hain
Khelta hai pani se Tan-badan bhigota hain
Jane kiske hatho se Gagarein chhalkti hain
Jane kis ki baho se Bijliya lapakti hain

If you have a special fondness for the off-beat songs that she
has sung I recommend you try YouTube and listen to a ghazal

by Kaif Bhopali, with Khayyam's music from the film *Shankar Husain* (1977). (The opening lines are: '*Apne aap raaton main chilmane sarakti hain/ Chonktain hain darwaze, seedhiyan dharkati hain*').

The time has come to pay one's homage to a great master of the ghazal: Khayyam. He has always followed his own path and when his compositions are sung by Lata Mangeshkar, the effect is electrifying. As the opening lines I have referred to above show, doors open magically and staircases begin to heave.

This same spookiness and haunting echo can be heard in some other numbers she has sung for Khayyam: '*Hai Kahin Par Shaadmani Aur Kahin Nashadiyaan*' (*Aandhiyaan*, 1952); '*Kabhi To Milegi, Kahin To Milegi Baharon Ki Manzil, Raahi*' (*Arti*, 1962); '*Badli Hai Zamane Ki Nazar, Dekhiye Kya Ho*' (*Majboor*, 1964); '*Vo Jo Milte The Kabhi Humse Deewanon Ki Tarah*' (*Akeli Mat Jaiyo*, 1963) and '*Kat-Te Hain Dukh Main Yeh Din Pahloo Badal-Badal Ke*' (*Parchhaiyan*, 1952); '*Khuda-e-Bartar Teri Zameen Par*' (*Taj Mahal*, 1963); '*Jane Wale Se Mulaqat Na Hone Payi*' (*Amar*, 1954) and '*Rasm-e-Ulfat Ko Nibhayein Kaise*' (*Dil Ki Rahein*, 1973). These are some of the delightful numbers they created together that will never be forgotten.

63

If you juxtapose the two mujra numbers created by Ghulam Mohammad ('*Thare Rahiyo O Banke Yaar*' and '*Chalte Chalte Yun Hi Koi Mil Gaya Tha*') from *Pakeezah* (1971), some interesting facts emerge. First, these are two beautiful examples (standing and sitting) of the courtly tradition of mujra singing. '*Thare Rahiyo O Banke Yaar*' is depicted in the film as a standing performance (*Khari mehfil*) where dance steps are more important than the words, perhaps because the legendary kathak guru Lachchu Maharaj choreographed it. Yet the subtlety of the lyrics is not altogether sacrificed to the dance steps. This may have been due to the fact that Meena Kumari (who performs the number on screen) was not a very accomplished dancer and the camera lingers repeatedly on her facial expression to make up for this lack. This fact is borne out by the musical prelude that has the sarangi, tanpura, tabla and Mishra Pilu and set to the beat of dadra.

The film version is an almost direct copy of a famous dadra of the Banaras gharana ('*Thare Rahiyo O Banke Shyam Ho*') which is set to Mishra Khamaj that has been sung by both Siddheswari Devi and Shobha Gurtu, doyennes of the Banaras gharana. In the film, however, it is introduced by a prelude set in the style of the Rajasthani maand folk tradition ('*Chandni Raat Badi Der Ke Baad Aayi Hai*'). This was the work of Majrooh Sultanpuri to enhance the dramatic situation in the film narrative.

> '*Chandni raat badi der ke baad aayi hai*
> *Ye mulaqaat badi der ke baad aayi hai*
> *Aaj ki raat vo aaye hain badi der ke baad*
> *Aaj ki raat badi der ke baad aayi hai*'

All these subtle nuances are perfectly rendered by Lata Mangeshkar: she pauses at the right places, she changes the pitch each time she comes to the recurring motif ('*Thare Rahiyo*') to make this one of the greatest mujra songs ever sung in a film. Even without the film in front of our eyes, she has captured the mood so unerringly that the song becomes a stand-alone number.

Let us now examine the other mujra song of this film ('*Chalte Chalte Yun Hi Koi Mil Gaya Tha*'), written by Kaifi Azmi. It is slightly different from the first and the singer's voice is accompanied by rhythmic claps to provide a beat. The orchestra is a collage of sarangi, flute, tanpura, ghunghroo, tabla and claps. It is set to the beat of the kaharuwa and the music is a delightful cocktail of Mishra Khamaj and Jhinjhoti. Finally, it is a fine example of a '*baithki mehfil*' (mujra performed while sitting). Lovers of classical music can understand why the ragas chosen were from the night and lend themselves to a perfect blending of moods. One must also mention that since by now Ghulam Mohammad was very ill, the composition was created by Naushad according to his directions. This accounts for the meticulous attention to the appropriate raga chosen keeping in mind the time of night (early or late) and mood of the composition. In both these aspects, there were few who could rival Naushad's knowledge of classical and folk styles.

Lata Mangeshkar has sung this at a very high pitch and while it sounds sweeter, it is difficult to say which one of the two mujra numbers of this film is better. As usual, she has managed to successfully bring out the mood of each song entirely in accordance with its ragas, its situation and its tradition. There is joy in one, pathos and longing in the other but each stands firmy in its place without giving ground to the other. In short, the two numbers bring out the emotional background of a courtesan where love, longing and fulfilment are imbued with both joy and sadness. As her voice soars to the highest pitch, she becomes the voice of the courtesan.

Reflect on the magic of the concluding lines:

Shab-e-intezar akhir kabhi hogi mukhtsar bhi
Yeh chirag bujh rahe hain mere saath jalte-jalte
(This eternal wait will end one day/ like these lamps that are
slowly dimming with me)

The throbbing pain of a trapped courtesan and her unfulfilled
desires are perfectly matched by the rising crescendo of
Naushad's background score.

64

Generally, the image that her fans have of Lata ji is that of
a serious, sober, reserved person. Her early struggles and the
burden of family responsibilities left little space in her youthful
years for her to indulge in the carefree pranks that many girls
like to play in their girlhood with friends and companions.
However, it is a joy to discover that underneath a disciplined
and very quiet exterior is a mischievous girl, a marvellous
mimic and a person who enjoys a good joke. She once narrated
an incident that must be included here. Asha Bhonsle and she
were once rehearsing a fun-filled, joyous duet for Shankar-
Jaikishan. Now while Lata ji was wrapped in her usual white
sari, her bubbly, younger sister Asha was proudly wearing a
gold necklace that she had just ordered for herself.

Suddenly, Lata ji noticed that two strangers were sitting
in the recording room with the music director. They were
probably friends of Shankar-Jaikishan who had wanted to see a

live recording or fans of Lata ji who wished to hear her sing live. Whatever the reason, these two (who looked like important government officials) attracted her attention. She pointed them out to her sister, saying that they looked like Income-tax officials and had probably come there to question her about the heavy gold necklace she was wearing. Asha fell for the gag and asked nervously, 'What should I do?'

'Why should you be nervous?' Lata ji retorted. 'After all, you have been earning well, so what if you have bought an expensive piece of jewellery?' As she saw the unease on her sister's face, she burst out laughing and told her she was merely pulling her leg. The two laughed heartily and that set the tone for the mood that colours the song.

The song was a frothy number, sung for Asha Parekh and a friend in the film *Professor* (1962). It is a great example of how the carefree life of two young girls comes across, '*Koi aayega, aayega, aayega. Hamare gaanv koi aayega, pyar ki dor mein bandh jayega . . .*'.

This little anecdote makes it even more entertaining.

65

One of Tagore's poems ('*Ami tomay jokhun shuniyechhilem gaan*') speaks of the haunting quality of a song he had once heard and the poet asks when will he hear such a voice again? Listening to Lata Mangeshkar's voice these lines become clearer to my mind. One wonders whether the ragas, the bhajans and the songs that Lata ji has sung can ever be sung by any other singer. When will we hear such a voice again?

66

I once asked Gulzar saab about his personal opinion of Lata ji's musical journey. His explanation of why he considers her among our greatest national treasures is worth repeating. Just as we inherit our traditions from our elders and they include a knowledge of the shastras, poetry, history and music among many other things, our great musicians leave behind them a huge collection of information and knowledge about various musical forms—thumris, dadras, khayal, bhajan, dhrupad and so on. If we view the last few decades of film music then we realize how much we have been bequeathed by the voice of Lata Mangeshkar, he added. She has created a separate tradition of music for us where even when she sang for someone else, she did not completely let us forget her own self.

If you observe closely, he went on, you will discover that Saigal, too, never surrendered his voice completely to anyone else. He may have sung for others but ultimately, he sang for himself alone. No matter that a song has multiple creative energies behind it but if Lata has sung it, then it becomes her song. She owns the song, and this is a great achievement, he emphasizes. Her voice, melody and discipline are as admirable as her dedication to her art. Like the stories of the *Arabian Nights* that endless delight, she has created for us a world that has enchanted listeners for the last 50-60 years.

Whenever I composed a song for her, I found myself asking how she would react to a simile I had penned. Once while recording a song I had written for *Devdas*, she came across a line: '*Sarauli se meethi lage*'. 'What is this *sarauli*?' she asked me. It is a very sweet mango that we used to suck as children,

I replied. Shall I change it? Oh no, she said I just wanted to know how sweet it was. Then, in another song for the film *Ghar*, there was a line that ran like: '*Aapki badmashiyon ke yeh naye andaz hain*' and the director was a little nervous about the word '*badmash*'. She may not like it, he told me. Let her see it, I advised him and if she objects to it, I'll change it to something else. Later, I asked her what she had thought of the lyrics of that song and specifically asked her about the word '*badmash*'. Was it offensive? Not at all, she replied, that is what gave it a tang: I loved singing that line. And if you remember, Gulzar saab said to me, she laughs as she sings it, giving it an entirely delightful air. This is what makes her such a great artiste, he concluded.

I don't think anyone has explained what makes her so great in quite this way before Gulzar saab drew my attention to this aspect. As someone who has worked closely with Lata ji right from his first film (*Bandini*, 1963), there are simply scores of his lyrics she has sung and acknowledged him as one of her favourite lyricists. In *Kinara* (1977), he wrote a song for her that said: '*Naam gum jayega, chehra yeh badal jayega, meri awaz hi pehchan hai . . . gar yaad rahe*', that describes her so perfectly. This song alone reminds us that her voice is truly immortal.

Let us briefly recall some of the wonderful songs he has composed for her: '*Jhir Jhir Barse Sawani Ankhiyan, Sawariya Ghar Aa*' (*Aashirwad*, 1968); '*Humne Dekhi Hai Un Aankhon Ki Mehakti Khushboo*' (*Khamoshi*, 1969); '*Na, Jiya Lage Na, Tere Bin Mera Kahin Jiya Lage Na*' (*Anand*, 1970); '*Roj Akeli Aaye, Roj Akeli Jaye, Chaand katora liye Bhikharan raat*' (*Mere Apne*, 1971), '*Din ja Rahein hain ya raaton ke saaye*' (*Doosri*

Sita, 1974), 'Do Nainon Main Aansoo Bhare Hain, Nidiya Kaise Samaye' (*Khushboo*, 1975), 'Ruke-Ruke se kadam, Ruk ke baar-baar chale' (*Mausam*, 1975), 'Ab ke na sawan barse, Ab ke baras to barsengi ankhiyaan' (*Kinara*, 1977), 'Aajkal paanv zameen par nahi padte mere' (*Ghar*, 1978), 'Jaane kya hai jee darta hai' (*Ek Pal*, 1985), 'Tujhse naraz nahi zindgi hairan hu main' (*Masoon*, 1986), 'Main ek sadi se baithi hoon' (*Lekin*, 1990), 'Dil Hoom-Hoom Kare, Ghabraye' (*Rudali*, 1993), 'Seeli Hawa chhoo gayi geela badan chhil gaya' (*Libaas*, 1994), 'Oo dil banjare khol doriyaa' (*Maya Memsaab*, 1994), and 'Bhej Kahaar piya ji bula lo' (*Maachis*, 1996). The thinking poet found a thinking voice to bring out the deep meaning of each lyric penned by him. After Sahir Laudhianvi and Shailendra, it was perhaps only Gulzar saab who was able to extract the best of Lata ji's emotional prowess.

The following are from one of Lata ji's favourite Gulzar songs:

Aaj agar bhar aai hain
Boondein baras jaayengi
Kal kya pata innke liye
Aankhein taras jaayengi
Jaane kab gum hua, kaha khoyaa
Ek ansun chhupaa ke rakhaa thaa
Tujhse naraaz nahin zindagi
Hairaan hoon main...

(If my eyes well up today, my tears will overflow. Who knows my dry eyes may need some tomorrow. I have saved a tear or two for just such a day. How amazing that Life hasn't turned its face away from you)

67

Raj Kapoor's film 'Satyam, Shivam, Sundaram' (1978) had its music scored by Laxmikant–Pyarelal. The film's title song that starts with, 'Ishwar satya hai, Satya hi Shiv hai, Shiv hi sundar hai . . . Satyam, Shivam, Sundaram', is composed and rendered as a prayer that uplifts and occurs several times in the film in different situations. It is as if these lines— which are the central message of the film—had to be remembered over and over again to bring out its purity and philosophy in its entirety.

Responding to its significance, Laxmikant–Pyarelal have used a variety of musical instruments, many of them audible in the opening itself. Before the words appear, there is a prelude where the flute, Hawaiian guitar, violin and even a temple bell are played. As it develops, there are others that join in: the tabla, manjira, surmandal, organ, ghunghroos, piano and the violin. The composers have very cleverly deployed the orchestra to bring the beginning and the end of the song into a harmonious togetherness. And above all, there is the divine voice of Lata Mangeshkar that holds its own and blends with each of these instruments.

Ram Avadh me, Kaasi me Shiv
Kanha Vrindavan me
Daya karo prabhu dekhu inko
Har ghar ke aangan me
Radha Mohan sharnam
Satyam Shivam Sundaram . . .

Lord Rama resides in Avadh,
Shiva in Kashi

And Krishna in Vrindavan
Bless me, my Lord, so that
I may see them in every courtyard of each house.
I surrender to Radha Mohan
Satyam, Shivam, Sundaram . . .

The base raga used by the composers is the majestic Darbari, which Lata ji embellishes with some marvellous twists and turns of her voice. Listen carefully to the whole song, paying attention to its words, music and orchestra and you will realize how Laxmikant–Pyarelal were finally able to place themselves where once only Shankar–Jaikishan could reach.

68

It is difficult to gauge the extent to which Lata ji's popularity extends across the country. She seems to be omnipresent whenever women pick up the dholak and sing wedding songs or folk music that have tunes inspired by some of her well-loved songs. This is certainly true of most of North Indian middle-class homes. One cannot say whether when Roshan or Shankar–Jaikishan composed a tune they realized how wide its reach would become.

Births, *haldi-ubtan, sohars*—each of these occasions in homes across the north has a Lata tune lurking behind it. This is perhaps because composers like Naushad were deeply influenced by the folk music of this region and generously used it when composing film songs. Interestingly, these were then used as 'shorthand' tunes when ordinary women used them to sing traditional songs. All they needed to say to each

other was, 'Sing this one like *Nagin's "Tan Dole, Man Dole"'*
(or whatever) and everyone instantly knew the tune! Hilarious
permutations of her songs are to be heard even at the all-
night *jagratas* organized on holy occasions, when a devotional
prayer is sung to the tune of what was originally a love-song
sung by Lata Mangeshkar!

Long before wedding sangeets or jagrans were handed
over to DJs, North Indian weddings were occasions for the
simple housewives, old aunts and young girls to sing traditional
wedding songs to the beat of a dholak played by a neighbourhood
'auntie'. As soon as a popular song was started, a ripple of
recognition went though the assembly as they remembered the
'tune' it had been set too. Everyone joined in then as they knew
every Lata song by heart.

As examples, I can quote a few permutations here.
'*Nainowali Ne Hai Mera Dil Loota*' (*Mera Saya*) was adapted
by women as a devi geet '*Bhawan Rangeela Ma Ka Sher Pila-
Pila*'. Similarly, Naushad's song from *Mere Mehboob* ('*Tere
pyar main dildar jo hai mera haal-e-zaar/ koi dekhe ya na dekhe,
Allah dekh raha hai*') becomes a fun-filled song at weddings
when the words are changed to '*Banni karo na ghuroor/ Tumko
jana hai zaroor/ Koi aaye ya na aaye/ Banna aayega zaroor*'.

69

Kumar Shahni used a beautiful love song composed by the
great Hindi poet Raghuvir Sahay in his film *Tarang*. '*Priye,
Aao, Sang So Jao*' (Come lie with me, beloved) is an exquisite
love song set to divine music by Vanraj Bhatia and Lata has
brought out each aspect brilliantly.

It can best be described as an off-beat composition that takes the thumri to another level of delight. Lata ji's voice coaxes and caresses each word so lovingly that it enhances the effect of Sahay's words in ways that are unimaginable. '*Chumban se chup kar jao/Piya aao/Sang so jao*' (Shut my mouth with a kiss/Come beloved, sleep with me). The way that Lata ji has sung these erotic lines remind one yet again how fine is the line that divides the erotic and the metaphysical. This is visible in the erotic sculptures of our temples, the sensusousness of our classical dance forms, where the viewer is transported to another level of consciousness as art transcends the erotic to reach the divine.

After listening to this song, one wishes that she had lent her voice to the poetry of some of our talented contemporary poets because if anyone has the power to popularize poetry, it is Lata Mangeshkar. It is said that she herself was so moved by this song that she asked for the recording to be played to her, a request she seldom makes for she rarely listens to her own songs.

70

Several scholars have tried to define exactly what makes Lata Mangeshkar such a unique phenomenon. Some draw our attention to her perfect understanding of classical music, others speak of her divine voice quality, still others are speechless at the manner in which she can control her breath, never letting one know where she pauses to draw a fresh breath.

In a sense, they are all correct in their assessments but one has to actually see her perform and meet her in order to understand what a great person she is in real life as well.

The great Marathi litterateur, Pu La Deshpande has a different take on this. 'Instead of analysing individual aspects of her singing, one should concentrate on how she manages to invest every song she has sung with something so special that it reaches a state of pure perfection. Many singers have tried to imitate her singing style but none has quite managed to reach there. I can only say that if you have seen a real work of art, then a copy will never thrill you and appear merely a print copy. She alone can take a song to a divine height.'

She never disappoints her listeners and once a song is given to her, you can be sure it is in the best hands. She understood instinctively how C. Ramachandra, or Salil Chaudhuri or Naushad wished the song they had given her to sing to sound. Majrooh Sultanpuri once said, 'It was not as if we invested something special in the songs she sang for us and if the same song had been given to someone else, they may have done a competent job as well. However, it was Lata alone who could make even an ordinary song extraordinary. That is what makes her different from every other singer I know.'

71

Sooraj Barjatya, the young filmmaker of Rajshri Productions once narrated a wonderful anecdote about his encounter with Lata ji. Fresh from his course in film studies abroad, when he was starting his first film, *Maine Pyar Kiya* (1989), he was bursting with new ideas. The film he was planning to make would be for a young audience, so he had decided to introduce new faces and use new talent to announce a break from the age-old formula of his production house. When he discussed his plans with his father, he was advised to use a name from the older generation to bind the new elements together and keep a tradition that had been a hallmark of their production house. 'Ask Lata ji,' his father wisely suggested, 'if she agrees to sing for your film, I can guarantee you will succeed.'

So he went over to request Lata ji to accept this offer. She heard him patiently and said, 'Beta, you are Tarachand ji's grandson and I am happy to know that you are going to be the third generation in your family to carry on this tradition. Of course I will sing for you, why would I not, when I have sung so often for your banner? Let me know when you want me for rehearsals and the dates you would like me to block.'

The story highlights not just her generous nature but also reminds one that her voice had not lost its appeal even after three generations had come and gone. She first sang for Rajshri Productions in *Arti* (1962), *Dosti* (1964), *Taqdeer* (1967), *Jeevan-Mrityu* (1970, *Mere Bhaiya* (1972) and went on for almost 30 years to give them one great hit after another, right up to the super hit '*Hum Aapke Hain Koun . . .!, 1994*'. Her voice lost none of its sweetness or youthfulness from one end of their relationship to the other.

72

Habib 'Jalib' was one of the many Urdu poets who decided to migrate to Pakistan after Partition. At heart a revolutionary poet, Jalib began to regret his decision within a few years of his migration. In 1976, he was picked up in Hyderabad (Sind) and put behind bars for his subversive verse. He was able to secure bail only after two years and went on to become a fairly well-known poet who later wrote for some Pakistani films as well.

He claims that it was only the prospect of being able to hear Lata Mangeshkar's sweet voice on the radio while he was jailed that helped him to survive that dark period. During his incarceration, he wrote a poem titled 'Lata', where he praises the pristine quality of her voice and compares her to Meerabai. Your fans outnumber the stars in the sky, he declares, while your voice lulled me when I tossed restlessly in those dark nights . . .

Tere madhur gīton ke sahāre
Beete hain din-rain hamāre
Terī agar āvaāz na hotī
Bujh jaatī jīvan kī jotī
Tere sachche sur hain aise
Jaise sūraj-chānd-sitāre
Tere madhur gīton ke sahāre
Beete hain din-rain hamāre

Kyā kyā tūne geet hain gaae
Sur jab laage, man jhuk jaae
Tujh ko sun kar jee uthte hain
Ham jaise dukh-dard ke maare
Tere madhur gīton ke sahāre
Beete hain din rain hamāre

'Mīrā' tujhmen aan basī hai
Ang vahī hai rang vahī hai
Jag mein tere daas hain itne
Jitne hain ākāsh pe taare

Tere madhur gītoṅ ke sahāre
Beete haiṅ din rain hamāre

As a prisoner
'*Tareekh ne khilkat ko to katil hi diye,*
 khilkat ne diya hai use '*Jalib*' *sa jawaab*'

Tere madhur geeton ke sahare/ Beete hain din-rain hamare/
Teri agar awaaz na hoti/ Bujh jati jeewan ki jyoti/ Tere sacche
sur hain aise/ Jaise suraj-chand-sitare/ Tere madhur geeton
ke sahare/ Beete hain din-rain hamare . . . / Meera tujhmain
aan basi hai/ Ang wahi hai, rang wahi hai/ Jag main tere das
hain itne/ Jitne hain akash main tare/ Tere madhur geeton ke
sahare/ Beete hain din-rain hamare . . .

(We have suffered our oppressive days and nights by
listening to your songs. If it weren't for your voice, the light
would gone out of our lives. Your pure notes are as eternal
as the sun, moon and stars. You are the embodiment of
Meerabai, the inheritor of her verse and devotion. Your fans
outnumber the stars in the sky . . .)

Jalib was not the only Pakistani poet to offered homage to Lata
ji's voice. Parveen Shakir wrote a poem describing how the
guards on both sides of the border broke off a skirmish when
the sounds of a Lata Mangeshkar song floated up from a nearby
shop. The point to be noted is that while individual singers from
various countries become cults in their own countries—it is the
Hindi poet Vishnu Khare who drew my attention to the fact that
Lata ji's voice transcends borders. All over the subcontinent—
and perhaps even in regions beyond—her voice has dedicated

listeners. 'In their time, Ella Fitzgerald in America, Um Kulsum in Egypt and Edith Piaf in France . . . were such figures. But the way in which Lata's voice has become the vehicle for carrying human emotions across South Asia is unmatched by any singer anywhere at any time in the world.' He goes on to add that '. . . We may differ on which one of her songs is the best but there is no dispute on the fact that her voice is the best.'

Majrooh Sultanpuri, Naushad—so many great composers and lyricists were moved to write poems in praise of her that it seems futile to debate the greatness of her presence in India.

Mujhse chalta hai sare-bazm sukhan ka jaadoo
chaand zulfon ke nikalte hain mere seene se
main dikhaata hoon khayaalaat ke chehre sab ko
sooratein aati hain baahar mere aaine se
haan magar aaj mere tarz-e-bayaan ka ye haal
ajnabee koyi kisi bazm-e-sukhan mein jaise
vo khayaalon ke sanam aur vo alafaaz ke chaand
bevatan ho gaye apane hee vatan mein jaise...

Jis ghadee doob ke aahang mein too gaatee hai
aayaten padhti hai saazon kee sada tere liye
dam-ba-dam khair manaate hain teri chang-o-rubaab
seenye nae se nikalatee hai dua tere liye
nagama aou saaz ke zevar se rahe tera singaar
ho teree maang mein tere hee suron kee afashaan,
teree taanon se teri aankh mein rahe kaajal kee laqeer,
haath mein tere hee geeton ki hina ho rakhshaan.

I create the world around me with my writing.
Because the words that spring from my heart

Display the characters of my imagination
As if they emerge from some mirror inside me.
Yet, I find today when I try to describe
The beauty of your voice has vanquished
All my words and images.
They are helpless when confronted with my memory
Of your songs.

When I hear you
A prayer arises unbidden for you in me.
I pray that you may always
Bring alive the lyrics and melody that I hear.
May you be ever adorned with your unmatched notes
May your notes reveal your face to me
And keep alive your fragrance inside me.

73

Describing the hallmark of a true shishya (student/follower), the great poet Malik Mohammad Jaisi once said: '*Guru birah chingi ur mela/Jo sulgayi layi soyi chela.*' Roughly translated into prose, it could be said to mean that the true shishya is one who can light a fire in his breast from the ember that his guru sparked inside him. Equally, it could be said that every shishya must open his heart fully to learn whatever he can from a guru.

Of Lata Mangeshkar it can be truthfully said that she has carried the memory of all her musical lessons from all those teachers and musicians she has encountered in her life. Foremost among these names is her father Dinanath Mangeshkar, and later Ustad Aman Ali Khan of the Bhendi Bazar gharana and Ustad Amanat Ali Khan of Dewas. She also humbly acknowledges her debt to those who nurtured her talent in the film world, Ghulam Haider, Anil Biswas, Naushad and Sajjad Husain come in this category.

It must be said of her that despite her enormous talent and stature in this world, she remained ever eager to learn from whoever had something to teach her. This endearing lack of arrogance is what makes her one of a kind.

74

She has been such a stickler for punctuality that she can account for each moment of her daily calendar. This must come from the strict discipline that drives her private and professional life. For me, interacting with her was a sober learning experience.

I had once fixed an interview with her at 7 p.m. However, for some reason I cannot now recall, I forgot the appointment and called ten minutes past the hour to apologize. She cut short my excuses rather sharply, 'You are late, Yatindra. I waited for a call from you ten minutes ago.' Ashamed of my lapse, all I could do was apologize humbly but I made a mental note that this must never happen again.

Through the scores of conversations we have had while compiling this book, she was always unfailingly courteous, easy to speak to and serene. I often forgot that I was in the presence of a person of her eminence. As one of these long interviews came to an end, I broached the subject of our next appointment. 'Call me tomorrow at 7,' she told me firmly, 'and I will let you know. And Yatindra, do keep in mind that the person you wish to portray has measured out her life in segments of three and four minutes. If you are late by ten minutes, remember that the radio will have broadcast three of my songs in that time.' Then, she broke into her tinkling laugh, blessed me and bade me goodbye. I was struck dumb by what she was trying to tell me: every minute of her long and eventful life is so precious that it cannot be wasted by those who do not share her discipline and passionate commitment to music.

75

Every song that she has sung for a Yash Chopra film has a special quality of tenderness, warmth, emotional intensity or pain. Perhaps the songs that were composed for her to sing in such films were structured to bring out this quality or perhaps she herself understood the underlying emotional subtext of a Yash Chopra film. To illustrate this, listen to a song she sang in his blockbuster film *Silsila* (1981): '*Yeh Kahan Aa Gaye Hum Yun Hi Saath-Saath Chalte*'. There is such freshness in her voice that one cannot miss it despite the distraction of the beautiful background music and Amitabh Bachchan's towering presence in one's memory, which makes this duet so different from the others sung on screen by the famous actor.

Music lovers will appreciate the soft beat of the congo drums that enhances the beat (*kaharwa*) of the tabla but even more exquisite is the diamond-like sharpness of Lata ji's Komal Nishadh that cuts through the air just like the glittering snow on the mountains in this scene. Yash Chopra fans know that he has a special feel for exotic foreign landscapes (tulip fields, ski slopes) and heroines clad in diaphanous chiffon saris cavorting there. If one listens to this song patiently, one can hear how Lata ji takes the opening words (*Yeh kahan*) to the highest octave (*taar saptak*) and leaves them hovering in air for a few seconds, to imprint the scene visually on the listener. One can only applaud the composition of Shiv–Hari, the lyrics of Javed Akhtar and the voice of Lata ji in bringing alive the tenderness of that moment. In fact, Javed Akhtar once remarked that a particular line that comes later in the song ('*Huyi aur bhi mulayam, meri sham dhalte-dhalte*') is unparalleled for bringing out the soft tenderness of the emotions depicted in the scene. No other singer could have caressed that softness (*mulayam*) so unerringly.

An added attraction is the sensitive use of Amitabh Bachchan's deep bass voice when he recites these lines:

Main aur meri tanhai aksar yet baatein kehte hain/ Tum hoti to kaisa hota/ Tum yeh kehti woh kehti/ Tum is baat pe hairaan hoti/ tum uss baat pe kitni hasti/ Tum hoti to aisa hota/ Tum hoti to vaisa hota/ Main aur meri tanhayi aksar ye baatein karte hain . . .

(When I am lonesome, I often wonder what it would be like to have you beside me now. Would you say this or that? Would you find this as wondrous?)

Chopra is thus successful in taking his viewer into a land of fancy, a place that every lover understands.

76

Lata Mangeshkar and Asha Bhonsle were undoubtedly the most popular female playback singers of the last seven decades. Interestingly, despite being sisters who grew up in the same home, they had clearly distinct voices. One was like a river of sparkling water, the other was like a dancing brook in mountains. One sister's voice remained steady and unchanged down the decades while the other moulded hers according to the changing times.

This is why while Lata's voice was sought by those composing devotional numbers and songs of love and longing, it was to Asha that they went when looking at a lively cabaret number or the saucier love songs. Their individual genius is best expressed by Gulzar who once declared: 'Lata ji's voice takes one to the moon. She is our Neil Armstrong, who first landed on the moon. Asha ji was also on the same flight but she sat by another window, so she landed just a little later.'

There are hundreds of songs they have sung together to produce unforgettable melodies and it becomes difficult to decide who outdoes the other. Here a few examples: 'Yeh Ruki-Ruki Hawain, Yeh Bujhe-Bujhe Sitare', composed by K. Datta in Daman (1951); 'Yeh Barkha Bahar, Sautaniya Ke Dwar, Na Ja More Sanware Piya' by Shankar–Jaikishan for Mayurpankh (1954) and 'Kar Gaya Mujh Pe Jadu Sanwariya' for Basant Bahar (1956); 'O Chand Jahan Woh Jayein' for C. Ramachandra in Sharda (1957); 'Sakhi Ri Sun Bole Papiha Us Paar' for Hemant Kumar in Miss Mary (1957); 'Ruthi Jaye Re Gujariya, Na Bole Re' for Vasant Desai in Do Phool (1958); 'Janeman Ek Nazar Dekh Le' for Naushad in Mere Mehboob (1963); 'Sajan Salona Mang Lo Ji' for Roshan in Dooj Ka Chand (1964) and 'Man Kyun Behka Ri Behka Aadhi Raat Ko' for Laxmikant–Pyarelal in Utsav (1984).

77

'Ram Shyam Gun-Gaan', a joint musical offering of devotional numbers by Pandit Bhimsen Joshi and Lata Mangeshkar, occupies a special niche in Lata ji's musical journey. Both the artists are doyens of their own style and reign over their own separate worlds. Pandit Bhimsen Joshi is a pillar of the Kirana gharana, while Lata ji's musical journey, which started with her father Dinanath Mangeshkar who traced his musical lineage to the Gwalior gharana, also reveals influences of her subsequent gurus (from Bhendibazar and Dewas). However, when they jointly present these devotional songs, they seem one in intensity and brilliance.

'*Ram Ka Gun-Gaan Kariye*' is a beautiful prayer that charms the listener with the clarity of their notes. In another piece, '*Baaje Re Muraliya Baaje*', they are able to seamlessly meld their voices in a joint offering. It is as if they instinctively divided the separate roles they would play while singing together. She takes the listener serenely forward, effortlessly negotiating the turns and twists of the composition with a searing sweetness, while he uses his grave voice to spin its own magic. The opening *alap* and concluding segment are his but the words (penned by Pandit Narendra Sharma) are a moving garland of lyrics that embody the best of Vaishnav bhakti poetry, and they cast their own spell on the listener.

> *Baaje re muraliya baaje.*
> *adhar dhare mohan muralee par*
> *honth mein maaya biraaje*
> *hare hare baans kee banee muraliya*
> *maram-maram ko chhuye anguriya*
> *chanchal chatur anguriya jis par*
> *kanak mundariya saaje*
>
> *The sweet flute plays again!*
> *The moment Mohan (Krishna) places his lips*

On it, He transforms it into something else
The simple bamboo flute
Becomes an instrument of healing
That soothes all pain
As gold glints from the ring
That He wears on the finger that glides over it

Lata ji faithfully echoes and supplements every note and taan that Pandit Bhimsen Joshi takes and delights in matching her own considerable musical prowess against one of India's finest classical vocalists. She told me once later that she tried to emulate the taans of Ustad Barkat Ali Khan as she sang along with Pandit ji for this album. The result is a delightful album where she is able to showcase her classical training and he is able to sing in a style that few classical musicians like to try.

As one listens enchanted to this album, one becomes aware that their deep understanding of a popular Marathi style (*bhaav geet*) lies behind this experiment. Fans of the legendary Pandit Bhimsen Joshi have been moved to tears by his soulful bhajans with which he liked to conclude his recitals. '*Jo Bhaje Hari Ko Sada Vahi Param Pad Paayega*', '*Rama Hari Ka Bhed Na Payo*' and '*Raghuvar Tumko Meri Laaj*' were encores requested at each concert he gave in the country. The songs he sang with Lata ji in this album enjoy the same level of popularity. It is astonishing how in the space of a few minutes, these great artists are not only able to present the full range and flavour of a raga but also fill it with such deep emotion. The credit for this is theirs but must go equally to the composer Shriniwas Khale and the lyricist Pandit Narendra Sharma.

78

Of all the concerts Lata ji has performed abroad, the ones that are the most memorable are those she presented in London. Both were held in the Royal Albert Hall, with the first one in March, 1974. This concert is also historic because it was a part of the efforts to raise money for the Nehru Memorial Fund. Later, in 1979, another Lata concert was held there along with Ed Welsh's famous Wren Orchestra.

She remembers both these occasions fondly because they were spectacularly successful and she classes them among the best-organized events abroad. 'It was a wonderful experience,' she tells me when recalling the first one. 'I had never experienced what I saw in the Royal Albert Hall that evening. The first thing I recall is how struck I was by the discipline of the audience. The show was scheduled to start at 7 p.m. and the public was in the hall well before that. Once the doors were closed, they were not opened for any latecomers. This was a totally new experience for me! As for the response I got, I can only say that it was overwhelming. And it was the same on all the three days I performed there.

'As a music lover, I look at the Wren Orchestra performance as another great experience. I could not get over how beautifully a collection of Western instruments was able to absorb the spirit of our Indian music and tunes. For some time, we became members of a single family.'

Lata ji had sent her music arrangers, Anil Mohile and Amar Haldipur, to London so that they could make notations of all the songs she was to sing, to provide the Western orchestra with score sheets to play along with her. Almost thirty-six years later, people who were present there can recall how perfectly the orchestra was able to replay the haunting romantic music that Naushad, Madan Mohan, Salil Chaudhuri, Shankar–Jaikishan or Laxmikant–Pyarelal had composed in songs such as 'Uthaye Ja Unke Sitam' (Andaz); 'Hum Pyar Main Jalne Walon Ko' (Jailer); 'Saathi Re, Tujh Bin Jiya Udas Re' (Poonam Ki Raat); 'Ehsan Tera Hoga Mujh Par' (Junglee) or 'Satyam Shivam Sundaram'. She concluded the concert with a Mirabai bhajan, 'Chala Vahi Des', and the orchestra signed off with a concluding melody based on it as a tribute to her.

Even today, listening to her Royal Albert Hall concerts on a CD is a very moving experience. Her 1974 concert has such hauntingly beautiful songs as Salil Chaudhuri's Bengali composition, 'Na, Mono Lage Na', and the soulful Punjabi 'Heer', 'Doli Chad Di Amaariyaan'. Her voice in Shankar–Jaikishan's song from Rajkumar, 'Aa Ja, Aayi Bahar, Dil Hai Beqarar, Oo Mere Rajkumar, Tere Bin Raha Na Jaye', will have your feet tapping. The songs, taken from some of her most popular numbers from the fifties and sixties, are unvanquished by time. The concluding number was taken from her album, Chala Vahi Des that the orchestra played to a crescendo. Her effortless voice matches the perfection of the orchestra to make this a truly historic occasion.

79

Lata ji has sung numerous romantic duets with Mukesh, Mohd Rafi and Kishore Kumar so these are the names that first come to mind when recalling her duets. While it is true that she has sung her most popular duets with these three, we tend to forget there are several equally beautiful numbers she has sung with Talat Mehmood, Hemant Kumar, Manna De and Mahendra Kapoor. Sadly, despite their popularity at that time, these are now often forgotten.

As a dedicated music lover, I feel compelled to remind readers of some of these neglected songs because I believe that, while there is no denying that she is best remembered for her duets with the voices mentioned earlier, there is a special quality in the duets she has sung with the latter voices, especially those with Talat Mehmood. The soft quiver in his voice and the sweetness in hers were an unbeatable combination. Think of Anil Biswas's *Seene Main Sulagte Hain Armaan Aankho Mein Udaasi Chhayi Hai* (*Tarana*, 1951); Ghulam Mohammad's *Aasman Wale Teri Duniya Se Ji Ghabra Gaya* (*Laila Majnu*, 1953); Madan Mohan's *Teri Chamkati Aankhon Ke Aage Yeh Sitare Kuchh Bhi Nahin* (*Chote Babu*, 1957) and Salil Chaudhuri's immortal *Itna Na Mujhse Tu Pyar Badha Ki Main Ek Baadal Aawara* (*Chhaya*, 1961) and you will be transported to another world. What a pity that that many of these gems lie forgotten today!

The same holds true of the duets Lata ji sang with Hemant Kumar. His calm, meditative voice had a depth that made these romantic numbers very special, while Lata ji's voice lent its own magic and appeared like a heavenly intervention into his grave world. What I wish to convey is the other-worldly aspect of this combination that is seldom heard in film music. I can think of some examples to make the point clearer: Vasant Desai's *Nain Se Nain Nahin Milao, Dekhat Soorat Aawat Laaz* (*Jhanak-Jhank Payal Baaje*, 1955); C. Ramachandra's *Jaag Dard-E-Ishq Jag* (*Anarkali*, 1953); Naushad's *Chandan Ka Palna, Resham Ki Dori* (*Shabab*, 1954); Kalyan ji–Anand ji's

'*Itna To Keh Do Hamse, Tumse Hi Pyar Hai*' (*Saheli*, 1965); Roshan's '*Chhupa Lo Yun Dil Main Pyar Mera*' (*Mamta*, 1966) and Hemant Kumar's own composition, '*Ari Chhod De, Chhod De Patang Meri Chhod De*' (*Nagin*, 1954). How can one forget such magic?

Let us now turn to those well-known duets she has sung with other playback singers. Although the majority of the duets composed by Shankar–Jaikishan with Lata ji featured Mukesh as the male voice, there are a few that she has sung for this duo with Manna De as well. These are memorable because sometimes these two voices reach a height that even Mukesh and she did not. The reason for this may be that both Manna De and Lata ji were trained classical singers and understood the nuances of musical compositions more deeply than most other singers. This is why when I recall some of these numbers, the reader will immediately agree with me: Anil Biswas's '*Ritu Aye, Ritu Jaye, Sakhi Ri, Man Ke Meet Na Aye*' Biswas's '*Ritu Aaye, Ritu Jaye, Sakhi Ri, Man Ke Meet Na Aaye*' (*Hamdard*, 1953), Shankar–Jaikishan's '*Aaja Sanam, Madhur Chandni Main Hum-Tum Milen To*' (*Chori-Chori*, 1956), '*Nain Mile Chain Kahan Dil Hai Vahin Tu hai Jahan*' (*Basant Bahar*, 1956), and '*Dil Ki Girah Khol Do, Chup Na Baitho Koi Geet Gaao*' (*Raat Aur Din*, 1967), Salil Chaudhuri's '*Ja Tose Nahin Boloon Kanhaiya, Raah Chalat Pakri Mori Baiyaan*' (*Parivar*, 1956), '*Daiya Re, Daiya Chadh Gayo Papi Bichhuwa*' (*Madhumati*, 1958), and '*Balma Mora Aanchraa Mehke Re*' (*Sangat*, 1975), Vasant Desai's '*Taar-Taar Baj Raha, Dil Ke Sur Bahar Ka*' (*School Master*, 1959), RD Burman's '*Chunari Sambhal Gori Udi Chali Jaaye Re*' (*Baharon Ke Sapne*, 1967) and Laxmikant–Pyarelal's '*Sham Dhale Jamuna Kinare, Aaja Radhe Aaja Tohe Shyam Pukare*' (*Pushpanjali*, 1970).

I also want to remind listeners of some lovely duets she sang with Mahendra Kapoor. From Ravi's '*Aaj Ki Mulaqat Bas Itni*' (*Bharosa*, 1963), Kalyanji-Anandji's '*Chori Ho Gayi Raat Nain Ki Nindiyaa*' (*Ishaara*, 1964), Chitragupta's '*Koi Aane Wala Hai Chaand Ki Doliyaa Pe Ho Ke Sawaar*' (*Mera Kusoor Kya Hai*, 1964) and '*Aaja Re Mere Pyaar Ke Raahi, Raah Niharu Badi Der Se*' (*Oonche Log*, 1965), to Madan Mohan's exquisite composition, '*Aapne Apna Banaya Meherbani Aapki*' (*Dulhan Ek Raat Ki*, 1966), this is an equally impressive list.

Most fans of Lata ji will agree with me when I say that her duets with all these three playback singers are perhaps even more beautiful than the ones she sang with Mohd Rafi, Mukesh and Kishore Kumar. While it is interesting to speculate why Talat Mehmood was chosen for a particular duet rather than (say) Mukesh, it is equally important to admit that no one else could have brought such lyrical beauty to the ones she has sung with him.

Sometimes, a song acquires a life of its own and this is more often than not due to the emotional depth that its singers are able to imbue it with. So, whatever prompted music composers to try out different voices for different songs, it is surely Lata ji's presence that remained a constant and an unchanging factor in their success.

80

Lata Mangeshkar rates Meena Kumari as her favourite actress and whenever she speaks of her, she emphasizes that she admired her for her dignity and gravity. She lists *Sharda* (1957), *Dil Apna Aur Preet Parayi* (1960), *Kohinoor* (1960), *Arti*

(1962), *Chitralekha* (1964), *Bahu Begum* (1967) and *Pakeezah* (1971) as her favourite Meena Kumari films. Meena Kumari's sensitive portrayal of women in all her films makes her an object of admiration in Lata ji's eyes. But, beyond that, Meena Kumari was an accomplished poet and a wonderful human being, she tells me. This is perhaps why Lata ji's songs sung for her on screen have a quality of empathy that is unmissable. Meena Kumari's personal life and its tragedies are unerringly interpreted by Lata ji in her songs.

Meena Kumari was a towering presence in the films of the fifties and sixties. She had converted her own tragic life into a finely honed talent and this, added to her elegiac poetic temperament, brought tremendous depth into her acting. It was said that she could make her eyes laugh while showing a bleeding heart. Her role in *Pakeezah* was almost a mirror image of her own search for a perfect and faithful lover all her life.

This brief list of Lata ji's songs for Meena Kumari will illustrate how perfectly the singer was able to capture the essential core of the legendary actress: '*Pee Ke Daras Ko Taras Rahi Ankhiyaan*' (*Aazad*, 1955); '*So Gaya Sara Zamana, Neend Kyun Aati Nahin*' (*Miss Merry*, 1957) '*Ajeeb Dastan Hai Yeh Kahaan Shuru Kahaan Khatam*' (*Dil Apna Aur Preet Parayi*, 1960); '*Kabhi To Milegi kahin To Milegi Baharon Ki Manzil Raahi*' (*Aarti*, 1962); '*Vo Jo Milte The Kabhi Humse Deewano Ki Tarah*' (*Akeli Mat Jayiyo*, 1963); '*Ruk Ja Raat, Thahar Ja Re Chanda*' (*Dil Ek Mandir*, 1963); '*Baharon Ki Mehfil Suhani Rahegi*' (*Benzeer*, 1964); '*Nagma-o-Sher Ki Saugaat Kise Pesh Karun*' (*Gazal*, 1964) '*Sansar Se Bhage Phirte Ho Bhagwan Ko Tum Kya Paaoge*' (*Chitralekha*, 1964); '*Duniya Kare Sawal To Hum Kya Jawab Dein*' (*Bahu Begum*, 1967); '*Oo Ganga Maiya Paar Laga De*' (*Chandan Ka Palna*, 1967); '*Roj Akeli Aaye*

Chaand Katora Liye Bhikharan Raat' (*Mere Apne*, 1971) and
'*Yuhin Koi Mil Gaya Tha*' (*Pakeezah*, 1971) . . to name a few.

Even this brief list shows us how the two seemed true
soulmates, made for each other.

81

Of the thousands of songs that she has sung over her long
career, there are some that bring out a playfulness and
mischievous aspect of the lyrics. Even though her sister
Asha Bhonsle was really the one whose vivacious personality
is associated with such numbers, there are some duets Lata
ji sang with her as well as with Geeta Dutt and Shamshad
Begum that must be remembered. Lata ji was better known
for her serious and grave personality, and her devotional songs
or love songs were able to project the emotional depth or
serenity of such compositions beautifully. And yet, she was
so multifaceted that whenever she had to sing lighter songs,
she delivered them with equal perfection. But since she always
made it clear that she was not comfortable with slightly risqué
or naughty lyrics, many composers did not dare to ask her to
sing a certain kind of song.

However, as the following selection of songs will show, she
can match the vivaciousness of Asha and Geeta Dutt note for
note. Among these songs are: C. Ramachandra's '*Mohabbat
Mein Aise Kadam Dagmagaye*' (*Anarkali*, 1953); Vasant Desai's
'*Sayyan Jhooton Ka Bada Sartaj Nikala*' (*Do Aankhain Barah
Haat*, 1957); Shankar–Jaikishan's '*Dil Mein Pyar Ka Toofan,
Na Samjhe Koi Nadan*' (*Yahudi*, 1958); '*Shishaye Dil Itna Na
Uchhalo*' (*Dil Apna Aur Preet Parayi*, 1960); '*Tum Jaise Bigde*

Babu Se Main Ankhiyan Bachaon' (*Jab Pyar Kisi Se Hota Hai*,
1961); '*Sayonara, Sayonara, Vada Nibhaongi, Sayonara*' (*Love
in Tokyo*, 1966); S.D. Burman's '*Jani, Tum To Dole Daga
Dayi Ke*' (*Dr Vidya*, 1962); '*Yeh Meri Zindagi Ek Pagal Hawa*'
(*Ziddi*, 1964); Chitragupt's '*Tadpaoge Tadpa Lo, Hum Tadap
Tadap Kar*' (*Barkha*, 1959); '*Tie Laga Ke Mana Ban Gaye
Janab Hero*' (*Bhabhi*, 1957); '*Dil Ko Lakh Sambhala Ji*' (*Guest
House*, 1959); Hemant Kumar's '*Sapne Suhaane Ladakpan Ke*'
(*Bees Saal Baad*, 1962); Kanyanji-Anandji's '*Bade Khoobsurat
Ho Tum Naujawaan*' (*Mahal*, 1969), '*Chhoti Si Umar Mein
Lag Gaya Rog*' (*Bairaag*, 1976); RD Burman's '*Aap Chaahein
Mujhko Aarzo Hai Kisko*' (*Pyaar Ka Mausam*, 1969), '*Bangle
Ke Peechhe . . . Kantaa Laga*' (*Samaadhi*, 1972), '*Baanho Mein
Chale Aao*' (*Anamika*, 1973); Laxmikant Pyaarela''s '*Zulmi
Hamare Sanwariya Ho Ram*' (*Mr X In Bombay*, 1964), '*Dil-
Vil Pyaar-Vyaar Main Kya Jaanu re*' (*Shagird*, 1967), '*Haaye
Haaye Ye Mazboori Ye Mausam Aur Ye Doori*' (*Roti Kapda
Aur Makaan*, 1974), '*Mara Thumka Badal Gayi Chaal Mitwa*'
(*Kranti*, 1981) and many others, including Bappi Lahiri's
'*Thoda Resham Lagta Hai, Thoda Sheesha Lagta Hai*' (*Jyoti*,
1981); Ram-Laxman's '*Dil Deewana Bin Sajna Ke Maane
Na*' (*Maine Pyaar Kiya*, 1989); Jatin–Lalit's '*Mere Khwabon
Mein Jo Aaye*' (*Dilwale Dulhaniya Le Jayenge*, 1995) and A.R.
Rahman's '*Jiya Jale Jaan Jale*' (*Dil Se*, 1998). Alas! She did not
sing any sexy cabaret numbers because one wonders what she
would have made of their mood!

It is believed that largely because she did not lend her voice
for sexy numbers that composers began to throng to Asha
Bhonsle. It is also worth noting that while most such songs
were screened as item numbers, the songs sung by the lead
actress still came to Lata ji.

It is safe to assume that this happened because she had the marvellous capacity to enter the spirit of the lyrics in a way that can only be described as an instinctive understanding of the composition and its screen presence. So whether it was a tender love song, a devotional bhajan or a lively dance number, music directors naturally gravitated to her.

While one can appreciate her distance from raunchy or risque songs, it is also what prompted some critics to say that she might have been a wee bit arrogant. However, if one listens to her lively rendering of '*Main Kya Karoon Ram, Mujhe Buddha Mil Gaya*' from *Sangam* (1964), one can say that, even while singing a supposedly saucy number, she managed to preserve the innate dignity of her voice.

82

By the fifties, the musical duo Husnlal–Bhagatram had created a name for themselves that could match the reputation of R.C. Boral, Khemchand Prakash, Anil Biswas and Naushad. Husnlal was a skilled violinist and Bhagatram was a wizard with the harmonium. He had been a student of the well-known classical musicologist, Pandit Dilip Chandra Bedi, who was a disciple of Bhaskar Buwa Bakhale of the Agra gharana. The Agra gharana is known for its complicated taans, sharp diction and musical skills and, although Husnlal–Bhagatram were not active practitioners of this style, they had imbibed its special techniques from their gurus. Their older brother, Pandit Amarnath, was also a respected name in music circles and considered adept at orchestration. Pandit Amarnath, now a forgotten genius, was once a well-known music composer. In fact, not many know that he scored the music for all the eight songs we have of Master Madan, a child prodigy who passed away at a tragically young age. These gems include ghazals and thumris of superlative quality.

For all these reasons, the music created by this duo was always a little different, both in slow and fast tempo compositions, and they had a great command over the use of the various musical instruments played in the background musical score. Occasionally, their compositions may sound a wee repetitive but this was due to the fact that they worked within the framework of a Punjabi beat and used a variety of instruments in their background scores. Their contribution to the making of the legend of Lata Mangeshkar is significant, particularly in her early phase. The compositions that she sang for them in *Badi Bahen* (1949) had created a stir and are remembered even today for two unforgettable songs, *'Chale Jaana Nahin Nain Mila Ke Saiyan Bedardi'* and the perky *'Chup-Chup Khade Ho Zaroor Koi Baat Hai'*, which she sang with Premlata. She very quickly learnt to handle the fast beats of their rhythmical scores even while delivering sad songs, an accomplishment that stood her in good stead when she sang similar numbers for Naushad, Shankarlal–Jaikishan and C. Ramachandra.

'Lut Gayi Ummidon Ki Duniya' (*Jaltarang*, 1949); *'Dil Hi Ho Hai, Tarap Gaya, Dard Se Bhar Na Aaye Kyoon'* (*Adhi Raat*, 1950); *'Agar Dil Kisi Par Lutaya Na Hota'* (*Gauna*, 1950); *'Tujhe Barbad Karna . . . Haye Dil Bhi Diya To Kisko Diya' Tha'* (*Meena Bazar*, 1950); *'Dard-e-Judayi Hai, Gham Ki Chhayi Hai'* (*Chhoti Bhabhi*, 1950); *'Thahar oo jane wale, Ek meri fariyaad'* (*Birha ki Raat*, 1950), *'Vo paas bhi rehkar paas nahi'* (*Afsana*, 1951), and *'Aye meri zindgi tujhe dhundhoo kahaan* (*Adal-E-Jahangeer'*, 1955)—to name a few—are some excellent

examples of her early songs sung for Husnlal–Bhagatram. It is difficult to believe that she had achieved such a high degree of excellence in just a few years and for this we have to give credit to Husnlal–Bhagatram's brilliant compositions and orchestral scores. Her association with them in the early years added an important dimension to her repertoire that needs to be acknowledged.

83

The eminent music composer Anil Biswas was once recording a song by Surinder Kaur and Lata ji happened to be present. Anil Biswas called out in an affectionate way to her, 'Latike! Come here and sing in the chorus. It will add to the song.' Lata ji says that perhaps he said so in jest but, because he was so senior, she went quietly and stood along with the rest of the chorus and sang along with them without demur.

She laughs as she recounts the incident to me. She says she felt that music directors were so certain of her performance and also because she seldom refused a senior colleague that they never hesitated to ask her for a favour. 'I don't know why Dada said that to me that day, but I felt I must not let him down . . . and, believe me, I really enjoyed singing in the chorus!'

What an amazing revelation from someone who was already the uncrowned queen of the music world by then! She could have laughed off Anil Biswas's offer but she did not. This recollection emerged during the course of our long exchanges and I felt I must include it in the story of her musical journey. The reason is that apart from her humility, this episode revealed to me the easy camaraderie that existed at one time in the world of film music. It was as if a mutual love and support for each other made them into a large, loving family.

84

Lata ji remembers with special warmth those actresses who became her friends. The pleasure that lights up in her eyes as she recalls those times pulls me back to the fifties and sixties that appear now to be a world remarkably free of petty jealousies and dishonesty. She laughs as she remembers a vamp of those days: Kuldeep Kaur. She may have played the evil woman on screen, Lata ji tells me, but she had a heart of gold. Another actress she was very fond of—Shammi—belonged to the same family as Nargis and was, in fact, named Nargis but was forced to change her name to avoid confusion. I learn from Lata ji that Mukesh once produced a film called *Malhar* in 1951, and that Lata ji sang a lovely duet for its composer, Roshan, with Mukesh ('*Bade Armanon Se Rakha*'). Shammi was the heroine of this film and the lyricist was Indivar. This was Shammi's first film as the lead actress and, because Nargis and Shammi were very close, Lata entered their cosy world and the three became close friends.

The same affection drips out of her voice as she remembers Mala Sinha, for the two of them could talk for hours, she says. Geeta Bali, Nimmi, Waheeda Rehman, Sadhana and Saira Banu are other friends she remembers with deep affection. Before she married Shammi Kapoor, Geeta Bali and she were very close but, later, as family affairs took away Geeta Bali's attention, they met less often although they remained friends right to the end. She was the playback singer for several of

Geeta Bali's films, of which the most memorable are *Albela* (1953), *Dulari* (1949), *Jaal* (1958), *Anand Math* (1952), *Jailer* (1958) and *Baradari* (1955).

85

There was a time when L.P. meant Laxmikant–Pyarelal rather than 'long-playing' record and just as the fifties were dominated by Shankar–Jaikishan, the seventies became the 'L.P. decade'. Most of the songs that Lata ji sang for them are still regarded among her finest and just as she was the first choice for S.D. Burman, Roshan, Madan Mohan and Shankar–Jaikishan in the fifties and sixties, she became the favourite singer for L.P. in the seventies. This ensured that she was now regarded as the voice of Indian film music as her name was branded on virtually every other song recorded for a film. Conversely, because she sang so often for them, L.P. began to be regarded as the most successful musical composers despite the fact that R.D. Burman, Kalyan ji–Anand ji had a strong presence as well.

Her support for them gave them an easy, struggle-free entry into this world and, from *Parasmani* in 1963 to *Ram–Lakhan* in 1989, they reigned over the film world with Lata ji delivering one hit song after another.

Hidden behind their long association is another interesting fact. For over three decades, film music was dominated by their musical collaboration. Just as we could say that Naushad ruled over the film music world after the success of *Ratan* (1944) by successfully using Lata's remarkable voice, she lifted the careers of Shankar–Jaikishan and Laxmikant–Pyarelal for she became the voice of this era. Their deft handling of the orchestration behind her songs often outdid what Naushad was previously renowned for. It was recorded by their biographer, V. Bichchu, that in 'Hansta hua noorani chehra' (Parasmani) L–P used an orchestra of 36 violins, where Naushad had once used 20 and Shankar–Jaikishan had taken 30 violins in their orchestra.

This points to the fact that in their early years, L–P were keen to register that their skill was a step ahead of the great Naushad and S–J team. This apart, the important fact to remember is that Lata Mangeshkar was the one vocalist they went back to for each of their 'hit' songs. One can perhaps say that her voice added immensely to their growing presence as composers who were virtually unassailable. It is impossible to list all these 'hits' here but just a selection will give the reader an idea of what I am trying to highlight.

Starting from their earliest playlist is Meghwa Gagan Beech Jhaanke' (Harishchandra Taramati, 1963), 'Jeevan dor tumhi sang bandhi' (Sati Savitri, 1964), 'Khabar Mori Na Leeni Bahut Din Beete' (Sant Gyaneshwar, 1964), 'Yeh rang-e-mehfil yeh jashn-e- baharan' (Mister X in Bombay, 1964), 'Neend Kabhi Rehti Thi Aankhon Mein' (Aasra, 1966), 'Ye Raat Bhi Ja Rahi Hai' (Sau Saal Baad, 1966), 'Udd Ke Pawan Ke Sang Chalugi' (Shagird, 1967), 'Allah Ye Kaisi Ada hai In Haseeno Mein' (Mere Humdum Mere Dost, 1968), 'Nigaahein Kyun Bhatakti hain, Kadam Kyun Dagmagaate Hain' (Baharon Ki Manzil, 1968), 'Saanjh Sawere Adharon Pe Mere Bas Tumhar hai Naam' (Maadhvi, 1969), 'Deeye Jalayen Pyaar ke chalo isi Khushi mein' (Dharti Kahe Pukaar Ke, 1969), come to 'Main dekhoon jis ore sakhi ri, samne mere sanwariya' (Anita, 1967) 'Kaise rahoon chup ki maine pi hi kya hai' (Inteqam, 1969),

'*Oo Ghat saanwari, Thodi thodi Baanwari*' (*Abhinetri*, 1970),
'*Zamane mein aji aise kayi nadaan hote hain*' (*Jeevan-Mrityu*,
1970), '*Sona laiye ja re, chandi laiye ja re*' (*Mera Gaon Mera
Des*, 1971), '*Palko ke dwaare pe nindiyaa khadi re*' (*Lagan*,
1971), '*Bhor bhaye panghat pe mohe natkhat Shyam sataye*'
(*Satyam Shivam Sundaram*, 1978), '*Pawan Jharokha Sang Mere
Gaaye*' (*Meri Bhabhi*, 1979), to '*Nindiyaa se jaagi Bahar*' (*Hero*,
1983), '*Mere pee ko pawan kis gali le chali*' (*Gulami*, 1985) '*O
Ramji, bara dukh deena tere Lakhan ne*' (*Ram-Lakhan*, 1989).
There are so many 'hit' songs that they have to offer film buffs
that it is impossible to list them all.

The unbeatable combination of her voice and their skill
at providing musical scores with carefully orchestrated music
in the background made it possible for Lata Mangeshkar to
vanquish almost all other playback singers to become the
uncrowned queen of melody in Bombay films.

86

Geeta Roy (later known as Geeta Dutt) and Lata Mangeshkar
first met each other while recording a song for *Shehnai* in a studio
of Filmistan Limited. The lyricist for the song was P.L. Santoshi
and the music had been composed by C. Ramachandra. '*Jawani
Ki Rail Chali Jaye*', their first song together, also featured the
voice of C. Ramachandra who sang under the pseudonym of
Chitalkar. This was some time in 1946 or 1947.

Lata ji remembers that meeting as if it had taken place just
the other day and her deep affection for Geeta Dutt is difficult
to miss as she recalls her late friend and colleague. 'When Geeta
spoke,' she recalls, 'she had such a strong Bengali accent that I

wondered how she would handle Hindi lyrics. However, I don't know how she could switch to a perfect Hindi diction when she stood in front of a mike! After her flawless performance was over, she went back to her rounded Bengali consonants,' she laughs.

The deep bonds of friendship they shared brought a magical quality to the songs they have sung together. Listening to them is like listening to two sisters or friends in conversation. If you don't believe this, listen to Vasant Desai's composition for *Goonj Uthi Shehnai* (1959) and the song *'Hoye . . . Ankhiyan Bhool Gayin Hain Sona, Dil Pe Hua Hai Jaadu-Tona/ Shehnayi Wale Teri Shehnayi Re, karejwa Ko Cheer Gayi, Cheer Gayi, Cheer gayi'*, or to Iqbal Queraishi's composition from *Panchayat* (1958), *'Ta-Thayya Karte Aana, Oo Re Jaadugar More Saiyyan/ Mere Dil Ki Lagi Bhujana, Oye Jaadugar More Saiyyan'*, where they bounce notes across the song as playfully as two friends playing with a ball.

Their consideration for each other is also reflected in their effortless matching of musical pitches—Geeta Dutt's lower pitch and Lata ji's high octaves. Despite their different voices, just listen to the brilliance of Shankar–Jaikishan's song from *Yahudi* (1958): *'Bechain Dil Khoyi Si Nazar, tanhaiyon Mein Sham Sahar, Tum Yaad Aate Ho . . .'*.

87

This episode is from 1962; Lata ji had been unwell for about three months but carried on recording through her pain. Suddenly, she took a 'turn for the worse, doubled up with severe gripes in her stomach and threw up several times. At this point, the family panicked and insisted she consult a doctor.

A thorough investigation and many tests later, their family doctor, Dr Kapoor, told the family that he was convinced she was being slowly poisoned. This suspicion was confirmed when their cook left abruptly without telling anyone and never returned to even collect his wages. After this incident, Lata ji's younger sister Usha took charge of the kitchen but the Mangeshkar family never breathed a word of this to anyone, nor did they seek help from the police. She tells me in her serene way, 'It's all over and what was done was done. What was the point of raising a hue and cry after it had happened? I felt I did not want the hassle of a police enquiry or publicity, so we did nothing. Someone must have certainly planted him in our house with some purpose.' According to her, she can think of no one who would wish to harm her, so why take names?

However, her confidence took a toll and, for some time after this incident, she was badly shaken. Her return to her old life was organized by Hemant Kumar when he made her sing that hauntingly eerie composition, 'Kahin Deep Jale Kahin Dil . . .'. She recorded this number in one shot and with it laid the ghost of another experience. She says she will never forget how Majrooh Sultanpuri would come by every day to check on her, something for which she remembers him till today with respect and deep affection.

After this revelation, the pain that lurks behind every syllable of that song suddenly takes on a new meaning for me.

88

In the course of an interview she gave to Doordarshan in the eighties, Rajkumari ji confessed: 'I can't say why Nayyar Sa'ab

made me sing "*Mori Nidiya Churaye Gayo*" (*Aasman*, 1952).
I always felt he had composed it with Lata ji in mind.' Truth
is that behind this artless and innocent revelation is a very ugly
and unhappy story. Now that he is no more, there is little point
in raking it up but fans of music like me will always wonder
why O.P. Nayyar and Lata ji fell out with each other and never
came together again.

O.P. Nayyar brought a dimension into film music that had
some important flourishes and a beat that was truly compelling. I
like to wonder how Lata ji's renderings of the songs he composed
for Asha Bhonsle, Shamshad Begum or Geeta Dutt would
have sounded. These are idle speculations of a music-mad fan,
nevertheless, just imagine whether a song like '*Yeh lo main haari
piya, hui teri jeet re, kahe ka jhagda baalam, nayi-nayi preet re*'
(*Aar-Paar*, 1954) would have sounded different in Lata ji's voice.

89

After the unforgettable music of Madhumati that she considers
one of her finest renderings, Lata ji believes that she got true
satisfaction from Lekin, which came out in 1990, at a time when
classical compositions were slowly fading into a new phase of
film music. In Lekin, Gulazar's lyrics, Hridaynath Mangeshkar
and Lata ji have used the mesmerizing combination of folk and
classical music to recreate a magic that is unrivalled.

In the songs from this film you can hear a wide range of
instruments: tanpura, surmandal, pakhawaj, ghungroos, tabla,
sarangi, violin, sitar, and sarod. Hridaynath has used this
extraordinary combination in various ways: each one a delight.
For lovers of the fifties and sixties music, the film brings to
mind such great composers as Pandit Ravi Shankar, Pandit

Pannalal Ghosh, Pandit Amarnath, S.D. Burman, Roshan, Pandit S.N. Tripathi and Vasant Desai.

Among its most memorable compositions is '*Suniyo ji araj mhari*' where Lata ji's voice soars effortlessly to the highest note (*taar saptak*), without wavering from its tender lyrics. Along with all the instruments, one can clearly hear the rare Ravanhatta and the veena as well! The effect is as if a hundred lamps have been lit up simultaneously.

Equally enchanting is the marriage of the pakhawaj and sarod in one interlude that brings a magical dimension of gravity and longing together. I would recommend that readers hear the perfect way in which the lyrics of '*Bisra diyo re kahe, bides bhijaye ke/ Hum ka bula lo babul, doliya livaye ke, Bhejo jee doli uthaye charon kahaar, suniyoo jee araz mhaari, oo Babula hamaar, Saawan aayo ghar layi jaiyo, babula hamaar*' (Why have you forgotten me after I left your home, Father? Send me a palki to call me back to you . . .) are matched with the background score.

90–92

It is not enough to just listen to Lata ji's voice; her singing invites you to delve deeper into her world of music. Her enunciation, pure and crystal clear, is in itself a joy to hear but even more is the way she emphasizes certain syllables, draws out emotions, takes in pauses and silences to make the listener aware of the entire emotional spectrum of a song.

It can be said of her that she has the capacity to coax every little feeling embedded in the lyrics that she gives voice to. Just as a viewer can gaze for hours at a favourite painting, one can go on listening to the magic of her songs without tiring.

Pick any song by her and you will find yourself immersed in some human condition; she has captured every kind of pain and pleasure that one has experienced and some that have no equivalent word to describe them. What can one say in conclusion but that listening to her simply opens one's eyes?

> *Din Aaye, Din Jaaye*
> *Uss din Ki Kya Ginti*
> *Jo Bhajan Kiye Bin jaaye*
> *Days come and go.*
> *Any day that passes without a prayer*
> *Needs no record*

93

If you wish to savour the best of Jaidev's compositions, you can do no better than listen to Lata ji sing Pandit Narendra Sharma's moving lyrics:

> *Jo samar mein ho gaye geet amar, main unki yaad mein/ Ga rahi hoon aaj shraddha geet dhanyavad mein . . .*

> (I sing in praise and gratitude of those songs that Time has made eternal . . .)

It is considered as one of her most moving patriotic songs and ends with the lines: '*Lautkar na ayenge vijay dilane wale veer/ Main geet anjuli main unke liye nayan neer*' (The braves who brought victory for us will never return/ My musical offering to them brims with my tears.)

She does not like mawkish songs, nor does she wish to sing such stirring patriotic songs that are composed for a mere dramatic flourish. Her love for the country and sorrow at the loss of brave soldiers comes from a much deeper recess. It brings before our eyes the fields and villages that they played in, the sisters and wives and families they left forever and the parents who saw their child snatched by death before them.

94

One of the most attractive qualities Lata ji has is her ability to be involved in the world around her and yet keep her inner core untouched by the vicissitudes of everyday life. She is the embodiment of womanly grace with layers of experiences locked inside her that she is often unwilling to share. For instance, if I ask her how she is as an opening sentence, she may say, 'Not so good today but in these times, that is good enough.' Make what you will of that!

Often, when I call her, she sends me a warm '*Namaskar*' before I have even opened my mouth to say, '*Pranam*'. Warm and intimate though our exchanges may have been, I was always aware that she never opened up on those topics that were hurtful or sad. I respected her dignified distance and, on such days, gleaned what I could from her silences.

95

One of the most charming aspects of her style is that she makes certain phrases special by investing them with a lingering memory. It is as if she opens a window for you to peep into a song that you want to hear over and over again to get an elusive fragrance. For instance, in '*Kheencho kaman, maro ji baan/ Rut hai jawan, Oo mere praan*' (*Jhanak Jhanak Payal Baje*, 1955), a duet she sang with Hemant Kumar, she leaves us with '*Kheencho Kaman, Maro Ji Baan*', with such piercing sweetness that you want to instantly rewind it and hear that bowstring pulled by her. Similarly, '*Jadugar saiyyan, chhod mori baiyyan*' (*Nagin*, 1954), she leaves us with the plaintive '*Jane de o rasiya, more man basiya, gaon mera bari door hai*', and you can picture the pleading heroine, pulling her wrist free of a lover's grasp.

I can give several examples, but will leave you with just two more examples. '*Pyaar ka hindola yahan jhul gaye naina/ sapne jo dekhe mujhe bhul gaye naina*' from the song '*Mila hai kisi ka jhumka*' (*Parakh*, 1960): '*Aji lakh pardon main chhup jayega, nazar ayeyga, nazar ayeyga*'; or '*Doli main dolega jiya, ki rani beti raj karegi*' from the song '*Mahalon ka raja mila*' (*Anokhi Raat*, 1968); '*Kesariya dharti lage ambar lalam-laal re, ang lagakar saayaba kar de mujhe nihaal re*' from the song '*Tu Chanda Main Chandni*' (*Resham aur Shera*, 1971) '*Main jab se unke saath bandhi, ye bhed tabhi jana maine, kitna such hai bandhan mein*' from the song '*Rajnigandha Phool Tumhare*', (*Rajniganda*, 1974).

Open these windows and they will provide you with hours of listening pleasure.

96

Her unerring talent in locating the throbbing emotion behind a song is actually a carefully crafted skill. She is a sharp observer of life in every situation and it comes as no surprise that she makes sure she gets to see R.K. Laxman's cartoons in the *Times of India* every morning to get a feel of the mood of the nation. She never allows others to tell her how to emote a particular composition, although she listens intently to each instruction she is given. Her inner voice is her best guide and takes her unerringly to the right pitch each time.

97

She is a divine voice that blessed our planet, like the mythological *gandharvas* who are described as celestial beings sent from time to time to Earth to dazzle us mere mortals with their art. One day, this divine presence will go back to the heaven that she came from and we will cherish each memory of that voice we heard.

98

This is then the story of a little girl who remained quaintly innocent throughout her life, despite the enormous reputation and respect she received for her work. However, she was also born to grow up quickly to take care of the people around her and grew into a mature and responsible elder sister to a large family. Somewhere between these two extremes is the story that I have tried to write to bring to my readers the saga of her musical journey. Perhaps my inept attempts at trying to explain are best embodied in a song she sang long ago: '*Suno choti si gudiya ki lambi kahani . . .* ' (Listen to the long tale of a tiny little doll).

99

Main hoon ghubaar ya toofan hoon/ koi batay main kahan hoon/ Dar hai safar mein kahin kho na jaaon main/ Rasta naya aa aa aa . . ./ Aaj phir jeene ki tamanna hai/ Kal ke andheron se nikal ke/ Dekha hai aankhain malte-malte/ Phool hi phool zindagi bahar hai/ Tay kar liya aa aa aa . . ./ Aaj Phir Jeene ki Tamanna Hai . . .

(Someone tell me whether I am a puff of dust or a rolling thunderstorm. I fear I may get lost in this journey, so unfamiliar . . . I want to live once again away from the shadows of the dark past/ As I rub my eyes/ I see a sea of flowers ahead of me/ I've decided I want to live . . .)

These unforgettable lines by Shailendra in *Guide* could have been written for Lata Mangeshkar rather than the heroine, Waheeda Rehman, in that film. Time and again, Lata ji has reinvented her music to become the voice of the nation. How fortunate we are to have her capture the times of our country and our lives in such melodious music!

Naam Gum Jaayega, Chehra Ye Badal jaayega
Meri Aawaaz Hi Pehchaan Hai, Gar Yaad Rahe . . .

PART 2

THE INTERVIEW

Interview with Lata Mangeshkar
(Selected Excerpts)

Yatindra Mishra (YM): Let's start with your music and your life. I am trying to plumb the depths of the life that created your unique musical persona so that I present those memorable incidents to those dedicated listeners of your songs who seek inspiration from your music.

How different is Lata Mangeshkar's inner world of music from the world outside?

Lata Mangeshkar (LM): I see them both as one. In all humility, I want to say that I have always viewed my music as a devotee looks to his God. I did not come to this industry to seek any personal wealth or fame and consider my entry into the world of music as a natural progression of my desire to serve my muse. This is why I look upon the fame and love I have received from my listeners and my country as divine benediction. The world I inhabit, this world of music, is the only world I recognize. Perhaps this may not be the answer you sought but it is what I sincerely believe.

YM: What memories of your father, Pandit Dinanath Mangeshkar, still fill you with happiness?

LM: There are so many. For instance, when as children we got into mischief, our father would call us and make us stand in front of him. He'd just look at us gravely and we'd dissolve into tears under his intense gaze. He never yelled or shouted but we all knew exactly why we had been summoned by him. He'd then ask, 'Understood?' and we'd nod to say 'Yes'. 'Now go and play,' he'd say and dismiss us. This is the man he was: he could convey so much even when remaining silent.

He was incredible and my most abiding memory of him is his complete absorption in his music. His drama company staged its shows after 9 p.m. so it was often 1 or 2 in the morning when he came home. These dramas had five acts and several long musical pieces set in classical ragas and ran for a long time. Once my father entered the stage, he was greeted by whistles, claps and cries for encores. He sang slightly loudly into the mike and I loved that. I also loved the way he would deftly switch from one raga to another by introducing a new note and then just as adroitly go back to the original raga. Another innovation he brought into his dramas was the introduction of Carnatic and Punjabi musical styles. He actually travelled to Karnataka to learn some musical compositions and put them in his dramas. Remember that this was the high noon of musical dramas and singing was a coveted talent.

On the days he was free, he organized musical sessions at home. When he sang on such occasions, it was not popular numbers from his musical dramas but pure classical compositions. HMV released some classical ragas sung by my father and as far as I remember there was Raga Jaijaiwanti that the Megaphone Company put in the market.

YM: Which were his favourite ragas?

LM: From what I can remember, Bhoopali, Yaman, Darbari, Darbari Kanhra, Jaijaiwanti, Shankara and Hindol. He sang Hindol with great feeling.

YM: Where did your father's players come from? I'd like to know more about the artistes that formed his drama company.

LM: Most of them were Marathi singers from small villages in and around Poona, Satara, Sangli, Miraj and Kolhapur. These were regions with a very vibrant musical tradition. For instance, tanpuras and sitars made by the skilled Muslim craftsmen of Miraj were sent all over India. Today, this skill is on the wane because most singers prefer to use the harmonium as an accompaniment rather than the tanpura. Satara was the seat of Shivaji's grandson Shambhuji Maharaj and all Marathi people look at it with great respect. Kolhapur is a very old centre for classical music and was made famous by ustads like Alladiya Khan sahib and his son Bhurji Khan sahib. In fact, a lot of the film industry's work was carried out in Kolhapur itself in those days and so it became an important centre of music, cinema and theatre. I clearly remember that I saw my first Ashok Kumar film, *Kismet*, there with my family and also V. Shantaram's *Shakuntala* starring his wife, Jayshree.

As for Sangli, it was my home until the age of eight. The royal palaces of Sangli and Kolhapur held musical soirees and my father's drama company was often cordially invited to perform there. I mean that in my travels with my father, I was always aware of the deep respect accorded to artistes and the love for music among the people. These were the places that nurtured the players who joined my father's drama company.

YM: Who did your father learn from and who among the artistes of those times were the people he looked up to?

LM: I was very young when my father sang on the stage but I remember him saying that his musical style was that of Gwalior. In fact, he had formally accepted the famous Gwalior gharana singer Pandit Ramakrishna Buwa as his guru and tied the traditional red thread (*ganda*) on his wrist to formalize the relationship. Although he was no mean musician himself, he spent time learning music from his guru. He was also very close to some stage and theatre artistes and among them Balgandharva ji and Ustad Alladiya Khan sahib must be mentioned because my father was especially close to them. Apart from these two great artistes, he counted several students of Ustad Alladiya Khan sahib, such as Kesarbai Kerkar and Mogubai Kurdekar as his friends. Like us, Kesarbai belonged to Goa and the Konkan region and my father and she got along very well. Nargis ji's mother, Jaddanbai, was another such friend.

YM: Apart from Balgandharv ji, did your father also share a relationship with the other great writers and composers of that time who wrote in Urdu and Hindi and considered famous in Gujarati and Parsi theatre? People like Narayan Prasad Betab, Amritlal Keshav Nayak, Agha Hashr Kashmiri, Jaishankar Sundari, Radheshyam Kathavachak and Master Fida Husain Narsi?

LM: No, none of these great names that you mention rings a bell. At least, I don't recall my father speaking of them or their work or recall Mai (my mother) mentioning them. However, since you mention Urdu and Hindi I do remember that before founding the Balwant Sangeet Company, my father worked in an Urdu play, titled *Taj-e-wafa*, staged by the Kirloskar Natak Mandali. He played a female role in that play and it ran for a long time in Calcutta. You may find it surprising that while he was there, Baba learnt Kathak and even danced in the first few months! He also learnt a bit of Farsi and Urdu during that time.

YM: I understand that as children you imitated film episodes at home. Can you recall any special incident?

LM: (Laughs) Play-acting was our favourite sport! Cinema was our most stimulating medium of entertainment in those days and children would keep a film alive for a long time by recalling its memorable scenes. I remember Prabhat Fims' *Sant Tukaram*, which had a scene where Tukaram ascends to heaven in a chariot sent by the gods. As he ascended, he sang, '*Ami jato amcha gava, amcha Ram-Ram dhyava . . .* ' (I am going to my village, and send a farewell Ram-Ram to all). We collected all the mattresses and pillows we could find in the house to create 'heaven' and I was perched on top singing Tukaram's farewell song. Below me were my 'disciples': my sister Meena, my cousin Pandharinath and Asha, who wailed asking me to take them along as they bade me a teary goodbye. (She chuckles at the memory). Usha was considered a baby then and not a part of this performance. Most of the films we saw were patriotic or mythological ones because my father did not allow us to see any other sort. Mind you, all this was done stealthily when my father was out of the house because we were afraid he would get angry at our obsession with films.

YM: After your father's death, who were the people who supported the family?

LM: I can think of no one who offered any material help. However, there was a doctor who ran a village dispensary, and whom we called 'mama' because my mother considered him her brother. He would come over once in a while to visit us and bring us some food stuff and small gifts. He was a Brahmin by birth but sported an Anglicized name—Dr Riswood. His kindness and civility are still a pleasant memory.

YM: Who helped you when you started working for the film world?

LM: Among those with whom I had a personal contact was Master Vinayak, the father of actress Nanda. He offered me some work under his banner of Praful Pictures. This gave me my first foothold in this world and the assurance that there were some people in it who were compassionate towards those in distress.

YM: Do you remember any of the films that you acted in?

LM: After my father's demise, the responsibility of the family fell on my shoulders. Apart from Mai, there were four siblings to take care of and to me the film world seemed to be the only way of earning instantly. Within a few days of Baba's death, Master Vinayak gave me a small role in his film, *Pehli Mangalgaur*. The film was released in 1942 and I acted as the younger sister of the famous actress Snehprabha Pradhan. Later, in 1943, *Majhe Bal* and in 1944, *Gajabhau* were screened. *Gajabhau* was a Marathi film but it had a Hindi song by me. Still later, *Bari Ma* (1945) was released and I have already spoken to you about it. The film featured Noorjahan as the lead actress. So altogether, I acted in 8 films (the others were *Chimkula Sansar* in 1942, *Jiwan Yatra* and *Subhadra* in 1946, and *Mandir* in 1948. In Bhalji Pendharkar's film *Chhatrapati Shivaji* (1952), I entered singing a song. Recently, some 10–15 years ago, I was shown on the screen as I sang a patriotic song in film the *Pukar* that starred Madhuri Dixit and Anil Kapoor.

I used to find acting and all the makeup I was forced to put on distasteful. That is why when I became a playback singer, I thanked God for releasing me from that torture. Truth to tell, I never found the idea of acting in a film attractive at all.

YM: Apart from your music what else did you learn from your father?

LM: Above all, how to live with self-respect. This gave me the courage to stand up for the values he had taught us to believe in. Let me give you an example: during 1947–48, one could buy saris only against a ration card. When I started out, our financial state was pretty grim, so I was able to just afford those rationed saris. These were plain cotton saris with a thin woven border and cost about twelve rupees. I washed them myself and carefully folded them and since I could not afford to get them ironed at a dhobi shop, I put them under my pillow at night so that their creases fell into place. When I wore them to go to work, no one would be able to tell that they had been pressed by my head on the pillow at night. I am proud that I never had to ask anyone for a loan and always lived thriftily within our meagre means. I think this comes from the lesson that my father had dinned into us and who showed us how to live with one's head held high. He also used to say do only that which you think is worth doing. Our family went from good times to bad: when my father earned well, we lived lavishly and then after his death we went through really hard times. My mother too had the same spirit: she never surrendered her dignity or sought help from anyone.

Another valuable lesson he taught us was how to accept change and adjust oneself to it. Mind you, many of these rules were made in a completely different time. Yet they have guided me throughout my life. Today I may have name, fame and wealth yet I still prefer to stay in the modest home I bought years ago because it has given us all so much happiness. I am

sure this had its own reward: my fame and wealth now come as
a reward for living by truth and dignity. Believe me, I never fail
to thank God that our family was able to be true to the values
upheld by my father.

YM: Your musical education was started in the 1940s, who
was your first guru?

LM: My musical education came to an abrupt end after
my father's death but I practised whatever I remembered of
his compositions. Master Vinayak once told me that I should
develop the musical training I had received from my father
under a teacher. He once invited Ustad Aman Ali Khan sahib
of Bhendibazar to his home and on 11 August 1945, I was
formally accepted as Ustad sahib's student. The first raga he
taught me was Hamsadhwani, although I had been introduced
to this raga by my father. He spent a long time refining my
singing and to date, it is one of my favourite ragas. The words
of the *vilambit* part were '*Patidevan Mahadevan*' and of the
drut laya were '*Lagi lagan pati sakhi sang*'. (She hums it). Later
he taught me Yaman Kalyan, Hem and Todi. A wonderful
teacher, he was very fond of me and treated me like his own
daughter. He came to Master Vinayak's house, Kumud Villa,
to hold my lessons because for some reason my sister Meena
and I were staying there. Concerned that I looked too frail,
he'd bring along a roti–omelette roll for me and watched me
eat it before the lesson started. These sessions went on for about
two hours and I sang along with him on my tanpura.

I realize today that I miss this beloved teacher almost as
much as I miss my father. Sadly, after a few months of teaching
me he left for his village and never came back. Master Vinayak
then found me another teacher: Ustad Amanat Ali Devasawale,
nephew of the famous singer Ustad Rajab Ali Khan. He was

renowned for having groomed several film personalities, among them Nargis' mother Jaddanbai. I understand that Nargis never showed any interest in learning music: apparently, she preferred tennis. She was consumed with the idea of joining the film world. However, much to my dismay, the Ustad had to leave for Indore for some personal reasons and once again my music lessons came to an end. In the 1970s, I learnt classical music from Ustad Bade Ghulam Ali Khan sahib and Pandit Tulsidas Sharma but by then I was so busy that I could hardly spare any time for sustained lessons. Even so, I went from the recording studios for these valuable lessons. Pandit Sharma taught me a composition in Ahir Bhairav, 'Guru Bin Gyan Nahin Avat', but after his sudden death, my lessons were once again over. Nevertheless, I always tried to keep all that I had learnt from these wonderful teachers whenever I did my riyaz (practice). In one sense, perhaps, my rushing from one recording studio to another in those busy days was a kind of riyaz in itself.

Beyond this, I must tell you that I attended every music concert I could and carefully listened to great artistes of the time such as Vilayat Ali Khan and Ali Akbar bhai and lapped up each performance and recording of Ustad Bade Ghulam Ali Khan. I have heard live concerts in Bombay by Ustad Amir Khan to learn how one took an alap or how it was played on the sitar. I believe all this was in itself an education in classical music.

YM: They say that Master Ghulam Haider played a seminal role in your early career and that you were deeply influenced by him. Can you elaborate on this?

LM: You are right. I hold him in very high regard. I recall an incident from my childhood that I often repeat. In 1941,

a film titled *Khazanchi* was released with its music scored by
Master Ghulam Haider. In fact, he had even sung a duet in this
film along with Shamshad Begum, '*Sawan Ke Nazare Hain*'.
The film was a big hit and sold so many records for its music
that it is some kind of a milestone of that era. The makers of
the film organized a competition for someone who would sing
two of its best songs before a panel of judges. My father was
still alive then and had gone to Bombay on some work, and the
contest was to be held in Poona. I went and entered my name
among the 114 other contestants. I still laugh when I remember
how each one of us was supposed to introduce ourselves to the
audience. When it was my turn, I declared confidently: 'Lata!
Dinanath Mangeshkar.' (Laughs). Everyone clapped at my
self-confidence. I think some of the applause was for my father
who was a much-admired singer of the time and some were
to boost my courage. I sang two songs as required, '*Laut Ayi
Papan Andhiyari*' and '*Nainon Ke Baan Ki Reet Anokhi*'. Both
these had been sung by Shamshad Begum in the film. I came
home with a dilruba as a prize. Years later, when I met Ghulam
Haider sahib, I told him that that was the first 'award' I ever
received. You'll probably laugh when you hear that instead of
being happy that I had won the first prize, my father was actually
displeased that I had taken part in a music contest. Perhaps he
was afraid that if I had not won that prize, he would have lost
face in his community. But what became evident to me later
was that I am different because I am Dinanath Mangeshkar's
daughter, not only because I was proud of this fact but also that
I owed it to his reputation never to let him down.

YM: How did your work with Ghulam Haider proceed?

LM: When I first sang from him (a Noorjahan song in the
film *Zeenat*) I was so nervous that I went off-key. He asked me

whether I had ever learnt music and I answered that Amanat
Ali Khan was my guru for about ten years. 'Then, when you
had such a fine teacher, why did you go off-key?' he countered.
I was terrified.

Later, when the film director Shashdhar Mukherji rejected
my voice as unsuitable for Kamini Kaushal in the film *Shaheed*,
he was most upset. He was quite angry with Mukherji although
he said nothing but told me quietly, 'Don't worry, you will sing
for my next film *Majboor*. I'm making this film for Bombay
Talkies, come along.' And both of us headed to Goregaon
station and waited for the train to arrive. Haider sahib was
holding a tin of 555 cigarettes and right there, on the platform,
he drummed a beat on the tin and said, 'Lata, sing in rhythm
with this.' He hummed the song for me, '*Dil mera tora kahin,
kahin ka na choda hai tere pyar main.*' I sang exactly as he had
wanted and in rhythm with his beat and he was delighted,
'Wonderful! This is exactly how I wished it to be sung.' This is
how we travelled from Goregaon to Bombay Talkies in Malad
and after two or three days of rehearsals, the song was recorded.
While singing for *Majboor*, I also met Mukesh Bhaiyya and our
duet, '*Ab Darne Ki Koi Baat Nahin*', was recorded. I think it
was because of Master Ghulam Haider that I was able to find
a firm foothold in the film industry. It was through him that
I came in contact with Khemchand Prakash and Anil Biswas.
My work became known and I started receiving offers from
music directors. Some would say she is a new girl but she has
sung for Ghulam Haider and Khemchand Prakash (laughs). So
I think I owe Master ji a lot.

YM: The music of the forties and fifties is quite unique. I
want to know what kind of recording studios there were because
you have often mentioned how you have recorded songs while

standing under trees. What were the recording arrangements in such cases?

LM: You will be surprised to learn that there were just two recording studios in those days: Famous and Central, both in Tardeo. There was a third one in Mahalaxmi, also called Famous but it was famous only in name. These studios had a small, hall-like room where the recording took place. Filmistan in Goregaon had a small studio and God knows why but we had to sit on the floor and record our songs. Do you know that we recorded the famous songs of *Nagin* and *Anarkali* on the stage of Filmistan? Only after shooting for the day was over and they became free, were we able to record our songs. Naturally, often these recordings took place very late at night or very early in the morning. I can't tell you how difficult it was for us to manage these odd timings. Often the floors were dusty and filthy and we had to record our loveliest compositions there . . . and the studio lights made the room so unbearably hot that, along with Bombay's humid climate and the fact that no fans could be switched on while recording, it was a great challenge to sing soothing or romantic songs! (She laughs and I join her).

It was much later that Mehboob Khan went abroad and brought back modern sound recording equipment and created a separate chamber in Mehboob Studios for recording music. This naturally became the favourite studio for Burman dada, Roshanlal and Naushad sahib. They were followed by Laxmikant–Pyarelal. Just imagine that in an industry that recorded hundreds of songs each year, there were just three–four proper studios for recording music!

YM: There were some outstanding sound recordists, someone like Minoo Katrak. How do you view their contribution?

LM: You are absolutely right: I have not just known but worked with some of the finest in this line. Minoo was a genius who worked in Tardeo's Famous Studio. There was another brilliant man, known as Kaushik Baba, in Mehboob Studios and one B.N. Sharma in Dadar's Bombay Labs. These were all men of exceptional talent and Minoo Katrak recorded for almost all of Raj Kapoor's films because Raj Kapoor took great interest in the music for his films and was very emotional about the subject. He liked Famous Studios only because Minoo Katrak was the sound recordist there. Madan Mohan ji also chose this studio for the same reason. The other well-known recordists were Mr Bose and Daman Sood.

Among the music directors, Salil Chaudhuri, Jaikishan and Pyarelal were great music arrangers. Personally, I like to work with Anil Mohile and have done several music shows with him.

YM: What were the working conditions like in those days? Did your life become easier after the first few years of struggle or were they were always difficult?

LM: I cannot say when life was easy and when it was difficult. I don't pay attention to such details but yes, I do remember how hard I had to work to become successful. Recording would continue from morning till late in the night and my whole day went in commuting from one location to another. My only concern was the music and song I had to record, nothing else mattered. Often it would be late by the time work ended and I was famished. In those days all that the studio canteens offered was tea and some biscuits. So all that I managed would be some cups of tea and a few biscuits and I remember often spending the whole day on just a few sips of water because there was no time to even run to the canteen to grab a cup of tea. My greatest concern was that I should be able to earn enough to feed my family, whether I was recording or at home that is all my mind was preoccupied with. You ask me about the good and bad phases of my life, but honestly all that I worried about was how much work I would be able to get. When one contract expired, I was worried about how to get another.

YM: I want to ask you about your financial situation. Did life become easier after 1950?

LM: Difficult to say. I have few memories of that time regarding all this. In 1949–50, we lived in Nana Chowk in two small rooms on a rent of Rs 300 a month. I had rented the place when I got my first bit of work with Master Vinayak. In 1960 or so, we shifted to Walkeshwar when I bought a three-roomed flat. In 1960, I put together money to buy this flat in Peddar Road in Prabhu Kunj, where we live now. I gave all the money I earned to Mai and she ran the house with it. Whatever she was able to save, she did that too.

It may surprise you to learn that playback singers were paid very modest sums for all the hard work they put in. In 1948, I was working on several films, including *Mahal*, *Barsaat*, *Andaz*, *Dulari*, *Bari Bahen* and *Girls' School*. They were all released during 1949–50 but I don't remember any great fortune that I was able to make. It was only after 1960, when my work had become known and appreciated, that I began to earn well. This was when films like *Anarkali*, *Baiju Bawra*, *Nagin*, *Amar*, *Naubahar*, *Udan Khatola*, *Basant Bahar* were released. Every music director now wanted me to sing for them and after *Anarkali* and *Nagin*, I never looked back.

YM: By the fifties, Akashvani had started to broadcast your songs and you became a household name. How did this affect your development?

LM: I had become pretty well known after *Mahal* and people began to write letters to find out more about the playback singer who had sung the songs in that film. This is when HMV decided to announce that Lata Mangeshkar had sung that song. Let me relate an interesting episode regarding this. It was around 1945–46, when the radio ran a programme of film and non-film music called *Aapki Farmaish*. This was the first time when the name of the person who had requested it was announced. To hear my own name being announced on the radio, I sent in a request for Begum Akhtar's ghazal, '*Deewana Banana Hai To Deewana Bana De*'. I tuned in every day not just to hear this wonderful composition but more to hear my name being announced on air (giggles). When they finally did, I walked on air for the next few days! Later, after *Barsaat* and *Bari Bahen*, the thrill of hearing my name on air was there but after 1950 or so, I was no longer so interested in either hearing my name or listening to my voice on radio. Truth to tell, the thrill I got from listening to my name after Begum Akhtar's song was unmatched.

YM: Both Mukesh and you were great fans of K.L. Saigal and there is a trace of his voice in both your voices. Do you agree?

LM: If we are both viewed as fans of Saigal, I am happy to hear that because I really respect Saigal's voice. I believe that no one could remain unaffected by his music because he was such an extraordinary singer. You are right: both Mukesh and I worshipped his voice and before I came to Bombay he was the only other singer apart from my father whose songs I liked to hear. I wanted terribly to meet him when I came here, pay my respects and request him to sing a song for me. Sadly, this never happened for he passed away soon after I arrived in Bombay.

In fact, when I bought my first radio the first announcement was that of his death. I was lying on the floor on a mat and listening to some songs when the news of his death was flashed. I was so shocked that I decided then and there to return the radio to the shop. In those days we had very little money for indulgences like a radio and the reason I decided to sell it at a loss was because I could not get over the coincidence of the arrival of a radio in my home and Saigal's death. I thought it was a bad omen and just could not get over it.

Mukesh Bhaiyya was luckier than I: Saigal had gifted him his personal harmonium. That harmonium is still in Mukesh Bhaiyya's home. Just listen to Mukesh Bhaiyya's first song from *Pehli Nazar* (music by Anil Biswas), '*Dil Jalta Hai To Jalne Do*', and you will think you are listening to Saigal sahib. I think this was Mukesh's way of honouring the artiste he so admired, he copied him because he could not coax the same magic out of his throat. What a marvellous tribute! By the way, Kishore Kumar was also a great Saigal fan.

YM: Did you never hear him live at a concert or see Saigal?

LM: No, never. I created a picture of him in my mind after listening to his songs whether from the film world or non-film compositions. My entire clan worships his voice and it was my greatest dream to sing one day along with him. And if that were not possible, then I wished for an opportunity to at least hear him perform or to be able to meet him one day. Sadly, that never happened.

YM: But suppose that you had been able to sing with him, which are the songs that you can think of?

LM: Saigal was not just someone I admired deeply, I think I learnt a lot from his style as well. I once curated a record titled *Shraddhanjali* to honour the voices that have affected my music and been a seminal influence in my career. I chose several Saigal songs for that album: 'So Ja Rajkumari'; 'Main Kya Janoo Kya Jadoo Hai' (Zindagi); 'Nainheen Ko Rah Dikha Prabhu' (Bhakt Surdas); 'Do Naina Matwale Tihare Hum Par Zulam Karen' (Meri Bahen); 'Dukh Ke Din Ab Beetat Nahin'; 'Balam Aye Baso More Man Main' (Devdas)—all of which I consider brilliant renderings by him. They sound fresh and appealing even after all these years. I also adore 'Sapt Suran Teen Gram Gao Sab Gunijan' (Tansen), set to a pure raga which endears it to me. There are so many Saigal songs that are branded on one's mind: 'Ek Bangla Bane Nyara' (President), 'Gham Diye Mustakil, Kitna Nazuk Hai Dil' and 'Chah Barbad Karegi Humain Na Maloom Tha' (Shahjahan) . . . Among his non-film songs that I love are 'Punchhi Kahe Hote Udas' by Kedar Sharma and Akbar Allahabdi's 'Duniya Hoon Main, Duniya Kas Talabghaar Nahin Hoon' are my favourites. I don't think any other singer can match up to him. Nor do I think it right to pick a few from the enormous range of his songs because each one is unique in its own way.

YM: Even so, if you had choose just one, which one would it be?

LM: Then 'Ab main kaha karoon, kith jaoon' from Dhartimata, composed by Pankaj Mulick.

YM: Which are his films you like the most?

LM: Zindagi, Dushman, Street Singer, Bhakt Surdas and Devdas.

YM: Did you ever see Gandhi ji?

LM: Although I never saw him, I heard him several times. I can vaguely remember that in the forties I heard him as he addressed public meetings in Shivaji Park and Chowpatty. The crowds were so huge that we couldn't see him but could only hear his voice from where we stood far away.

YM: Did you ever wish you had been able to sing at one of his prayer meetings?

LM: Not really, because I was so young then and no one knew me as a singer. I had just started my career and those years were full of struggle for me and my family. Then Gandhi ji passed away in 1948, long before I could muster up the courage to meet him personally. Certainly, I would have loved to sing for him (who wouldn't?) but the opportunity never arose.

YM: Later, did you ever feel dedicating something to his memory in a song?

LM: Do you know, when I compiled a record called *Ram Ratan Dhan Payo*, I took most of the songs from his prayer book. In those days, we had toyed with the idea of making a film on Gandhi ji and Sandeep Kohli, Madan Mohanji's son (then working for Music India), encouraged me to pick the hymns and songs that Gandhi ji liked. Pandit Narendra Sharma also helped me in sourcing these songs, so we included songs by Narsinh Mehta, Tulsidas and Mirabai that were dear to Gandhi ji. Pandit Sharma also decided to include some quatrains from the *Ramcharitmanas* since Gandhi ji regularly read this work as well as some verses from the Gita. So this is how we created our homage to Gandhi ji. I must also tell you that this album (*Ram Ratan Dhan Payo*) reached unprecedented levels of popularity and I was flooded with hundreds of appreciative mails and messages. Till today, I receive fan mail for that album!

YM: What are your memories of his assassination?

LM: I remember clearly that I was in Goregaon's Filmistan Studios attending a Silver Jubilee party for *Shehnai*, although, as you know, I keep away from parties and social celebrations.

I had been persuaded by Rai Bahadur Chunnilal ji (Madan Mohan's father) to come and I slipped away early to catch the local train home. When I reached, I noticed that the station was strangely empty and people were scurrying home. Outside the station, there was a lot of confusion and noise and I remember that someone shouted, 'Gandhi ji has been assassinated!'

I was shocked and went home with a heavy heart. After I reached, I just went to my room and the tears would not stop. I felt as if everything had collapsed and there was a strange darkness descending on us. It was a spontaneous outpouring of grief and even today, I can clearly recall how devastated I had felt.

YM: What are your memories of 15 August 1947?

LM: This is another day I remember well. We spent the morning at home but that evening the whole family (including my mother) went out to see the celebrations. There were fireworks and the whole city had been lit up. I remember we even went around on a truck for a while to see the spectacle. There were many others like us who were cheering and waving madly. My mother made some special sweets that we all ate together and distributed in the neighbourhood. I was thrilled that we were alive to see the day when our country became independent.

YM: After Independence came the Partition. What about those memories?

LM: That was a very painful time for the entire country. Don't forget that some of our most talented film people left India for Pakistan. These included Dalsukh Pancholi (who made *Khazanchi*), composer Master Ghulam Haider and Noorjahan. I was very fond of Ghulam Haider sa'ab and we shared a special bond, so I was very upset by his departure

from Bombay. But we must remember that this pain
affected both countries equally and that even though we lost
several talented men and women, their absence was filled
by others who came in from there. In those days, we never
believed that the borders would become so intimidating and
somehow the feeling was that art knows no boundaries and
we are all one large, loving community of performers and
creative people.

YM: Is there any unfulfilled childhood dream in your life?

LM: I can't think of anything special but I will share
one small dream. As a child whenever my father went for a
performance, he would proudly pin all the medals he had
received over the years on his chest. This was the done thing
at that time and I can remember seeing Kumar Gandharva,
then regarded as a child prodigy, on one such occasion sitting
in a sherwani and his medals flashing on it. I used to dream
that one day I would enter a stage for a performance, proudly
flashing such medals.

YM: It is said that you never went to school, then how did
you learn to read and write?

LM: This is not quite true. When we lived in Sangli, there
was a small school called Muralidhar Pathshala near our house.
My cousin Basanti used to go there and when she was in the
third class, I tagged along with her one day. The class teacher
asked who I was and I leapt up and proudly announced 'I am
Master Dinanath Mangeshkar's daughter.' The teacher said,
'Oh, he is a very famous singer. Can you sing something for us?'
I replied with confidence, 'I can sing several ragas: Malkauns,
Hindol, what would you like to hear?'

So she took me to the staff room and I sang a composition
in Hindol that everyone liked very much.

Then, one day, I hoisted my baby sister Asha—who was just ten months old then—on my shoulders and took her along as well. When we reached the school, I put her in my lap while we waited for the teacher. When he arrived, he frowned at me and said a little sternly, 'Babies are not allowed into the classrooms here.' I was furious, picked up my baby sister and marched straight out. After that, I never went to that school again. Also, we often had to go to Bombay and it was never possible to attend regular school again.

In those days, a young boy called Vitthal used to work in the house. He asked me to teach him the Marathi alphabet so that he could learn to read and write. This how I learnt to read and write Marathi so perhaps you could say that Vitthal was the person who taught me to read and write in Marathi. Similarly, we once went to Kolhapur for a few months and my cousin Indira taught me Hindi. Later, when we moved to Bombay, Master Vinayak encouraged me to attend regular Hindi classes along with his children, who had a Hindi tutor Lekhraj Sharma at home.

Ram Gabare was a director with Prabhat Films who taught me English. I felt since this language was spoken and understood all over the country, I must learn it. In the early days, when I commuted by the local train, I always carried a Marathi or Hindi novel to read on the way and this is how I improved my vocabulary. During the fifties, I came in touch with a Sanskrit scholar named Pandit Hardikar and I started to take Sanskrit lessons from him because I wanted to read the Bhagwat Gita . . . However, I must tell you that although I learnt these languages from different teachers, I worked very hard to refine my language skills at home. Today, I can say with confidence that my Marathi, Hindi and Urdu are very good and in addition to these, I also know a smattering of Punjabi. I can understand Sanskrit pretty easily and I even tried learning Bangla once from Basu Bhattacharya, Bimal Roy's assistant and later a director of eminence himself. Salil da also sent me to learn Bangla. I tried to learn Tamil and even learnt the script but found that the language is not easy to speak.

YM: How did you learn to speak such elegant and beautiful Urdu?

LM: (Laughs). Urdu was the dominant language in the film industry when I entered this world, or perhaps you could call it Hindustani because it was a lovely mixture of Urdu and idiomatic Hindi. If you recall the early lyrics of Shakeel Badauni, Qamar Jalalabadi, Arzoo Lakhnavi and Sahir sahib, you will understand what I mean. At that time, all playback singers were required to have perfect diction. Years ago, on the sets of *Bari Ma*, the scriptwriter Ziya Sarhadi sahib called me and said, 'Beta, you will have to work on your *talaffuz* (pronunciation). Come and sit with me and I will refine your accent.' However, this never happened and once Dilip Kumar told Anil Biswas after I sang a song composed by him, 'The tongue of a Marathi singer brought up on a diet of homely *dal-bhat* can't possibly do justice to the spices that make up Urdu.' I kept quiet then but his taunt really cut me to the quick. I took this as a challenge and went to Mohd Shafi, who used to assist Anil Biswas and Naushad sahib. I told him, 'Shafi Bhaiyya, tell me how to improve my Urdu pronunciation so that I can prove to everyone that I can handle ghazals and Urdu lyrics.' He arranged for a Maulvi ustad, Mehboob, who came regularly for a month and I carefully listened to his every advice and correction. Today I thank Dilip Kumar for that remark because it drove me to become proficient in one of the sweetest languages of the world. If he hadn't brought my deficiency to my notice perhaps I would have never been inspired to learn Urdu from a maulvi because the more I learnt from him, the deeper became my appreciation of ghazals and lyrics. I have read all the great Urdu poets Ghalib, Mir, Momin, Zauq, Sauda and Daagh. I am confident now that whenever I sing a lyric that has an Urdu word, my pronunciation is faultless.

YM: How much importance have you given to practice (riyaz)?

LM: I believe that riyaz is very important but it should be done in the correct manner: patiently and according to the teachings of a guru, and in solitude. My teachers also taught me that one should pay attention to the duration: this means that it should not be either too long or too short. A wise practitioner should always bear in mind how much and for how long one can play with notes to understand their nature.

In the beginning, from about 1942–47, I kept my practice sessions as I had always done. I sat with a tanpura—I always did my riyaz with a tanpura—and practised different notes and scales. After the death of Master Vinayak and the closure of his drama company, I had to travel long distances every day in search of work and travel on local trains from Dadar to Malad to Andheri. I still got up early to do my riyaz but after I started getting more and more work and took up playback singing as a career, I had to reduce the time I used to devote to it. However, there wasn't a single day when I did not practise by myself. When I look back I find that all my work was also a kind of riyaz as I sang for different people in different scales and with different notes and rhythms.

Nowadays, I find it difficult to sit down with a tanpura because after my knee replacement surgery this became a

casualty. I find it impossible to sit on a chair and sing or
play a tanpura and no matter how painful it is, I still prefer
to sing or record while standing up before a mike. I may
need to spend a little extra time with the composer or duet
companion to get it right but I still think I sing as I have been
for the last seventy years.

YM: Did you have a special ritual you followed for riyaz?

LM: Nothing special but I did get up at the crack of dawn
and finish my practice by 6 a.m. Along with my trusty tanpura,
I always kept a book of compositions by my guru while my
father's notebook with his notations sits in my prayer room
and I fold my hands before it each day. My father never taught
compositions but taught ragas and made me understand the
notes and their inner qualities. He would educate me on how
each raga is sung and why it is sung at a particular time of the
day. I always kept these lessons in mind as I practised. Apart
from the tanpura he never allowed any other accompaniment
at practice sessions. His belief was that a singer should carry
the rhythmic patterns in his mind and sing according to that
inner beat. His lessons in elaborating a raga are unforgettable
but he was different from my later teachers. Aman Ali Khan
sahib liked to teach compositions and made me practise those.
I think the first raga he taught me was Hem but I learnt so
much more than the raga from him. My second guru, Amanat
Ali Khan sahib taught me both ragas and compositions like
kajris and ghazals. I still remember a ghazal I learnt from him,
first sung perhaps by Begum Akhtar: '*Sach-sach bata e dil, tune
kahin sarsubz hote dekhi, ulfat ki sarzamin bhi.*'

YM: Which is your least favourite raga and the one you like
most to sing?

LM: I am perhaps that rare singer who does not particularly care for Bhairavi because most singers love to sing it. I don't know why it fails to move me and a reason for that is that I sang so many compositions in this raga for Shankar–Jaikishan that if ever someone composes a number in Bhairavi for me to sing, I am unhappy.

My favourite raga is Pahari although it is mostly used for thumris, not a full concert. Perhaps a reason for this is that my father introduced this raga into Marathi theatre for he started the trend for using classical ragas in Marathi stage musicals. I love his composition, *Chhodo-Chhodo Bihari Hari*. Pahari is generally used while singing thumris, dadras and *chaiti–kajris* but Bismillah Khan sahib used to play a number of Pahari tunes and I loved each one. They say Banaras artistes use Pahari very imaginatively.

YM: Now that you mention Banaras, have you ever visited it and what do you think of its tradition of light classical music: thumri, dadra, tappa, chaiti, kajri and baramasa?

LM: I went once to Banaras in 1950 or 1951 for a music conference where I had been invited to sing. I spent just a day or two but I do remember a visit to Siddheswari Devi's house. I had just begun to acquire a name for myself but her love and respect is a cherished memory. I begged her to sing me a typically Banarasi number and she readily obliged me with several . . . I was transfixed. I think her daughter Savita Devi also sang but she was very young and had just started learning. I also met Girija Devi and kept up our relationship after that. Over the years we have met several times and often when she came to Bombay for a performance, she would come over and we would enjoy each others' company.

I have heard a lot of dadras and thumris but not enough kajri and baramasa. Shobha Gurtu, who lived here in Bombay, sang in the Banarasi style and I loved her music. We often met and had a mutual admiration society.

YM: If you had chosen classical music as a career, who would you have liked to sing as?

LM: Like Bade Ghulam Ali Khan. What a colossus of a man he was! He brought a touch of genius to anything he lent his voice to. His music never fails to move me and as for his thumris, they are pure magic. In 1962, during a programme in Calcutta, both of us participated in the same conference. As I was going to the stage, I found him sitting in the wings. Sandhya Mukherji, a famous Bengali singer, was also present. As soon as he saw me approach, he called out, 'Come here, beta, sing with me.' I was so taken aback. How can I sing with you, Khan sahib, I asked. I am too humble to sit beside you. He strummed the surbahar he was carrying (his performance was slated for later) and gestured with his hand that I should sing with him. I was so terrified that I almost lost my voice. 'Khan sahib,' I replied. 'I am not so ill-mannered that I will share the hallowed space beside you. I should listen to you sing rather than sing along with you.' It was not that I could not sing with him, it was just that we had been brought up in a tradition which taught us that one should always give a senior artiste his due. Whenever he came to Bombay, I tried to visit him and spend time in his company.

YM: It is said that he once remarked, after listening to you, 'Damn, that wretched girl (kambakht) never goes off-key!'

LM: (Laughs delightedly). This was his generosity, I am sure. Else, compared to a giant like him what am I? Perhaps it is due to the blessings I have received from such senior artistes that I was able to achieve what I have. I consider this my greatest wealth.

YM: I think that the years 1950–55 were the most important in your career. This was the time when films like *Albela, Malhar, Aawara, Baghi, Azad, Devdas, Mayurpankh, Naubahar, Baiju Bawra* and *Shri 420* were released. Their music marked a paradigm shift in film music. Do you agree?

LM: I think you are right. I agree that the kind of film music one heard in the films until 1950 changed after that. These were followed in the next few years by *Madhumati, Patrani, Chori-Chori, Jhanak Jahank Payal Baje, Udan Khatola, Kathputli* and *Dekh Kabira Roya*. These films and their music directors changed the earlier trend set by Zohrabai Ambalawali, Amirbai Karnataki and Suraiya. Although we had recognized the changes that Shankar–Jaikishan brought with the music of *Barsat* and *Awara*, the full extent of this momentous change was not visible to us then. Those responsible were Shankar–Jaikishan, Anil Biswas, C. Ramachandra, Naushad sahib and Master Ghulam Haider because all of them experimented with new tunes and rhythms.

YM: Kumar Gandharva once said of you that if you wish to hear the purest Gandhar that emanates from the strings of a tanpura, listen to Lata Mangeshkar's '*Aayega Anewala*'. To what extent is this true?

LM: I am honoured that an artiste and connoisseur of his eminence said so. Do you know that my father Dinanath Mangeshkar once declared, 'Gandhar flows naturally from Lata's throat.' When you tune a tanpura, you can distinctly hear gandhar above all the other sounds. (She demonstrates this by humming). My father also used to say that Laxmi and Sarawati take permanent residence inside anyone who holds the pure gandhar and never go away. If both my father and Kumar Gandharva have said so, then I think I must consider this a special benediction. Both of them were such effortless singers and so tuneful that this observation holds a special significance for me. Your remark suddenly reminded me of what my father had said of my voice so long ago!

YM: Any regrets?

LM: Just that I had to enter the world of films as a child artiste to play the younger sister or brother of the lead actors at a time I should have pursued my classical music training. Later, as I moved to playback singing, the pressure of work and recording schedules again came in the way of sustained musical grooming. I wish I had been able to spend more time in learning classical music from gurus and ustads. This has always been a lingering regret.

YM: Yet when virtually every great classical music practitioner in the country has praised your work, why do you still have this regret?

LM: That is not the question: I am immensely grateful for the appreciation given to my music by these great artistes. However, I still feel I was unable to do justice to the training I received in my early years. It is a different matter that this training was to become my strength as a playback singer but what I really wanted was to be known as a major classical music singer and that did not happen for several reasons. Mind you, it is quite possible I would not have made the name there that I made as a playback singer in films so perhaps it is futile to speculate on what did not happen. Even so, while I am deeply grateful to God for giving me so much fame in this world and accept with all humility the role that destiny had charted for me, I occasionally regret I was not able to achieve what I think was my deepest wish.

YM: What are your favourite ragas?

LM: I have a special fondness for two ragas: Bhoopali and Malkauns. My guru, Ustad Aman Ali Khan had taught me a bandish in Bhoopali that I love till today. (Sings it) '*Ab maan le ri pyari*'. I love Bhoopali also because it is a morning raga and the time when bhajans are sung in most homes and temples. I have grown up listening to these and perhaps this is why it is so close to my heart.

YM: You have sung a beautiful composition in Bhoopali for *Bhabhi ki churiyan*, '*Jyoti kalash chhalke*' is Bhoopali a favourite raga?

LM: Bhoopali and Malkauns are very dear to me but Bhoopali perhaps because it is the raga in which most morning bhajans are sung. It starts our day in a manner of speaking. I have sung '*Chala vahi des*' and '*Sanvari rang rachi*' for Hridaynath in this raga. And you are right in saying that '*Jyoti kalash*' is among my favourite songs. I have spoken to you about how beautifully it has been picturized in the film. You see, in most Marathi homes such as ours, the day began with washing down the courtyard and open spaces of a house and then decorating the threshold with rangoli. The tulsi plant was watered and worshipped. This whole ritual was known as '*sada*' and this is what '*Jyoti kalash*' demonstrates in song. It was composed by Sudhir Phadke, a thorough Maharashtrian, who understood this tradition very well and I was able to do justice to it.

As for favourite ragas, I love some quality or the other in most ragas, but I have a soft spot for Yaman, Jaijaiwanti, Madhuwanti, Bahar, Malhar, Durga, Hamsadhwani and Pahari. However, I have sung so many ragas in my career that it is difficult to pick just one.

YM: V. Shantaram's film *Amar Bhupali* (1951), Vasant Desai had composed a song in Bhoopali for a scene about this sada ceremony: '*Ghanshyam Sundara Shridhara Arunodaya Jhala*'. How do you view the Bhoopali of this song?

LM: I am delighted to be reminded of this song. I was speaking of the Hindi film songs in Bhoopali to you else I would have started with this one. Vasant Desai had created a beautiful composition in Bhoopali ('*Ghanshyam Sundara Shridhara Arunodaya Jhala*'), based on an epic tale in Marathi literature. It is a superbly created song and the picturization on screen (of an early morning pastoral scene) is very moving. You must try and see it if you can.

YM: We often wish that you had been able to record an album of pure classical music. One would love to hear a Bihag, Yaman, Rageshri, Bahar, Jaijaiwanti or some such raga from you.

LM: I have already explained how this was never possible given the fact that I had to earn money from my playback singing to support my family. Whether I wanted to only sing for films was not an option available to me in these circumstances. Gradually, as work occupied all my time, my riyaz got curtailed and that was that. However, I can say with honesty that whenever I was asked to sing a filmy composition set in a raga, I remained completely focused on the purity of the raga.

When I came to Bombay, several all-night concerts of classical music used to be arranged by music lovers. Despite the fact that my day began almost at dawn and ended late at night, whenever I could steal some time for myself, I attended these concerts then snatched a brief nap before starting my punishing recording schedule, fresh as a daisy! Such was my passion for classical music that I could never tire of it.

I remember once listening to Bade Ghulam Ali Khan's Shudh Kalyan till late in the night, like a demented person. I have never been able to forget that divine sound and lapped up whatever I could of his voice at these concerts. Similarly, I was once so enchanted by Nazakat Ali-Salamat Ali's qawwali that I lost track of time.

Now that you ask me, I would have definitely chosen either Shudh Kalyan or Malkauns had I ever recorded a classical raga.

YM: In the four decades before you entered the film industry, there was a galaxy of playback singers—Suraiyya, Rajkumari, Zohrabai Amabalawali, Amirbai Karnataki, Kanan Devi, Parul Ghosh and Shamshad Begum. Keeping the quality of their singing in mind, did you decide that you had to be different? Or was there a silent watershed being formed that subtly changed the trend of playback singing after you entered it?

LM: Look, even today people who are interested in this phenomenon speculate whether that style of music was germane to the kind of films being made then. So let's leave that alone. Among the names you mention, Noorjahan's voice stands out. I used to listen to her records diligently to figure out how one can be a successful playback singer. I learnt from her how one pitches a sad song and how a happy, joyous number should be presented. To put it better, I learnt that one must immerse oneself totally into the mood of the lyrics and become someone else. This is an intrinsic part of my style now and if the song is a tearful one, I even introduce a sob into it to make it authentic. I try and make the song as real to the situation on screen so that if it is a sad song, one must not just see it on screen but also feel it in one's heart.

I would say, I did not just learn from Noorjahan's style but understood the subtleties of film songs and how to bring out the essential mood and theme of every song.

YM: Several artistes try and copy the artistes they admire. Did Noorjahan's voice appear the most ideal voice to you then?

LM: More than her voice, I was impressed by her expression of lyric into music. This was a pioneering style in those days. Saigal sahib, on the other hand, was an artiste of a different mettle. Although his scale and range was a male singer's, his songs bring out the emotional content of lyrics brilliantly. Just think of '*Dukh Ke Din Ab Beetat Nahin*' from *Devdas*: to me it is a mirror image of the scene on screen which is that of a maudlin drunkard seeped in his misery. I used to wonder how Saigal sahib had managed to hiccup and sob while singing and that too in key! Throughout my formative years, I tried to seek out this quality in the two artistes I have mentioned and give my own songs a different style.

YM: Any singers whose voices you did not like? What about those who sang to fit a dramatic situation but failed to bring any musical depth?

LM: I have not thought very deeply about this so it would not be fair to name such singers. However, our film music started moving away from a creative involvement of the singer and the film. As time went on and new films came to be made, some music composers started importing western trends or Indian folk music to and created situations in a film to include these numbers. The singers who preceded me came from a different tradition and so it would not be fair to compare these discrete streams.

YM: Have you even felt that you would like to try and sing something differently from how you sang it years ago?

Have you reviewed past performances and wished to change something?

LM: No, not at all. What I sang then was for that time. You must understand that old film music does not have the scope to change according to current trends. Of course, this is not to say that everything that I sang then was perfect forever and could never be improved. When I look back, I see many that did not become hits but that was due to several factors, not my singing alone—the lyrics, the tune, the film—all these are contributing factors to the popularity or not of a number.

I find it interesting that when radio programmes air what they call old forgotten songs (*Bhule bisre geet*) they are all those that were well-known even now. Another amusing fact is that many films, dismissed as B grade or C grade and declared box-office disasters, have brilliant songs and when these records are commercially released, they become super hits. I have sung for several mythological and patriotic films that weren't well-known but their songs are evergreen. My only focus is to sing as well as I can for every film, how that film pans out or whether it is a box-office hit or not is someone else's concern.

YM: Have you ever considered that if A.R. Rahman, Jatin–Lalit, Shankar–Ehsaan Loy had been around when your most memorable songs were sung (*Mahal, Barsaat, Bari Bahen*), what would have happened. How would '*Hawa Main Urta Jaye*' been composed?

LM: (Laughs). This is an interesting fact to speculate. How can I say what it would have been when I can't quite get my head around this imaginary scenario? I can say, however, that the outcome would have been quite spectacular. Yet isn't it also true that if something like '*Mere Khwabon Main Jo Aye*' (*Dilwale Dulahaniya Le Jayenge*), which is a lovely song, had been composed by a Naushad, Shyam Sundar ji or Anil Biswas, it may have been different? It is true that each decade brings its own rhythms and choices but please remember that in those early years when I recorded my most memorable songs, there was virtually no technological input. We had to sing and compose background effects and music with the most basic kind of material and the kind of hi-tech gadgetry now available to our composers could have taken those to another level. Conversely, if today's composers had to contend with those handicaps they would have to really struggle to produce any music at all! I think it is quite something that we were able to produce music comparable to what is being produced today even while we were so backward technologically. I am extremely proud of that.

YM: When did you first meet Noorjahan?

LM: It was perhaps 1944 when I first met her. I was working for Master Vinayak's Prabhat Films and she was the lead star in their film *Bari Ma*. She had come to Kolhapur where two songs had to be picturized. A small room in the studios had been decorated for her where she stayed with her little son, Akbar. I was working there while she was outside after her make-up was done, waiting for the outdoor shoot to begin. Master Vinayak called me there and introduced me to her, saying 'This is Lata who works with us. She has a very sweet voice, you must hear her.' She looked at me very lovingly and asked me to sing something for her. I was in awe of her voice and personality and was quite nervous as I sat down before her. After all, I was just 14 years old then and because I used to sing mainly in classical ragas, I sang a short classical composition. She then asked me to sing something from a film and I sang two of her own songs. She was delighted, 'Mashallah! God bless you and keep you happy, beta. Never give up your practice for I can tell you will go very far. One day, you will be a great singer.' I met her several times after this. Once, during the shooting of *Bari Ma* she spread a sheet on the floor and wept while reciting her namaaz. I was mesmerized by her complete absorption in her prayers but found the courage to ask her why she was crying while praying. 'Do you have some problem?' I asked. I will never forget her answer, 'I have no problem nor was I crying because I want something very badly. I was merely asking His forgiveness because I am only human and may have committed a wrong even if I did it unknowingly. If I have hurt someone or been the cause of someone's sorrow, I asked Him to forgive me. That's all.' She added, 'Lata, you must always ask for His forgiveness for any wrong you may have done.' Her advice touched me so much that my respect for her deepened. Do you know that I even had a small role in *Bari Ma*?

YM: Do you believe that film music has popularized some ragas?

LM: I think there is no harm in assuming that this is a little true. Of course, the popularity of a raga will always depend on the film song it is set to. Knowledge of a raga while singing is important but more critical is the mood and personality of the raga and how it reflects the situation in a film. It is here that the singer plays a big role. A singer has just a limited time span to give the composition all that it deserves. The end result should be such that a connoisseur can say, 'What a beautiful rendering of a Bhairavi or Bhoopali that was!' I cannot claim that film music popularized classical ragas but their frequent use in various compositions made ragas such as Yaman, Bhoopali, Hindol, Pahari—among many, many more—a place in the heart of the common listener.

YM: Among the hundreds of films you have sung for, are there any that you would like to be specially remembered?

LM: It is very difficult to choose a few out of the hundreds that I have sung. But *Andaz, Madhumati, Baiju Bawra, Awara, Nagin, Parakh, Basant Bahar, Woh Kaun Thi, Chori-Chori, Azad, Bees Saal Baad, Tere Ghar ke Samne, Hum Dono, Ganga Jumna, Mother India, Guide, Mera Saya, Chitralekha, Mamta, Mughal-e-Azam* and *Pakeezah* are some that stay with me. *Jahanara* is another one although that film flopped at the box office. Kamal Amrohi's *Mahal* will always be close to my heart and I love all its songs even those sung by others. All my three—'*Aayega Anewala*'; '*Mushkil Hai Chahat Ko Bhula Dena*' and '*Dil Ne Phir Yaad Kiya*' will always remain my favourites.

YM: How come you don't name C. Ramachandran's *Anarkali*, whose music belongs to the same era and which got you such acclaim?

LM: You are right about those songs giving me a name and all that but I feel that the mood of the songs in it did not match the age it was supposed to be set in. There was somewhere a dissonance between the age of *Anarkali* and the music composed for it, which I felt was too modern for it to sound credible. So although they won me accolades, I cannot get myself to remember them along with the rest I named as my favourites.

YM: How much did a song earn you in the early years?

LM: (Laughs). As far as I remember, during the phase of 1948–57, I used to be given anywhere between 200 and 500 rupees for a song. In 1964, after Raj Kapoor's *Sangam* was screened I started getting 2000 per song. Now you can calculate how many songs and how much I have earned.

YM: Did you ever feel tired while recording?

LM: Of course! When I sang the same song many times during a rehearsal, I often felt exhausted. This used to happen when I recorded for Shankar–Jaikishan for instance because their rehearsals and recording sessions often went on till very late in the night. But it happened with other music composers as well. I recall that during the recording of songs for Dev Anand's *Jewel Thief*, ('*Hoton Pe Aisi Baat*'), the rehearsal and recording went on for so long that I was wiped out. Dev Anand was also there and something or the other would start off another round. Either Burman dada could not understand the words or his son, R.D. Burman then his assistant, would discover a fault. If you hear the song carefully, you'll realize that it had a huge amount of background music and the tempo is very slow.

Bhupendra and I were so tired that it became difficult to go on doing retake after retake. Morning turned to evening and we were still not there. Late in the night when it was still being recorded, Dev Anand suddenly got up and insisted that the recording be wound up and completed. He realized that all of us singers and players had reached a point of exhaustion and there was no point in prolonging our agony. So he told Burman dada that since the song was going quite well he should now stop finding faults with minor issues. This kind of thing often happened and left us tired. Also, when there were chorus singers, even if we were fine it sometimes happened that one of them went off-key and the whole song had to be re-recorded.

YM: Did anything distract you from the words and tune?

LM: No, I tried to keep my mind completely focussed on how to make the song sound its best. I blanked out all my personal problems when I sang and if I had something really difficult to deal with or was not well, I rang my music director and requested the recording be postponed to another day. Nor did I ever sing half-heartedly: I tried to give each song my best and since this was the only thing that mattered to me, I just concentrated on making each song special.

YM: What gave a song its star quality in your opinion?

LM: This is impossible to say because no one can predict what will make a song popular. In fact, often the song you feel is special sinks without a trace and vice-versa. For instance, Hemant Kumar scored the music for *Nagin*. Of all the songs in that film, the one I liked the least was '*Man Dole*' and yet that was the one that went on to top the popularity charts! Another example is Madan Mohan ji's number '*Jiya Le Gayo Ji Mora Sanwariya*' from the film *Anpadh*. I did not think much of it when I sang it but not only did it go on to become very popular it is counted among Madan Mohan's best compositions. So there you are!

YM: How do you distinguish outstanding songs from popular ones?

LM: Well, there is no real distinction between them as such because several songs that went on to become popular had beautiful lyrics, tunes and singing behind them. For instance, the songs composed by Madan Mohan for *Woh Kaun Thi* and *Mera Saya*. All the solos and duets I sang in these became hugely popular. There is no law that a good song cannot be popular as well. Occasionally, however, some good songs are unfortunately not able to become as popular as they deserved.

I have never recorded a song with an eye to its ultimate acceptance by the public. My focus was always to be as true to the situation of its picturization and its mood. Sometimes I have not felt as moved by a particular composition and even if later went on to become a hit, my feelings for it did not change. There are some devotional numbers that I may have loved but others did not find them as moving and then there are those that grow on one after the first hearing.

YM: You have been in situations where you have sung in 3–4 shifts during a day. Did you ever sing for one half-heartedly so that you could go on to the next shift because you liked that composer's work more?

LM: No. Not only do I not play favourites, I also believe that the right to choose or reject a performance belongs to the composer. This is why I concentrated on doing full justice to the composition I was asked to sing. It does not matter, whether the composer is a big name or a newcomer, every song deserves to be given one's best effort. This is what I sincerely believe.

Again, I never gave unsolicited advice on any changes to be made. After all, this right is that of the composer and it is very disrespectful to say I want to sing it differently. However, there were some composers with whom I shared a special relationship and could suggest that they could try a different approach, people like Burman dada, Shankar-Jaikishan and Salil da. At practice sessions in Madan Mohan's home, I did occasionally suggest some changes but as a rule I do not interfere with compositions given to me. Nor have I ever rejected a piece because I did not like it all that much.

YM: Yet isn't it true that you are very sensitive about words and lyrics and that you have asked for some changes there?

LM: Yes, if I felt that there were some vulgar undertones in the words and unpleasant innuendoes, I would refuse to sing them. At times, I may have annoyed some lyricists but gradually the industry accepted that I would just not sing vulgar songs. Even so, I often had some arguments with Jaikishan and Shailendra ji when I objected to a particular word or phrase. If I pointed out a word that upset me, they would try and change it to my liking. Shankar-Jaikishan liked me to sing their main songs and Raj Kapoor's team would only seek me out for their films. Every song was run by all of us before it was recorded.

YM: Marathi Natya Sangeet had a strong influence on the film music of the early years even though film music had some outstanding non-Marathi singers and composers at that time. Since you yourself came from the home of a Marathi stage singer, what did you feel about this changing trend?

LM: You are right. As a child I heard my father's Marathi songs in his plays like *Ayodhya Ka Raja* and *Sant Tukaram* that were steeped in the Marathi tradition of singing. One of the best known composers of this style was Govind Rao Tambe; he composed the music for my father's play *Manapman*. I also remember Prithviraj Kapoor's play *Sikandar* from about 1941 that had a strong touch of Marathi natya sangeet in its music, as in the number '*Khilo Khilo Matvari Kaliyon*'. When I started to sing for films, this tradition was already changing as Master Ghulam Haider, Naushad, Anil Biswas and Shankar-Jaikishan introduced a new idiom into film music. C. Ramachandra experimented with touches of western music in a film called *Shehnai*. I worked with all these composers but it was only in the work of Sudhir Phadke and Vasant Desai that I got an opportunity to sing traditional Marathi natya sangeet.

Much later, in the sixties, Shankar–Jaikishan composed a song, '*Bagar Bum Bum Bum Baje Ghunghroo*' for a film called *Kathputli*. It was a dance number and became very popular. Someone must have told Jaikishan about a Marathi natya sangeet song, '*Bagar Bum Bum Bum*', dedicated to Shiva's tandava. I think he picked and replicated its musical phrase for phrase in the opening for this song, while the rest of the composition was his. The song was written by Hasrat Jaipuri and Shankar got his favourite percussionist Dattaram to set the beat to that compelling phrase of *bum bum bum* . . . Later, when my brother Hridaynath composed the music for *Lekin*, I sang a song ('*Main Ek Sadi Se Baithi Hoon*') which was a complete remake of one of my father's compositions from his play *Manapman* ('*Bhali Chandra Ase Dhari La*'). All the taans I have taken in that song from *Lekin* echo my father's voice. These are some songs that I can recall immediately but there are many more.

YM: Which was your busiest year and what is the maximum number you have recorded in a single day?

LM: After *Barsaat*, roughly from 1950 onwards, I feel as if I recorded songs day and night. This went on till the sixties and even up to the eighties. There was so much work that I could not even take a day off to celebrate Diwali and holidays were out of the question! Then, I gradually stopped recording on Diwali and cut down on the number of assignments I took on. I could afford to pick and choose by then but there were some old friends like Raj Kapoor, Raj Khosla, Yash Chopra and Subhash Ghai who would just not take no for an answer. They insisted that I sing at least one song in their films and I could not refuse them.

YM: Do you believe that music has a goddess as its presiding deity?

LM: Of course, I believe that Saraswati is the goddess of knowledge and music. I pray that she always blesses me. However, our clan prays to its own deity, Mangeshi. All the people of the region we come from worship this god and there is a beautiful temple dedicated to him in our native region in Goa. We also hold Amba (the goddess of my mother's clan) and Mangeshi (from my father's clan) as our presiding deities and are considered devotees of Shiva. We consider Shiva the god of the arts because one can please him by singing the Shiv tandava stotra said to have been composed by him. Ravana was able to please Shiva by playing the veena. There are many such mythological stories that reveal the tender and sensitive side of this god.

We believe that our gods themselves practised our art forms. The iconography of our temples and the deep respect for music and dance are a living example of how highly we regard our arts. Just reflect on how many of our gods and goddesses are associated with dance and music traditions. Some of our instruments are named after them: Narad veena, Saraswati veena and Rudra veena. I know of so many royal homes where children were formally groomed in classical music although the girls of such families were not allowed to perform on a public platform. We owe a huge debt of gratitude to these royal traditions for preserving our classical art traditions during colonial times.

Our magnificent temples were endowed by these royal patrons and I believe that this is what made such families truly noble. The tradition of teaching the young some form of art is slowly receding, which is a pity because such an education made them better citizens and human beings. If I had not been groomed by my father in the arts, perhaps the person I am now may never have been created.

YM: In your opinion, is style more important or influence? What makes an artiste great?

LM: The first influence on any artiste is that of the guru: the evolution of an individual style comes much later as one acquires maturity and confidence. When you follow the teachings of a particular gharana, you are moulded by its fundamental traditions regarding *swara* (note) and *laya* (rhythm). In my initial years, the Kirana gharana played a very important role in shaping my voice and music. If you study the evolution of Ustad Abdul Karim Khan's students— Roshanara Begum, Hirabai Barodekar, Saraswati Rane—you will find the distinct stamp of the Kirana gharana in their style. However, they all had their own distinctive attributes as well, and followed their own trajectory as they matured. So you will never hear Kesarbai Kerkar imitating Roshanara Begum even though they belonged to the Jaipur-Atrauli gharana of Ustad Alladiya Khan. Kesarbai's devoted student Dhondutai Kulkarni sings in her style. I have never personally heard Dhondutai but this is what many say of her. So even though they all learnt from the same gurus, they brought something unique to their musical persona, adding a touch here or an elaboration there. The important thing to remember is that they never stray far from the fundamental grooming of their gharana. So you may be influenced by many styles and teachers but you eventually evolve your own way of singing.

I strongly believe that the tradition of surrendering oneself to a guru's teaching is an important part of one's education. Nowadays this strict adherence to a particular gharana is slowly fading and this is a pity because you cannot imbibe the experience of that rich knowledge tradition except by sitting at the feet of a guru. Unless you are prepared to submit to the rigorous discipline of the gharana tradition, I feel mere talent will not take an artiste very far.

YM: Of all the composers you have worked with, which are the ones that you had to work hardest for?

LM: The composers who reserved their most difficult compositions for me were Anil Biswas, Madan Mohan, Salil

Chaudhuri and Sajjad Hussain. They cared little for commercial success and so were bold in trying out new ways of making music exciting and appealing. Sajjad Hussain's '*Ai Dilruba Nazrein Mila*' (*Rustom-Sohrab*) was a very challenging number for me. Salil Chaudhuri introduced such freshness into film music that was always difficult to bring out. The same goes for Madan Bhaiyya, whose ghazals were as difficult to sing as they were pleasing to hear. These were highly creative composers who knew classical music well and so appreciated and expected a higher level of performance from their singers. My brother Hridaynath was another person whose compositions were very complex and a challenge to sing.

YM: Have you ever wished that film music was composed keeping in mind an individual singer?

LM: This may never happen given the direction being followed by our film music nowadays. In Saigal's time, it was his voice rather than the actor's that became paramount when composing. Today, I don't think anyone gives serious thought to matching a voice to a song. There was a time when a composer kept the special quality of a Mukesh, Hemant Kumar, Rafi, Kishore da or me and all of us understood perfectly why a particular song was earmarked for a particular playback singer. In those days, we wanted our songs to be heard forever while today all that seems to matter is whether the young will rock to a tune for a few days before they move on to another number that takes their fancy. Naturally, demand dictates supply: if immediate stimulation is all that people seem to want, then that is what they will get.

Times have moved on from when a film situation was carefully considered before composing a song and its lyrics. I can only laugh at the trend that now seems to be fashionable.

A song today must have a dance beat for listeners to rock to. So where earlier we had solo numbers full of soul (a lullaby, a sad song, a devotional bhajan or a romantic number), today we have saucy duets where the lyrics hardly matter, just the background music and noise will do.

YM: Does this mean that the rigour and tradition of the earlier years of film music is vanishing?

LM: Yes, I am convinced that where singing was a calling for us, today it is regarded as a profession. This is true of both singers and composers. Music directors such as Naushad sahib and Roshan would lovingly craft a melody over weeks; others were brilliant at instantly hitting the right note and all these became evergreen numbers because they were inspired compositions. Just recall the lyrics that we had then. Do you know that Salil Chaudhuri hummed the Bengali lines behind a famous song in *Parakh* for Shailendra and he wrote out the first few lines ('*O Sajana, barakha bahar ayi . . .*') in ten minutes?

It is rare to find such synergy today. Perhaps many younger singers and composers feel that because I belong to an earlier age, I haven't really moved with the times. But this is not true: I have sung with many younger and new composers as well and some of their music is very sweet and tuneful. All I can tell you is that the passion and respect that we had for our art made the music of our times so popular down the ages is hardly visible any more. I cannot get myself to appreciate those to whom this is merely a career and who sing just with their vocal chords, not with their heart and soul.

YM: Does this sadden you?

LM: Of course it does. I strongly feel that many of today's talented younger singers (Suresh Wadekar, Alka Yagnik, Kavita Krishnamurthy, Sonu Nigam) would have reached even higher if they had the benefit of the great composers we had. Similarly, our talented composers would have had such a brilliant choice before them if they had a Mukesh, Kishore Kumar or Rafi sahib to direct. Just imagine where we would be today! I pray that one day we are able to blend the best of both worlds so that we can create the magic of the music of those unforgettable films (*Madhumati*, *Baiju Bawra*). But I fear this will remain a dream.

YM: If you recall Hemant Kumar's music in *Nagin*, it is the songs that come to mind before the lead stars of the film. This is no longer true.

LM: You are absolutely right. This is how I remember old films: through their music. Another fact to remember is that most of these films had a message embedded in them and every viewer took that message home with him. So music and social messages were the two pillars on which our most memorable films were built. Think of any great film of that time and this will hold true: *Do Ankhen Barah Haat* is a perfect example. Another is Raj Kapoor's *Awara* whose story is about an orphan and how his life takes a turn after he falls into bad company. Think of a song like '*awara hoon, ya gardish main gira asman ka tara hoon*' and a host of other lilting tunes from there come crowding back.

YM: So the message of a film and its music go hand in hand.

LM: Right. When V. Shantaram made *Jhanak Jhanak Payal Baje*, he based it on the kathak dance form. His intention was to remind the public (then in the throes of a westernization of musical tastes and crazy about rock and roll) that we have a tradition of rhythm that is far grander. Vasant Desai and Bharat Vyas were the music director and lyricist respectively, while Pandit Gopikrishna, the renowned kathak dancer, choreographed the dances that were central in the film. I rate the songs I sang with Hemant Kumar in this film among my finest. Even if you set that aside, who can forget the thrilling notes of Ustad Amir Khan in the eponymous number in it?

An artiste's challenge is how to successfully convey this passion or message across to audiences. I think it is equally true of writers and readers. When a creative piece fails to move people, the artiste often questions whether this was because of his or her inability to transfer the mood appropriately.

YM: How did you first meet Madan Mohan?

LM: Long ago, while shooting for Filmistan's film *Shaheed*, I was called by Ghulam Haider to sing a song. I was thrilled at this invitation from an important personality but when I reached the studio, I was told the song was a duet I had to sing with someone called Madan Mohan. This is when I learnt that he was the son of the owner of Filmistan, Rai Bahadur Chunnilal. I must confess I wondered whether he would be a proper singer and that perhaps he was my partner in this song because he was the owner's son. So felt a little let down. I went to Ghulam Haider and he introduced me to a young man, Madan Mohan. He looked a perfectly decent and well-mannered person. After all, he came from a very well-respected family. The song we were to record ('*Pinjare Main Bulbul Bole, Mera Nanha Dil Dole*') was to be picturized on a brother and sister and he sang it so sweetly with me that I told him, 'You sang really well.' He replied, 'But not as well as I should have. You see, I am on my way to becoming a music director and I would like you to sing for me.' That was our first meeting, although that song was later removed by the director of the film.

The first film Madan Mohan scored the music for was *Aankhen* and for some reason I was unable to sing for him.

So he came over once on Rakhi and declared, 'Lata, do you remember the time we sang as brother and sister? Now come and tie this rakhi on my wrist. From now on, you are my younger sister Lata and I am your Madan bhaiyya. Promise me that you will sing in every film your brother scores the music for.'

This relationship endured till the end and even today, I regard his wife Sheela bhabhi as my sister-in-law.

YM: What made his music so special?

LM: The fact that he first recorded each song he composed in his own voice and when he called a singer for a rehearsal, he played the song he had in his head. I never saw this in any other music composer. He was such a perfectionist!

YM: And how do you remember C. Ramachandra?

LM: Oh he was a completely different person! Like Anil Biswas and Master Ghulam Haider, he broke new ground. He did not know much about classical music but he took one note as his base and composed a whole song around it, occasionally mixing two ragas—a no-no with most purists. He used the orchestration of western music so competently that your feet began tapping whenever you heard his music. So in this sense, he followed the line of Marathi bhava sangeet (mood music) and Latin American music. This fusion would bring a new dimension to music is what he believed and perhaps he was right.

YM: And Naushad sahib?

LM: He was another unique composer and very strict about his music compositions. He wanted a singer to just follow his directions completely, no deviations were allowed from the tune he set. He did occasionally consult me or Rafi sahib but eventually he did his own thing. So, even though it became tiresome to sing strictly by the book, one honoured his direction. Mind you, others like Madan Mohan and Jaikishan always allowed me to put in an extra flourish of my own and encouraged me to do so but Naushad sahib was very different from them.

YM: Shankar–Jaikishan, which of the two was more talented?

LM: Definitely Jaikishan, although no one denies that together they created magic. Shankar first started out as a table player in Prithviraj Kapoor's Prithvi Theatres. Later, he met up with Jaikishan who was equally adept at playing the harmonium. Shankar brought him over to Prithvi Theatres as well and later they started their own banner and started composing for Raj Kapoor's films. I was associated with them from their very first film and soon they became known as a very hard-working duo. Since I was familiar with their style and they were comfortable with me, we shared a great relationship. Perhaps Jaikishan had a more subtle touch but together they were inseparable. Their music is so sweet and tuneful.

YM: Can you explain how Jaikishan was better?

LM: There are several examples but let's take the music of *Hariyali aur Rasta*. If you hear the title song, which I have sung and which was composed by him, it is both tender and tuneful. Shankar made '*Bol Meri Taqdeer Main Kya Hai*' and if you hear them together you will see the difference. This difference is audible in almost all their films and perhaps I say this because I find Jaikishan's style closer to my own preference. After all, music is a personal choice.

YM: What do you have to say about Sudhir Phadke's music?

LM: Sudhir Phadke has hardly composed for Hindi films and is better known in the Marathi film world. He was very talented but Asha has sung more for him than I. However, it is true that '*Jyoti Kalash Chhalke*' is considered immortal. Even more than that are the songs he has composed for *Malti Madhav* and in that my favourite is '*Bandh Preeti Phool Ki, Man Leke Chitchor, Door Jana Na*'. There are few songs in Hindi films that can match this one. Another special quality of his songs is that they are all set in pure Hindi; witness the classical vocabulary of '*Jyoti Kalash*' and you will see what I mean.

YM: His *Sajani* (1959) has one song, (*Ja re Chandra . . .*) which outpaces the lyrics of *Malti Madhav* and *Bhabhi Ki Chooriyan*. It is a brilliant composition and beautifully rendered.

LM: Those are Pandit Narendra Sharma's lyrics and what can one say of his style except that it is brilliant? It is a shame that the film was never a commercial success because all films are assessed by their commercial or box office appeal. In those days, there was no television and if people did not hear the song in a theatre, it just faded away. Those who could hear it on the radio went and bought a record to hear at home so even if the film did not work, often the music made it popular. This is why even though all the three Phadke films you mentioned were not commercially successful, their music became hugely popular. This is also true of mythological and patriotic films which is why often music directors were hired for a higher salary than even actors and actresses because if the songs were a hit, the producer could earn his money from their sales.

YM: Can you think of any song that appears perfect to you in terms of situation, lyrics and composition?

LM: There are several I can think of, so to choose just one is tough. However, there is one that I can name. Take, for example, '*Piya Tose Naina Lage*' from *Guide*. We had really worked hard on this song and Burman dada's pursuit of perfection and countless rehearsals made it something else. It is a trifle longer (7 minutes) than the average film song and is a dance number. When I saw the finished screen result with Waheeda's brilliant dancing through all the four sections of the song, I was thrilled that our efforts had paid off. Vijay Anand had picturized this number beautifully for the screen because I think he had a special talent for choreographing such sequences. In this respect, Bimal Roy, Mehboob Khan, Raj Kapoor, V. Shantaram, Kamal Amrohi, Hrishikesh Mukherji and Guru Dutt must also be mentioned as directors who brought something special to song picturization. The other songs from *Guide* are also very pleasing numbers.

LM: Did you have a particular sari, piece of jewellery or something that you carried as a lucky charm while recording?

LM: In the beginning, yes. There was a necklace from my father's drama company's stuff that I had a soft spot for. It was a very fine ivory piece and I felt that because it was my father's, it would bring me good luck. When it broke, I had it cast in gold to preserve it. Nothing else comes to mind but if I wore a new sari, earrings or bangles and the song did not go well, I would set them aside. I am sure others do this too.

Once, while in America, I wore I sari for my first show and it was a grand success. So I wore the same sari for the following 8 performances of that tour, dry-cleaning it before each performance. In fact, the organizers asked me why I wore the same sari at each show and I told them because I considered it lucky. Let me tell you a funny story: I once saw Chitragupta ji limping and asked him, 'Have you hurt your foot?' and he told me it was because he was wearing a broken pair of slippers. But why, I asked him, can't you afford a fresh pair? It was then he sheepishly confessed that it was his lucky pair and he always wore it for recordings. 'Ah,' I ribbed him, 'this means you trust the slipper more than your singers!' And both of us laughed at this superstitious streak in ourselves.

YM: Does a singer's mood change with the hours of the day?

LM: Of course, what you feel in the morning is a different mood from what you experience by the end of day. This is so beautifully understood by our classical music where each raga is supposed to be sung at a particular time of the day. Those of us who grew up in that tradition find it awkward to break this rigid timetable but in the film world, where a song is sung in 3 minutes and one raga is fused with another, these questions cease to matter.

YM: Have you ever been so influenced by a particular raga that it haunted you?

LM: Yes, very often. It happens even with songs that enter your head and you can't get rid of them but I remember once hearing a Shudh Kalyan by Bade Ghulam Ali sahib and being so moved that I hummed it for many days.

YM: V. Shantaram's films had a very unique kind of music, what did you think of films like *Do Aankhen Barah Haat*, *Jhanak Jhanak Payal Baje, Navrang, Toofan Aur Diya* et al.?

LM: In my opinion, the music of V. Shantaram's films represents the best of our musical tradition. His films always carried an important social message and had extraordinary scripts. Vasant Desai was his favourite music composer. As you know, he was a formidable musician and because of his knowledge of classical music, he brought a special element to his compositions. There was a strong touch of Marathi bhava sangeet in his style. I was very impressed with his work because it was so close to my own tastes.

Of all Shantaram's films, *Jhanak Jhanak Payal Baje* is the one I like most, although some of the music of his Marathi films is even better. *Do Aankhen Barah Haat* also had some great experimental touches, such as in the song '*Tak Dhum Dhum, Tak Dhum Dhum*'. Then there was my duet with Manna Dey, '*Umad Ghumad Ke Aayi Re Ghata*', a thrilling number that brings alive the sound of a thunderstorm. Shantaram was very sensitive to the music of his films and in this respect a lot like Raj Kapoor, Guru Dutt and Bimal Roy. This is why the music of their films still reaches out to audiences everywhere.

YM: Is it true that he made *Teen Batti Char Rasta*, a film based on your life and that the character of Kokila played by Sandhya is you?

LM: Yes, that role was developed with me in mind, although V. Shantaram never spoke of this to me or asked me. It was only when the film was screened that people began to draw correspondences between that character and me. Truthfully, though, I don't think I am not at all like that character at all.

Raj Kapoor also scripted his *Satyam Shivam Sundaram* on my life and in the beginning he wanted that I play that role in the film. However, I did not think it proper and declined to do so. I told him I will lend my voice to the film's character that was supposed to be me but would not play the role. He was a little disappointed but gave in. When the film was eventually made, the role was given to Zeenat Aman.

Gulzar sahib used to say that he wrote the lines '*Naam gum jayega, chehra badal jayega, meri awaz hi pehchaan hai . . . gar yaad rahe*' with me in mind. And I feel he has expressed my emotions perfectly. After all, my voice is what makes me Lata Mangeshkar and this is perhaps equally true of all the other singers (Mukesh, Saigal and Kishore Kumar) as it is of me.

YM: Your songs in *Mahal* composed by Khemchand Prakash have overshadowed the other songs you have sung for him. *Ziddi* and *Asha* (both released in 1948) are hardly ever mentioned. Can you tell us something about these forgotten films?

LM: Certainly. I did three films with him although *Mahal* will always be remembered as the finest of them. 'Chanda Re Ja Re Ja Re' (*Ziddi*) is among the songs I am very fond of. The way I have sung the last verse, without pausing for breath, appears a challenge to me now. As for the music Khemchand ji scored, what can I say except that it was beautiful? Even though the *Mahal* songs are remembered as his best compositions, I think that 'Jadoo Kar Gaye Kisi Ken Ain' (*Ziddi*) which is my first duet with Kishore Kumar, is also a lovely number.

YM: In *Usha Haran*, you sang for the first and only time for a female composer, Saraswati Devi. You sang two songs for her of which one ('Mere Nagan Main Chandni Chamke Chamcham') was with Rajkumari. Can you tell us something about that?

LM: I don't recall the words of the songs I sang for her but I do remember Sarawati Devi very well. She was the only female composer when I joined the industry, although Jaddanbai preceded her. However, Jaddanbai had left this work before I came. Sarawati Devi was an impressive Parsi lady, always pleasant in her interactions with singers, who had managed to carve out a space for herself even among such stalwarts as Naushad, Anil Biswas and C. Ramachandra. She had a deep understanding of music and gave her complete attention to whatever she did. She once told me she had heard my father in his Marathi stage performances. She refined my voice and enunciation in the same way that Anil

Biswas was to do later and gave me invaluable tips on how to handle a song.

YM: *Saiyan* (1951) with music by Sajjad Husain is considered an important film in your repertoire of film songs. How did you view his work?

LM: I sang a sad but very lovely composition for him in that film ('*Woh Raat Din, Woh Sham Ki Guzri Hui Kahaniyan*'). All I can say of his work is that there was never another composer like him. He was the only composer I knew who took care of every part of a song's composition by himself—from direction to arranging its background orchestra. He was a perfectionist and all the other songs I sang for him in that film were beautiful. I rank my duet with Talat Mahmood ('*Dil Main Sama Gaye Sajan, Phool Khile Gulshan-Gulshan*') among my favourite songs. Similarly, my songs from his film *Sangdil* are wonderful and I rate the sad songs I have sung for him as my best.

YM: What about his other film, *Rustom Sohrab* (1963) where you sang '*Ai Dilruba Nazrein Mila*'?

LM: You are correct, there can be no denying that this was the best song of that film and I rate it among the most difficult songs I have ever sung for any composer. This was probably the result of his meticulous planning and the countless rehearsals he made us do. It is unfortunate that some of his best songs were victims of technical errors and because of the archaic recording techniques prevalent at the time, they could never be re-recorded. He was such an original creator and it is a great pity that he could not present his best to the industry.

YM: Is it true that to an artist the outside world ceases to matter?

LM: I can only speak of musicians and singers and when I heard Ustad Bade Ghulam Ali Khan sing, it seemed to me as if nothing mattered to him but his music. I found the same deep commitment and veneration in the gurus I learnt from. Even at the height of his career, I saw this in Pandit Ravi Shankar. So I feel very strongly that unless you can surrender yourself totally to your art, you will not attain perfection. Let me give you an example from my own life from the time when I was recording an album of Meera bhajans, titled *Chala Vahi Des*. I was very unwell those days and the recording went on for 8 days. I suspended all my other recordings until I could finish it. The day I recorded the last song for the album, I was admitted to hospital and underwent a serious operation the next day. I cannot describe the pain I was in during the recording but whether it is a recording or a stage show, when I perform I give it my all. I remember going to Pandit Narendra Sharma who was listening to my recording and he had tears in his eyes as he said 'You did it, beta. I know what pain you suffered but no one who listens to that album will ever find out how you suffered as you sang.'

Nothing in life comes easily and unless you have the capacity to suffer for it, you will never achieve what you want. That and an unshakeable faith in the Almighty give you the courage to go on.

YM: It is said of you that you tried to match your voice to the actress you were singing for. But there were so many different personalities in the early years: Nargis, Madhubala and Meena Kumari on one hand and Nalini Jaiwant, Kamini Kaushal and Nirupama Roy on the other! How did you manage this?

LM: I wanted to understand the personality I was supposed to bring out when I sang. However, as you know several actresses from those early years (like Nalini Jaiwant) were also accomplished singers and until I began to lend my voice for her, she preferred to sing her own songs. Kamini Kaushal had a very thin voice, and it matched my own voice quality then. For the rest, I would carefully match their voice and personality when I sang for them so that the listener who heard the song on radio could make out that this song must have been sung by a Meena Kumari, or Waheeda Rehman on screen. In fact Waheeda Rehman once remarked that one can clearly make out that whether a song was sung on screen by Nutan or Nargis. I used to pay attention even to the lip movement of the actress because that makes a difference to the sound. I also paid attention to how a particular actress takes an alap—all these details made it possible to sing for different actresses without sounding the same. I find it amusing that many actresses are not aware that when a voice reaches the upper notes, the mouth opens wider, but that is their art and who am I to make such observations? My concern was how well I could match voice and personality. However, there were some notable exceptions: for example, Nutan in *Seema* in the song, '*Manmohana Bare Jhoote*'. She sang along to make the veins of her neck stand out when the song soared. Similarly, in *Abhimaan*, Jaya Bhaduri was careful to pay attention to the song and its rhythm when it was being picturized. In both cases, it appears as if the actress on screen is actually singing the song.

YM: While singing what were you particular about?

LM: Keeping my voice and the kind of songs that were composed for me, my main concern was that it should sound natural. If anything came in the way of that I rejected it. For instance, I do not like theatricality and unnecessary noise in the background score. I feel strongly that a song should be as pure as possible. What did not come naturally to me became an anathema. I placed a great emphasis on the correct pronunciation of the words and to the lyrics of a song and left the composition to the musician. Occasionally, I felt disappointed that a song turned out differently from what I had been led to believe because they tinkered with it but that was rare.

YM: Do you go to a movie theatre to watch films?

LM: I used to love going to the movies but that was when there was no television and all. For the last 15 years or so, I have not been to one but there was a time when I loved to see English films. In our childhood, cinema was our only entertainment but our father was very strict about which kind and how many films we could watch. These were mostly black and white ones and I loved watching Saigal films.

I must have been 5–6 years old when I saw Greta Garbo's *Mata Hari* in Sangli. I loved it, just as I loved all Hitchcock films. Since I also liked murder mysteries and thrillers, I saw all Agatha Christie films and loved *Death on the Nile*. I was a big fan of Yul Brynner and Ingrid Bergman. I can't remember how many times I saw Ingrid Bergman and Charles Boyer's *Gaslight*, which is my all-time favourite. I saw it first in Metro Theatre. Another great favourite was *The King and I*. Many years later, when I went to New York for a stage show I saw the stage production of *The King and I*. *Sound of Music* is another film I loved and was mad about *Singing in the Rain* as well. Another film I remember with fondness is *The Ten Commandments*. Among the Hollywood stars, Peter Ustinov, Bette Davis, Gregory Peck, James Stewart, Cary Grant and Richard Burton are some of my favourites. I have always loved James Bond and liked Sean Connery and Roger Moore the most as the famous spy. And how can I forget *The Guns of Navarone*, *Dr Zhivago*, *The Magnificent 7*, *A Passage to India* and that golden oldie, *The Three Musketeers*? I've seen them all many, many times.

YM: What are some of your favourite Indian films?

LM: As I said, for the last 15 years or so, I mostly watch films on DVDs but in the early years, whenever I found the time, I took the whole family to Metro Theatre to see a film but if a smaller cinema theatre was screening a good film, I went there as well. I can't remember many of them but the Marathi films of V. Shantaram like *Amar Bhoopali* and Bhalaji Pendharkar's *Chhatrapati Shivaji* stand out in my memory. I also enjoyed Bengali films, especially those starring Soumitra Chatterji and Uttam Kumar. I have also seen some of Shivaji Ganeshan's Tamil films although I can't recall their names now.

Among the Hindi films I enjoyed were Prithviraj Kapoor's *Sikandar*, Ashok Kumar's *Kismet* and Dilip Sahib's *Madhumati*. I like almost all of Amitabh Bachchan's films, particularly *Trishul*. Whenever it comes on TV I sit down to watch it yet again (laughs). He is such a wonderful actor, just think of *Sholay*, although all the others have acted equally well in that film. That is another film I can watch over and over again.

I never missed a Hrishikesh Mukherji film and my favourites were *Anupama* and *Anuradha*, with Leela Naidu and Balraj Sahni. What a film *Anuradha* was! Perhaps I felt drawn to it because it dealt with the struggles of a singer's life. Hrishida's *Khubsoorat* also had a very subtle message and Rekha was lovely in it. Not one of his films was ever vulgar. Bimal Roy is another director whose films are brilliant. His *Sujata*, *Bandini* and *Devdas* are classics in my opinion. Both *Bandini* and *Sujata* convey important social messages. His *Parakh* is another such film that satirizes greed. Salil Chaudhuri was both the scriptwriter and music composer for the film, which is among my favourite scores.

I really admire Yusuf Bhai (Dilip Kumar) as an actor and have seen *Devdas*, *Madhumati* and *Mughal-e-Azam* countless times. Just recall the songs of his film *Kohinoor*: how well he emotes in each song! Do you know that to lend his role authenticity he actually learnt how to play the sitar for this film? He is equally adept in comic roles I think and speaking of comedies, that is a genre I love. Whenever I feel low, I pull out *Padosan* to cheer myself

I like entertaining films that are not sad, like *Seeta aur Geeta* and *DDLJ*. Among some recent films, I loved *Veer-Zara* because Yash Chopra was able to do full justice to the emotions in the story. There are so many others and I can't recall all of them.

YM: You haven't mentioned Raj Kapoor and Dev Anand among the people you admire. Is there a reason for this?

LM: Not at all. I consider each film made by Raj Kapoor an important milestone and his early films, *Barsaat*, *Awara*, *Shri 420*, *Boot Polish* and *Jagte Raho* are simply brilliant. Each carries a message that attaches itself to the viewer's mind and as for the music of these films, I think it is unmatched. In fact, Raj Kapoor used to joke that his films became box office hits because of their music. I don't know another director who was so particular in choosing the songs he picked.

I often felt that he made us work so hard that it appeared as if the core of the film was created in the music room rather than in studio. He was an equally accomplished actor: look at the work he did for others in *Chhalia*, *Anari*, *Dil Hi To Hai* and *Teesri Kasam*.

Dev Sahib was another polished performer. He'd often come and join us at Burman dada's home for song rehearsals and we really looked forward to these occasions because he was so handsome (giggles). Of the many songs I sang for him, he liked 'Rangeela Re Tere Rang Main Yoon Ranga Hai Mera Man' (Prem Pujari). I liked almost all his films but Guide, Jewel Thief, Hum Dono were special. Although most people think that Guide had the best music among his films, I think Jab Pyar Kisi Se Hota Hai and Tere Ghar Ke Samne, with its title song and 'Dil Ka Bhanwar Kare Pukar' are unforgettable. The latter is a duet I sang with Mohd Rafi and I included it in the Shradhanjali album we compiled in memory of Rafi sahib.

Dev sa'ab was a very gregarious person and loved meeting everyone. Once when asked why he walked so fast, he replied, 'If you want to keep pace with the changing world then you must walk fast. Else you'll get left behind'. His joie de vivre and energy were really admirable and he kept it at that pace right till the end. Burman dada was the composer of his choice in almost all his films and he once shared an interesting story with me. It seems Burman dada could just not find the tune he was looking for while composing a particular song and finally told him, 'Let's leave it. I'll think afresh tomorrow morning.' Then, at two in the morning, an excited Dada rang him up saying, 'Dev! I've found the notes for that song. Listen!' So this is the enthusiasm he brought out in people he worked with. How many of that calibre can you see around you today?

YM: Why have you always shunned colour? You always wear white and I wonder what you do on Holi. Can you share some special memory?

LM: As children we celebrated Holi with abandon, but that was only as long as my father was alive. We would play in the water till late in the evening. Now I have stopped playing that kind of Holi because what is called Holi now is so different from the beautiful way it was celebrated then. It began with the ritual burning of Holika and the distribution of sweets and sprinkling the ashes of the bonfire on each other the next day. We called it *gudbud*. On the fifth day after Holika came Rang Panchami and our parents would sprinkle us children with saffron water. My mother made sweets that we got as Prasad after offering it to the household gods. Now tell me, where is such Holi to be found today?

In our house Dussera and Diwali were considered more important festivals.

YM: What about Raj Kapoor's famous Holi celebrations? Didn't you ever take part in those?

LM: I don't think anyone in the film industry could afford to ignore that celebration. I was warmly invited each year but I think I just went 3–4 times to Raj Studios in Chembur where it was held. The reason was that I disliked colour on my body and when I did go I made Raj Kapoor promise he would not force me to play with coloured water or be dunked into the pond of coloured water that was a mandatory ritual. If anyone tried to run away from that, his men would physically toss him or her in. I once saw Sitara Devi being tossed in but that spunky dancer enjoyed it and did a great dance after it as well. What I remember the most is the marvellous spread that accompanied his Holi party. The tables offered every kind of food and drink and Raj Kapoor personally took his guests around as they went from table to table. Anyone who was associated with the film industry was there and high or low, everyone was offered equal hospitality. Truly, I have met few hosts like him in my life.

On the subject of festivals, when I first entered the film industry and started my career, I used to personally visit all my music directors and greet them with sweets. I started off at daybreak in order to be able to make all the rounds. Once

I reached Naushad Sahib's house at 5.30 in the morning and found him at his gate looking very worried. 'Is all well with you, Lata?' he asked anxiously. 'Oh, I just came to offer you my good wishes and some sweets for Diwali,' I answered. Then he insisted I come in and share a cup of tea with his family before I went ahead. 'Lata,' he said later as we sipped tea, 'you know all of us should give you sweets on Diwali so that we replenish the sweetness you have spent on our compositions.' I was so touched.

In those days, my mother would make all the sweets (laddus) and savouries at home and distribute them to our neighbours. Sadly, few homes do that now. Today, we all give and receive boxes of readymade sweets or dry fruits and consider our work done. And, of course, bombard the neighbourhood with noisy crackers for days: that is how we celebrate this wonderful festival!

YM: As you became more busy, did all this change?

LM: There was a time when I was so busy that I didn't even register what day it was. I worked through Diwali and every other holiday.

YM: So many films have a festival as the main theme. For example, Janamashtami, Raksha bandhan and songs that celebrate Holi or Bhai Dooj. They are still played when these festivals are near. Did you ever play these songs to celebrate the mood they captured?

LM: No, I rarely listen to my own songs. Sometimes, when such a song is being played in a car or elsewhere, all I can recall is the circumstances during the recording: how tired I was, how many rehearsals we had to do. I get lost in the memories of that time and forget to listen to the song itself. There are some that I didn't like too much when I recorded them but they grew on

me hearing again and again. I am not aware of any special songs
that are sung on festivals although weddings were traditionally
celebrated with song and dance. Now even that is almost gone
and film songs are played on amplifiers.

YM: How much should a singer reveal of herself in a song?

LM: Interesting thought. I do try and visualize a song
when I record it to leave something of myself in it. After
all, I must not be erased completely from its music. At the
same time, one must be careful to not overshadow the person
it is being picturized on. However, I always kept in mind
the person for whom I was the playback singer: Nimmi,
Madhubala, Nargis or Waheeda Rehman. I did leave my
own imprint somehow even while keeping all this in mind.
The liberation to sing as oneself comes only when you are
recording non-filmy music, and I have been able to do this
in my albums of devotional numbers when I sang purely as
myself, as Lata Mangeshkar.

There is another kind of situation, when a song is being
picturized in the absence of a human presence. For example,
in 'Aa Ja Re Pardesi' in the film Madhumati. I was merely told
that it would be picturized on Vyjayanthimala but even if it
had been someone else, I don't think I would have sung it
differently. This is true in all the so-called haunting songs I
have sung for films like Kohra or Bees Saal Baad. In 'Jhoom
Jhoom Dhalti Raat' (Kohra) the song is picturized on a woman
who is inebriated and just her back is shown, not her face. The
same happens in 'Kahin Deep Jale Kahin Dil' (Bees Saal Baad)
where the woman's face is never shown, but her presence is
suggested through images and movements. In 'Naina Barse'
(Woh Kaun Thi) and 'Ai Mere Dil-E-Nadan' (Tower House)
you will find the same quality.

In *Mahal*, the first of such films, I sang without being aware of the subtleties of this situation because I was so new and young. I followed the instructions of the composer and tried to put in the expressions he wanted. I had no idea what the song would seem when seen on screen. In fact, this is one genre where the existence of the heroine or her personality ceases to matter: the song is the main focus.

In the case of background songs, I always tried to study the feeling behind the lyrics and keep the mental state depicted intact in my singing. The joy or sorrow determined the emotional pitch of the song for me. Even the enunciation of words and the lowering of the voice to a mere whisper became important to me in such a situation.

YM: Did it ever happen that your own emotional state was at complete variance with the mood of the song you were recording?

LM: I am able to create a mood suitable for a song no matter what I may feel personally at that point. In any case, I never allow my personal moods to take control of me. So when I record a song I keep all extraneous thoughts out from my voice. I simply merge myself into what I sing and instinctively follow the words and tune to create a suitable mood.

YM: Ustad Bismillah Khan and you have collaborated in a wonderful song (*Dil Ka Khilona Hai Toot Gaya*). Vasant Desai was the composer for that film (*Goonj Uthi Shehnai*). What was that experience like?

LM: You have opened the floodgates of a very pleasant memory with this question. As far as I can remember I sang along with his shehnai in this song and he had set the tune for the song. This was Bismillah Khan's own composition although Vasant Desai had persuaded Khan sahib to play little melodies

on his shehnai throughout the film. I know that Khan sahib
was very pleased to have me sing along with his shehnai. As
for the plaintive and high notes used by him, how can I tell
you what inspired him to do that? However, I consider this as
much his song as mine . . . (hums it).

> *Dil ka khilauna haae tut gaya*
> *Koi lutera a ke lut gaya . . . haae*
> *Dil ka khilauna haae tut gaya . . .*
> *Hua kya kusur aisa saiyya hamaara*
> *Jaate hue jo tune hamen na pukaara*
> *Ulfat ka taar toda*
> *hamein majhadhaar chhoda*
> *Ham to chale the le ke tera hi sahaara*
> *Saathi hamaara ham se chhut gaya*
> *Dil ka khilauna haae tut gaya . . .*

YM: What about Pannalal Ghosh's unforgettable flute in *Basant
Bahar* (1956) in the song '*Main Piya Teri Tu Mane Ya Na Mane*'?

LM: That is also among my favourite songs and I was thrilled
to record it with him. I always feel there are two singers in that
song: Panna babu's flute and I. I think I am really fortunate
to have performed with such great artistes and consider these
opportunities greater than all the awards I have received. Ali
Akbar Bhai played in *Seema* with me ('*Suno Choti Si Gudiya
Ki Lambi Kahani*') and when I look back I am so proud that
we worked so hard to make each song special. Both these songs
were composed by Shankar-Jaikishan of whom it was said that
they did not care to look for classical music in their songs. I am
convinced that the blessings of these great ustads have taken
me where I find myself today.

There have been other great artistes with whom I have sung or been accompanied. Rais Khan sahib's sitar playing had an unmatched sweetness and he has accompanied my singing many times. The same is true of Abdul Halim Jafar Khan sahib. Pandit Ram Narayan's sarangi was in a class of its own as was Sultan Khan sahib's. Whenever I have to sing these songs on stage, I find myself as nervous as when I actually recorded these songs with them.

YM: Let's turn our attention to folk music now. What did you think of Naushad sahib's folk compositions?

LM: Naushad sahib belonged to Lucknow and in his early days of struggle, he worked in a shop of musical instruments. This is where he acquired his deep knowledge of folk music. As a composer he made brilliant use of this and brought a new dimension to Hindi film music. I was very close to him and he taught me a lot. However, it would be wrong to slot him only as a connoisseur of folk music. He had an equally deep understanding of classical music and few could equal his understanding of that genre. If you look carefully, you will find touches of pure classical music in almost all his compositions. However, as far as his folk music is concerned, my favourite compositions in this genre are two songs from *Ganga–Jamuna* ('*Dhoondo Dhoondo Re Sajana*' and '*Na Maanu Na Maanu Na Maanu Re*'). I think they are perfect compositions from any point of view. There is also '*Mohe Panghat Pe Nandlal*' from *Mughal-e-Azam*, a near-perfect number. After Ghulam Muhammad sahib passed away, Naushad sahib completed the musical score for *Pakeezah* where he merged a range of folk compositions (Avadh's famed kajri, thumri and dadra) with the background of kothewala music to create magic.

His work has carved a permanent place for itself in film music. I sang '*Pyare Babul Tumhari Duhai*' in *Pakeezah* for him, which is a *vidai geet*. This was released only on disc and another of my favourites is '*Peeke Chale Yeh Chale Hum Hain Sharabi*'. When you sang for him, you understood completely why he merged folk and classical together. When recording a number for *Andaz*, Naushad sahib once said to me, 'Lata bai, I've made this song for your friend. That is how you have to sing it.' I knew he meant it was to be sung in the style of Noorjahan and that was exactly how I sang. This was his greatness: he managed to extract exactly what he wanted from his singers.

Another wonderful film from the point of view of its music was *Shabab*, which has one of my favourite numbers as it is yours: '*Jo Main Janti Bisrat Hain Saiyan*'. I love that song too and another one of his compositions that is a favourite of mine is '*Jogan Ban Jayoongi Saiyan Tere Karan*' and '*Marna Teri Gali Main*'—both from *Shabab*. There is also my duet with Hemant Kumar, '*Chandan Ka Palna, Resham Ki Dori*', a beautiful lullaby. All these went on to become hugely popular. Moreover, they were all picturized on my favourite actress Nutan who used to give a most natural performance when singing on the screen. All her film songs appear to have been actually sung by her. I agree with you that although he is best known for his mega-hits like *Mughal-e-Azam*, *Andaz*, *Baiju bawra*, *Mother India* and *Ganga–Jamuna*, Naushad sahib's best music is actually to be heard in *Shabab*, *Amar*, *Sohni Mahiwal* and *Udan Khatola*.

YM: According to you, who are the most classically pure composers?

LM: Anil Biswas, S.D. Burman, Madan Mohan, Naushad sahib. To some extent I would also include Khayyam sahib who has a deep understanding of classical music.

YM: What about Roshan sahib?

LM: How could I forget that name? His knowledge of classical music was tremendous because he had learnt from the famous Allauddin Khan sahib of Maihar. He played the dilruba beautifully and was equally adept at both the sarangi and harmonium. He is the only composer who made me sing in pure classical ragas. For example, 'Ai Re Aali Piya Bin' (in Yaman) in Raga-Rang; 'Garjat Barsat Sawan Aayo Re' (in Malhar) and 'Ai Re Jane Na Doongi' in Chitralekha, inspired by Kamod. Roshan made some beautiful compositions for me: in Naubahar, Mamata, Tajmahal, Zindagi aur Hum, Bahu Begum, Chitralekha, Raga-Rang, Taksaal, Arati, Malhar and Anokhi Raat.

YM: Ghazal composition is also an art and while we remember the work done by Madan Mohan and Naushad sahib in this genre, what did you think of the music set for ghazals by Roshan. And Khayyam?

LM: You are absolutely right: both Roshan and Khayyam matched Naushad and Madan Mohan in this sphere. You forget qawwalis although strangely I never sang for any of their qawwalis.

YM: Looking ahead, what kind of voice do you think will dominate film songs? And who would you choose as a role model for the future singers?

LM; Look, it is difficult to predict what the future will bring and how films will develop. All I can say is that I sincerely hope that we should encourage those who worship muic to come to this field.

As for role models: I leave it to you to say what kind of female voice you would like to hear (laughs) but if I were to choose a male voice, then it would be someone who can sing like Kishore Kumar.

YM: Why did certain voices disappear from the playback world after just a few songs? Why did singers such as K.C. Dey, C.H. Atma, Parul Ghosh, G.M. Durrani and Geeta Dutt vanish?

LM: Each of these voices was associated with a certain style of singing, so whenever the film suited their style, they gave wonderful performances. I would place Geeta Dutt at another level: she worked hard at her singing and whatever she sang is unforgettable. She earned a big name while she was alive and even today she has a dedicated band of fans who love her songs.

As for the rest, some were good at bhajans, some at bhatiyali or sad songs and so on. Burman Dada liked to give K.C. Dey his folk songs in the bhatiyali style because he excelled at them. Dada himself sang rarely but when he did (Bandini, Sujata and Aradhna) he brought magic to the atmosphere. So both K.C. Dey and Durrani gave great performances but they seem to have had a limited repertoire. Parul Ghosh had a really sweet voice and she should have been given more songs but even the small number she sang is unmatched. Even today, when I hear her 'Papiha Re Mere Piya Se Kahiyo Jaye' from Kismet, I am transported to another world.

Let's now come to C.H. Atma. His problem was that he always imitated Saigal's style and as you know I have a 'thing' about imitators. What is a copy will always remain a pale shadow of the real is what I have always believed. I say this also to all those who try and imitate my style and voice: develop your own style, I tell them, why copy what is available? This is true of all imitators whether in art, literature or music. You may get limited success but it will never grow into a major voice.

YM: You have sung from almost all our religious texts, but why did you never choose some verses from Valmiki's Ramayan?

LM: I can't really say why but since the Ramcharitmanas is more popular, I preferred to choose verses from there. However, I have sung selections from the Tulsi Ramayan and was helped by Pandit Narendra Sharma in choosing them. Mukesh has sung the entire Ramayan and done a brilliant job, I think. After that, I thought why try and improve something so perfect?

As for the Bhagvad Gita, I would have liked to sing all the chapters but because of technical problems at that time, I was able to just do small extracts from it that would fit a disc.

YM: How did you think of singing from the Gita?

LM: I have always been very deeply influenced by its teachings. Once, the legendary musician Vasant Joglekar rebuked me: 'Lata! Will you always only sing film songs? Sing something that will be remembered by generations of listeners. Sing from the Gita: ask your brother Hridaynath to compose it.'

I began to give his advice serious thought and that is how the Gita came to be recorded. I cannot tell you what peace and satisfaction this project brought me.

YM: Among the duos who composed film music, who do you rate the best?

LM: Without a doubt, Shankar-Jaikishan, although Husnlal–Bhagatram before them were also very popular. However, gradually their music began to sound the slightly stale and this became a reason for the rising popularity of Shankar–Jaikishan. After them, I would rate Laxmikant–Pyarelal and then Jatin–Lalit. However, I must mention that S–J's style was copied by many: for instance, Laxmikant–Pyarelal, Kalyan ji–Anandji and Dattaram.

YM: Which music composer made the best use of western music?

LM: All music composers have used western tunes and styles at some point or another, but the best example of it (in terms of orchestration and use of musical instruments) was R.D. Burman. Salil Chaudhuri, C. Ramachandra and Shankar–Jaikishan have all used orchestration but S.D. Burman used western musical instruments not Indian substitutes. In this he was assisted by his son, R.D. Burman who knew a lot about western music.

YM: Who followed the Indian tradition most faithfully while composing music?

LM: According to me, the music composed by Jaidev, Khayyam sahib and Hridaynath Mangeshkar carried a distinct stamp of our Indian music. Jaidev and Hridaynath have composed some beautiful raga-based songs and Hridaynath was a disciple of Ustad Amir Khan. Among the others, Anil Biswas and Chitragupta ji also composed very lovely pieces in this style.

YM: What about Vasant Desai?

LM: Of course he must be included here, because he was very partial to raga-based music. However, his style bore a deep stamp of Marathi music and culture. So if you call him an expert in that tradition (of Marathi Natya and Bhava Sangeet), I would agree with you. Sudhir Phadke is another name you can add here. I would say that every music composer brings the culture and tradition of his own state into his music: Naushad's music can be traced to his Awadhi roots and the Lucknow-Banaras tradition. Jaikishan was a Gujarati, so you can hear traces of Gujarati folk music in his compositions and Khayyam sahib brought Punjabi and Pahari tunes into our film music.

YM: Do you think that the era of Naushad, Shankar-Jaikishan and S.D. Burman in the same light as we view the age of Gandhi and Nehru as the golden era of Indian politics?

LM: This is an interesting way of assessing their contribution! I must tell you that I have been present for 70 years of the last century of film music, so perhaps I am in a position to speak with reasonable authority on this topic. I can see how far we have come from the music of those early years and can spot the watershed changes. Let us keep personalities out of this equation for the time being: from the 1930s to the 1940s, our film music was a mixture of Bengali, Marathi and Gujarati styles. At one end of this era stood Saigal sahib and at the other we had Noorjahan. I can only think of these two names from that time.

Now let us come to influences and the composers who brought these into the industry. One was Master Ghulam Haider in his film *Khazanchi* in the forties, the next were Shankar-Jaikishan with their music of *Barsaat* in the fifties and R.D. Burman with *Teesri Manzil* in the sixties. *Khazanchi* brought the vigour of Punjabi music although Naushad, Anil Biswas, C. Ramachandra, Roshanlal, Hemant Kumar, Madan Mohan and S.D. Burman gave some memorable compositions during the same period. Yet, films such as *Kismet, Ratan, Baiju Bawra, Anarkali, Bawre nain, Nagin, Woh Kaun Thi* and *Guide* began to reflect the changing trend in composing music.

Shankar-Jaikishan's was the only team that changed the entire scene with their music in *Barsaat*. In my opinion, no other music composer matched the deep impression they left on the music of those times. So these, according to me, are the watershed moments of this long musical journey.

For a long time, S–J's style dominated our film music and you can hear this in the music of Laxmikant–Pyarelal and Kalyan ji–Anandji. I often felt that both these tried to imitate S–J's style. This is why the next big change came with the music of R.D. Burman and if you analyse the music of the sixties and seventies, no one came close to his creative experiments. Whether it was *Teesri Manzil*, *Caravan*, *Amar Prem* or *Aandhi*, each bore the stamp of R.D. Burman's special style. Today, I think such a phenomenon is visible in the compositions of A.R. Rahman.

I say this not because there have not been other competent composers but because, like R.D. Burman, he is a bold experimenter and that places his kind of music in a special niche by itself. Rahman has a very good understanding of words and tunes and is brilliant at arranging musical scores.

YM: After R.D. Burman, there was a great demand for disco numbers in films. One feels that this was over-mined by Bhappi Lahiri and film music began a downward spiral, as can be seen in the music of the eighties. True?

LM: The problem with his music was that he tried to imitate R.D. Burman and never quite succeeded.

YM: The film industry was never kind to those like Khayyam and Jaidev who chose a different path. Even though they were great composers, they got very few offers. There were others too: Sapan jagmohan, Raghunath Seth, Kanu ray and Vanraj Bhatia. Why did they not enter mainstream cinema?

LM: You are absolutely right. This is indeed a pity because all the names you mention were exceptionally talented composers. They were limited to art house films and were unable to modulate their talent to commercial films. Perhaps this is the reason.

YM: How do you prepare your voice to sing different kinds of music? When you are, for example, told that this is going to be a devotional number or a lullaby in the film, do you have to make a mental adjustment?

LM: I internalize the situation of the song within myself before recording it, so you are right: I do prepare myself. Every song has a different mood whether it is a love song, duet, bhajan or whatever. As an example, let me tell you that when I was recording Meera bhajans for Hridaynath, I became completely enraptured in her life and times. You could call me Meera-mad. I would spend hours trying to figure out what she must have felt as she wrote a particular bhajan, what she must have undergone when she was thrown out by her husband. It is only after all this that I was able to sing with confidence in her voice.

A different situation was created when singing a duet with someone. Or when recording a sad song, you had to be conscious of the mental pain suffered by the artiste on screen. I also kept the individual actress on whom the song was being picturized because each actress had her own personality. Great discipline is required to fulfil all these demands and a distracted singer will never be able to bring a song alive is all I can say.

YM: So do you agree with the fact that your voices are largely responsible for the development of the character on screen?

LM: This is quite true. Often the actress creates her screen persona according to the direction given by the songs she sings in a film. Mere words and tunes cannot breathe the life that a human voice can and the background orchestra can only set the mood. The feelings come from the playback singer.

This is particularly true of sad songs: how long a heroine will cry on screen depends on the song she emotes to. Although, come to think of it, no really sad person will sing a song. I mean it is hilarious if looked at realistically: the voice chokes, the eyes and nose stream . . .how can one possibly sing in such a state? Frankly, you can't even talk, let alone sing! When I thought of all this, I had to work very hard to make the effort to bring out the pathos of the song. Often I had violent disagreements with those composers who would ask me to sob while singing.

Let's leave these extreme situations aside for now, but when I sang a sad song I always tried to make it as close as I could to the feelings behind the situation on screen. It must look and sound natural.

YM: In film music, no composer was told that a dadra or kaharwa (rhythmic patterns on perscussion) was to be played. On the other hand, percussionists were told to bang out a 'Pakeezah', 'Anarkali' or 'Sargam' beat. In fact, Shankar-Jaikishan's favourite percussionist, Dattaram, is still remembered for his signature 'Dattaram theka'. What do you have to say on this?

LM: Look, film music is different in the sense that the lyrics are the crucial element. So while dadra and kaharwa are the most common rhythms used in it, sometimes the patterns were altered to fit the lyrics in properly. And Dattaram was not the only percussionist who was a master at this, there were others as well who were clever at adapting rhythmic patterns. There was a Marathi player called Lala who was a master naal player and was always called whenever it had to be played for a song. Another one, called Sattar, was a brilliant tabla player. In fact the two scored the music for a few films under the moniker of Lala–Sattar.

Shankar-Jaikishan's orchestra had a great mandolin player called David. Salil da's musical group had an oboe player called Surkhe. In fact you can hear his oboe in all Salil da's compositions. So there were many very talented musicians who played for different composers in their orchestras. In the eighthies, the South Indian ghatam (clay pot) was used a lot in Hindi film songs. In the sixties, a clay violin was popular.

Similarly, wood sticks (used in garba dances) became popular and were polished to provide a 'tak-tak' beat. Every composer had one such master player in his group.

YM: In the fifties and sixties, several musical instruments were very popular: the mandolin, piano, accordion, clarinet and organ. What do you have to say about this?

LM: Look, I have told you how every composer had a special player in his group. Shankar-Jaikishan were very fond of the mandolin, Naushad saab composed all his songs on a piano and it features in most of his songs. The organ was the most popular as far as I can remember and it was used to provide the chord, which was a great help to us to find the correct pitch.

YM: What was your relationship with chorus singers like? Were they kept away from the main singer?

LM: Once upon a time, there was just a single group of chorus singers and they were used by all the music composers, from Naushad to Burman dada and all. Naturally, we became familiar with each other and I felt very comfortable with them because most of them came from backgrounds similar to mine. We even visited each others' homes and when my sister Meena got married all the chorus singers came to our home and sang wedding songs. This state of affairs continued till about the eighties and then it changed as some of them stopped singing and some went away elsewhere.

After the eighties, the chorus bits were separately recorded and not along with the main singers. Earlier, the men and women chorus singers sang as we recorded and some of their names still come back to me as I recall their voices. Kavita, Gandhari, Kalyani, Suman and Rekha had exceptionally sweet voices I remember. Kavita and Gandhari were sisters and sang together. Rekha was married with children. They were so humble that, as there was a chronic shortage of chairs in recording studios then, they would squat on the floor to wait. Often I joined them as well. We continued to remain in touch even after they left singing. I don't know what the situation is like now: I have no idea.

YM: What happened if the accompanists goofed up; did that bother you?

LM: Although this did not happen all that often, it did pain us that we had to re-do a song because of someone else's mistake. Often, the second take was not as good as the first I had sung. When I started my playback singing (around 1947 or so), songs used to be directly recorded on the film. Later, the director and recordist would listen to the recording and decide if it was fit to be included. Often we had to re-do the entire song because of a recording flaw. This happened a lot in my early days. Also, because the music was sold under the HMV imprint, we had to re-record the same song for them for copyright reasons. If you listen carefully to Naushad sahib's '*Uthaye Ja Unke Sitam*', you will realize that the song is much longer in the film than it is on record. This is because the record version had to be a 3-minute piece, so often they trimmed a verse or a musical interlude to fit it into their time slot. This is how we recorded all the *Barsaat* songs, for instance. The same happened in *Andaz* and some others that I can't now recall. We singers thanked God when the tape came to be used for now the whole version was saved on tape and could be cut and chopped without our having to sing it over again!

As you can imagine, this was both tedious and difficult. We were expected to carry every memory of the original recording faithfully in our heads to make a disc copy. As time went on, I got used to this and overcame my nervousness over this trial.

YM: Which music composer do you think composed music perfectly suited to your voice and temperament?

LM: This is difficult to say because each one of them made beautiful compositions for me. All I can say is that I respected each one of them, and tried to keep in mind what they expected of me. Sometimes, I recorded three songs in one day, each for a different composer and I am happy to tell you that I never mixed up their styles. For instance, when I sang for R.D. Burman, I set aside the fact that he was S.D. Burman's son and gave his composition the quality he wanted me to. So how can I pick one out of so many?

YM: Does the music of Salil Chaudhuri stand out for any special reason?

LM: Salil da had a unique style of his own and although his music appears simple when you hear it, it was actually quite difficult to sing. His music spanned a huge range of genres: classical ragas, folk music and western music. However, one can easily pick out his songs from the others because they all bore the stamp of his creativity. Take 'Itna Na Tu Mujh Se Pyaar Barha' for instance, which he based on a symphony of Mozart, set in G-minor. 'Mere Man Ke Diye' from the film *Parakh* has touches of church choir music. You can find such flourishes from western music in many songs he composed. In fact, he was the one who educated me about western music. He'd take me to Bombay's Rhythm House and help me choose Mozart, Beethoven, Chopin or Tchaikovsky's music for my listening pleasure. I owe my love for western music to him and it led to my building up a private collection for myself.

YM: According to you, who were the film directors who best understood the importance of music in cinema?

LM: I think Mehboob Khan, Kamal Amrohi, Raj Kapoor, Vijay Anand and Yash Chopra were those who were most sensitive on this subject. Not only did they have a genuine understanding of good music and singers, they were excellent at making the best use of music in their films.

YM: How is it that you only sang 5 songs for Guru Dutt?

LM: There was no special reason but you forget that he had an outstanding singer at home: his wife Geeta Dutt! So there was really no need for me to be present in his musical framework. Also the kind of voice that suited his lead actresses matched Shamshad Begum and my sister Asha's voices. All these singers, particularly, Geeta Dutt, have left an unmistakable stamp on all the songs they sang for films such as *Pyasa*, *Kaghaz Ke Phool* and *Sahib Bibi aur Ghulam*. I loved the way he made a song seem so natural on screen: think of '*Aji, Dil Ne Kiya Aisa Jadoo*' from *Mr and Mrs 55*. The song just springs out of the scene! His genius was evident to all who worked with him: I sensed it immediately when I recorded '*Badle Badle Mere Sarkar Nazar Aate Hain*' for him.

YM: How do you view Raj Kapoor's work?

LM: Raj Kapoor had no equal, I think. He could play any musical instrument—the violin, piano, table or mandolin—and had a deep understanding of music. His brother Shammi Kapoor was also very musically inclined and even took regular lessons in classical music.

I consider Raj Kapoor a perfectionist and he worked really hard to get the kind of music he wanted in his films. He would constantly suggest changes and keep at it until he was satisfied. I remember when we recorded '*Ghar Aya Mera Pardesi*' for *Awara*, all of us—Manna De, Shankar–Jaikishan and I—were made to do it over and over again until we were exhausted. The recording that started at 9 that morning was finally approved at 3 in the morning the next day! It was precisely this pursuit of perfection that gave each one of his songs that quality of depth and soul.

The largest body of his music was composed by Shankar–Jaikishan and after them by Laxmikant–Pyarelal and Ravindra Jain. Above all, there was an element of his own creativity in all the songs he chose. He worked along with the composers and was not satisfied until he had tinkered with the song himself. Never did he approve of a song as it was presented to him: this was an important part of his style.

YM: Mehboob Khan's *Mother India* (1957) was an unforgettable saga of courage and empowerment and the music of the film matched its central themes. Your songs in that ('*O Mere Lal Aaja*' and '*Nagri Nagri, Dware Dware*' as well as the wonderful '*Duniya Main Hum Aye Hain To Jeena Hi Padega*' with Shamshad Begum and your sister Meena have retained their freshness down the ages. How do you respond to the stirring call of these numbers?

LM: As far as the songs of this film are concerned I think they are an inalienable part of the story and the ones you mention are placed in the most moving segments of the film. There are other beautiful compositions as well but these three are in a separate category I think. Think of '*Umariya Ghat-Ti Jaye Re*' and '*Dukh Bhare Din Beete Re Bhaiyya, Ab Sukh Ayo Re*'; their lilting folk rhythms are also mesmerizing but in a different way from those three. They were taken from Gujarati folk music because that was the location in the film and also because Shakeel Badauni had put his heart into those lyrics. A singer could not help but respond to those lines.

Mother India is one film that has as many songs by me as by Shamshad Begum so that the personality of every character is brought out. Personally, I am very partial to '*O Mere Lal Aaja*' and '*Nagri Nagri Dware Dware*' and even now my heart fills with sorrow as I listen to their plaintive lyrics and music. I felt very depressed after they were recorded and even after all these years, that same feeling is evoked each time I hear them. I realize now that Mehboob Khan was able to blend story and music so perfectly that they have become imprinted on our hearts.

YM: Shankar–Jaikishan liked to pitch their songs at a very high note ('*Rasik Balma*', '*O Basanti Pawan Pagal*', to name just two). There is a long list of such numbers. How did you deal with their demand?

LM: That was their signature style and something that made their music special. I was a bit wary of singing at such a high pitch because you have to be careful to modulate your voice else it sounds screechy. So I dreaded these numbers. I did my best yet often Jaikishan would urge me to try yet a higher octave. Often we had violent arguments about this demand and I used to ask why they composed songs in that impossible pitch. I felt that lowering the pitch would actually make the song sweeter and also be less hard on my voice. During the recording of '*Aji Rooth Kar Ab Kahan Jaiyega*', I asked him whether he had any idea what I went through when singing such high notes. 'Don't you have any compassion for my throat?' I asked angrily. 'I go through hell when singing these compositions, no matter how wonderful they may be.'

Jaikishan was a little perturbed and tried to explain how he felt that I could sing even higher notes and that the higher I went, the sweeter my voice became. 'Your voice blossoms like a flower at those notes,' I remember him saying to pacify me. However, I feel that my voice is best when it is at an even pitch. You will be surprised to know that whenever I was sent requests from the audience during my stage shows, most of them were for these high-note compositions. So perhaps they had a point!

Many of the songs I have sung for Burman dada or Madan Mohan are also similar and sometimes I felt as if these composers deliberately tested my capacity to take my voice higher and higher. That lovely *Hum Dono* number '*Prabhu Tero Naam, Jo Dhyaye Phal Paye*' (Jaidev's composition) is another example. I asked Jaidev why he had done this to me, as the song begins on a low note and then soars to an impossible pitch. Do you realize, I asked him, how difficult it is for me to span these octaves? 'Oh come on, Lata ji,' he laughed. 'We both know you can handle this pitch with ease. Besides,' he added, 'if you won't sing these numbers, who else will I go to?'

YM: Which of the songs sung high are your favourites?

LM: There must be several but I rate S–J's composition '*Rasik Balma*' (*Chori-Chori*) my favourite. Another number also composed by them is '*Jao Re Jogi Tum Jao Re*' (*Amrapali*); Madan Mohan's '*Sapnon Main Agar Mere Tum Aao*' (*Dulhan Ek Raat Ki*) and Roshan sahib's '*Ae Ri Jane Na Doongi*' (*Chitralekha*) are some others I like very much.

YM: When recording technology was not as advanced, you had to sing with the orchestra and also speak some dialogue. Going back to the original track must have posed problems. How did you manage all these difficulties?

LM: Few people understand this problem and as far as I am concerned, breaking off a song to speak a dialogue did not bother me too much. All I did was to make sure that I knew exactly where the break came in the song and prepare myself in advance. I never lost my pitch either after such a break. In the days of single track recording, we had to also be aware of the notations of our co-singers, if it was a duet, and of the orchestra and ensure that we were all in tune with each other. It was difficult no doubt but it also made such sessions challenging and exciting. Each time I did such a number, I came away feeling very satisfied and happy. If you recall a song ('*Sharabi-Sharabi Mera Naam Ho Gaya*') in the film *Chandan Ka Palna* (music by R.D. Burman) a Meena Kumari starrer, I had to speak a few lines in the song. If you hear it today, you will not be able to make out whether it is Meena Kumari or me who is speaking those lines. Sometimes, one was asked to laugh or chortle in a song, and I did that too, without going off-key or missing a beat!

YM: This is an awkward question but I have to ask: in a long musical journey of almost 70 years, there were occasions when you stopped singing for a particular music director for some time. Later, when the misunderstanding was cleared up, you sang for him again. This happened at various points of your career with C. Ramachandra, S.D. Burman, Vasant Desai, Jaidev and Shankar–Jaikishan. Was there any music composer who never left your side and never looked for an alternative to your voice?

LM: I am glad you asked this question and no, there is nothing awkward about it. I can only think of Madan Mohan who stayed with me throughout. It was not as if he did not use other singers for both Geeta Dutt and my sister Asha have sung some unforgettable numbers for him, but my place in his music remained unchanged all through his life. Even when I was too busy to give him exclusive time or was unwell, he would wait patiently until I reached the studio.

He was the only composer who really believed that the only alternative to Lata was Lata herself! This is why I respect him so deeply.

I don't deny that other music directors and I had our ups and downs but it was not always because of me. I also can't deny that this hurt me deeply at the time, because I am human after all. However, I also believe that in life you don't have control over every event and when fundamental differences arise, there is nothing that can resolve them except time. I must add that when our differences were resolved, there was no lingering ill-will between me and people like Burman dada and Jaidev. As far as Shankar–Jaikishan were concerned, Jaikishan often told Shankar that the songs that are meant for Lata's voice should not be given to others and as long as he was alive, they sorted this out amongst themselves. After Jaikishan passed away, this partnership broke up and Shankar could never capture the magic they brought to music when Jaikishan was alive. At the height of their career, S–J was called the Silver Jubilee *jori* because each film that had their music went on to become a hit. This place was then taken by Burman dada, Kalyan ji–Anandji and Laxmikant–Pyarelal and the era of the S–J glory came to an end. I am proud that I sang for all of them for as long as they were around and there was no bitterness in either of our hearts.

List of favourite duets:

- With Mukesh: '*Sawan Ka Mahina Pawan Kare Sor*' (*Milan*)
- With Mohd Rafi: '*Awaz Deke Hamain Tum Bulao*' (*Professor*)
- With Hemant Kumar: '*Chhupa Lo Yun Dil Main Pyar Mera*' (*Mamata*)

- With Talat Mehmood: '*Dil Main Sama Gaye Sajan, Phool Khile Hain Chaman-Chaman*' (*Sangdil*)
- With Manna De: '*Chunari Sambhal Gori, Udi Chali Jaye Re*' (*Bahron Ke Sapne*)
- With Kishore Kumar: '*Kora Kaghaz Tha Yeh Man Mera*' (*Aradhana*)
- With Mahendra Kapoor: '*Chhod Kar Tere Pyar Ka Daman*' (*Who Kaun Thi*)
- With Shashad Begum: '*Bachpan Ke Din Bhula Na Dena*' (*Didar*)
- With Asha Bhonsle: '*Man Kyoon Behka Re Aadhi Raat Ko*' (*Utsav*)
- With Geeta Dutt: '*Ta Thayya Kar Ke Aana, More Jadugar More Saiyan*' (*Panchayat*)
- With Usha Mangeshkar: '*Dagabaaz Ho Banke Piya*' (*Burma Road*)

YM: Which Indian actress do you rate as the best?

LM: I love both Meena Kumari and Nargis. Meena Kumari was such an accomplished actress that her eyes and face could emote without a single word of dialogue. Have you seen her in *Sharada*? She is outstanding there. Her work in *Chitralekha, Arti, Bahu Begum* reveals what a great actress she was. I loved her in *Dil Ek Mandir, Dil Apna Aur Preet Parayi* and *Baiju Bawra*. If you met her privately, she came across as a very sober and decent human being. She always kept a diary near her so that she could jot down her own poems or write down a poem someone brought to her notice.

If you ask me, I feel my voice was best suited to her, Nargis, Madhubala, Saira Bano and Nutan. The song I sang for Meena

Kumari in *Bahu Begum* ('*Duniya Kare Sawal*') is among my favourites.

YM: Would you not add Waheeda Rehman, Vyajayanthimala, Mala Sinha, Sadhana and Nanda to the names you mention?

LM: All these actresses emoted beautifully and lip-synced with my songs very well, especially Waheeda Rehman, Vyajayanthimala and Sadhana. I chose the earlier names because their voice quality (pitch etc) was closest to mine. Take Nutan, for example, she had a very soft voice; Saira Bano's voice was very thin and fragile: all these are qualities that I think are close to my own voice. Of the names you mention, I would say that Sadhana has done full justice to my songs. Her lip movement was excellent.

As for Waheeda Rehman, she brought depth to all the roles she played on screen. Whether a dancer's or a serious tragic role, she did justice to every character she played. I think her work in *Guide* is enough to prove this point. There have been few dancers to equal Vyajayanthimala, and her. Waheeda was an all-rounder, I think.

Another dancer that comes to mind is Asha Parekh and some of my most popular songs were picturized on her: '*Chham Chham Nachat Ayi Bahar*' (*Chhaya*), '*Raat Ka Samaa, Jhoome Chandrama*' (*Ziddi*), '*Koi Matwala Aya Mere Dware*' (*Love in Tokyo*). Her dances on all these numbers are wonderful. However, I think my sister Asha's voice was a better match for her but like Waheeda and Vyajayanthimala she was an accomplished actress.

To answer your question, in my opinion, Vyajayanthimala was the best dancer of them all.

YM: Of the dance numbers you sang, which is your favourite?

LM: There are several but there some that are special to me: 'Hoton Pe Aisi Baat Main Chhupa Ke Chali Ayi' (*Jewel Thief*), 'Piya Tose Naina Lage Re' (*Guide*) and 'Raat Ka Samaa, Jhoome Chandrama' (*Mujhe Jeene Do*). Remind me of some more . . .

YM: 'Jhan-Jhan Jhan Payal Baaje' (*Buzdil*); 'Pawan Deewani Na Mane Udaye Mora Ghunghata' (*Dr Vidya*); 'Julmi Hamare Saanwariya Ho' (*Mr X in Bombay*); 'Radha Na Bole Na Bole Na Bole Re' (*Azad*); 'Ghari-Ghari Mora Dil Dharake' (*Madhumati*); 'Na Maaro Nazariya Ke Baan' (*Pehli Jhalak*); 'Jao Jao Nand Ke Lala Tum Jhoote' (*Rangoli*); 'Raat Dhalne Lagi' (*Teesri Kasam*); 'Kajra Laga Ke Bindiya Saja Ke' (*Jal Bin Machli, Nritya Bin Bijli*); 'Look Chhup Badra Main Chamke Jaise Chanda' (*Ganga Maiya Tore Piyari Chadhiybo*); 'Ho Re Ho Re Jhanan Ghunghar Baaje' (*Ganga Jaumna*); 'Aya Aya Atariya Pe Koi Chor' (*Mera Gaon Mera Des*); 'Yeh Galiyan Yeh Chaubara' (*Prem Rog*), 'Nindiya Se Jaagi Bahar' (*Hero*); 'Morni Bagan Main Bole Aadhi Raat Ko' (*Lamhe*); 'Mayi Ri Mayi, Mundair Pe Teri' (*Hum Aapke Hain Kaun*). I haven't taken any of your mujra songs we'll talk about them later.

LM: You are right, some of these songs are lovely and have wonderful dance numbers filmed on them. Please may I request you to delete one song? The one from *Mera Gaon Mera Desh*— 'Aya Aya Atariya Pe Koi Chor'—I just don't think it fits here. (We both laugh).

YM: Let's just go back to the actresses for a bit: among them we forgot to talk of Madhubala. I want to know what you thought of her.

LM: Madhubala was stunningly beautiful but I always thought she could have been more restrained because I think she occasionally overacted a bit in her films. By the way, she was the first actress who insisted that her contract had a clause that I would sing the songs to be filmed on her. Later, others started to include this clause as well. I feel very strongly that if she had not started this trend, I would have lost out on several songs.

YM: After this generation, who else comes to your mind?

LM: Rekha. She is a superb actress and what a dancer! How many could have done what she did in *Umrao Jan*? It is among my all-time favourite films. Despite being a South Indian, her Urdu is flawless and she brings magic to every role she plays. Think of her role in *Utsav*, how brilliantly she handles the nuances in that role. I loved her in *Silsila* as well. I think there is no one to touch her in this generation.

YM: You mean after the age of Nargis–Nutan–Meena Kumari, the next best thing to happen to Hindi cinema was Rekha? What about Hema Malini?

LM: You are right, she is in the same league as Rekha. She has always appeared to me as a very classy and cultured person and carries herself with great dignity in all her roles. You may not be able to recall individual roles but her persona is that of a dignified, cultured woman. And how beautifully she has aged!

YM: There were some actresses who appeared in just a film or two but left an imprint. Like Leela Naidu and Suchitra Sen, both of whom you have sung for. What about them?

LM: I remember Leela Naidu in just one film, *Anuradha*, which I consider a classic. Hrishikesh Mukherji's direction and Ravi Shankar's music have made it immortal. So I can't really assess her range as an actress, even though she has emoted beautifully in the songs of that film.

I have seen Suchitra Sen more in Bengali films and she is undoubtedly a great artiste. Her role as Paro in *Devdas* with Dilip Kumar as *Devdas* makes me wonder why more directors

did not avail of such talent. Mind you, her Hindi was a bit
wobbly and you could hear a Bengali speak when she opened
her mouth but she was so good that one overlooked that flaw.
Mamata was another wonderful film with her playing a double
role. Her acting as a *tawaif's* daughter is at a different pitch
from her role as the mother in the film. Roshalal's superb
music in the film was also largely responsible for the success of
that film and Suchitra brought out their loveliness each time.
Gulzar's *Aandhi* is another of her memorable Hindi films. I
love all the songs there, particularly, '*Is More Se Jaate Hain*'.

YM: Of the contemporary generation, which is an actress
you admire?

LM: Madhuri Dixit is a natural actress and because her
work is consistently good. The others I like are Juhi Chawla,
Kajol and Rani Mukherji. All of them are very good I think.
I like to think that instead of a Waheeda today we have a
Madhuri and Kajol keeps alive the tradition of her aunt Nutan
and mother Tanuja as a thinking actress. Rani Mukherji has
also made a place for herself with her capacity to get inside a
role: I loved her in *Black*.

YM: You admire actresses who can dance well and act.
What about Sridevi, who can do both well and for whom you
have sung in *Chandni* and *Lamhe*?

LM: Without doubt, she is a very accomplished performer.
I have loved her work in both the films you mention, especially
her dance number in *Chandni* where she has danced just to
music. She incorporates some classical dance steps there very
competently, I think. In *Lamhe*, her performance to my song
'*Morni Bagaan Main Bole Adhi Raat Maan*' is also worth
mentioning. Sridevi understands the correspondence between
words and movement very well.

YM: Were you always satisfied with how you sang?

LM: Look, as I have told you over and over again, I always prepared myself to sing to the best of my ability. I never cut corners or sang half-heartedly. So yes, I have that satisfaction. It is a different matter that some songs are more memorable than others. I once went to visit Meena Kumari and found her trying out dance steps with 'Mausam Hai Ashiqana' playing in the background. She stopped as I entered and told me, 'If we can bring even a fraction of the quality that you put into your songs, the screen lights up. There is already so much expression and emotion in your songs that we need to do little else. I feel I don't have to work very hard because you have done the real work for me in a song.' I was thrilled with this praise coming from an artiste of her calibre.

YM: What do you like doing when you are happy?

LM: I don't think I am the kind of person who lets moods overtake her. Earlier, I used to love to travel, not abroad but to visit the famous places in our country like Jaipur, Udaipur, Madurai or Kashmir. Sadly, because work kept me chained to Bombay I wasn't able to fulfil this ambition and this is the price I paid for my success.

YM: What kind of person puts you off and you like to avoid?

LM: There are 2–3 kinds of people I just can't stand: those who flatter and those who lie. The third kind is the person who loves to boast about himself: they insist you hear them sing. Mostly, they are terrible singers and that really puts me off. I hate the fact that they have reduced something as sacred as music to such a low level. I can still deal with a person who knows he is bad and wants to improve but the one I hate above all is the sort who thinks he is superb and has no shame at all in promoting himself. I stay miles away from such people.

YM: How do you assess a person's worth?

LM: I feel you judge a person by the moral values he displays. These moral values are planted in us in our childhood and every person keeps them within to act as touchstones throughout life. To me, any person who respects his parents is a good human being.

YM: When you stand before a microphone what are you mindful about?

LM: For one, I never sing directly into a mike because that can distort certain sounds, like bh, ph, and fa. Sometimes, a music director tells me to soften my voice or begin in a soft way, gradually raising my volume as the song proceeds. I always pay attention to such instructions.

You see, I learnt very early on that one's voice on a microphone can take on a different tone. You will notice that even in my stage shows, I prefer to sing a little distance away from the mike. I think this makes my voice sound sweeter.

YM: Do the younger singers come to you for advice on how to modulate their singing to bring out its best qualities?

LM: (Laughs). No, not even one has ever come to me for advice or help. I have not seen the kind of interest in this generation of singers we had in knowing how to improve our style by seeking out senior artistes, music directors and accompanists for tips. This just does not happen now.

I learnt from Ghulam Haider, Anil Biswas, Naushad sahib (who taught me so much more than just how to improve my singing style). Master Ghulam Haider drilled the importance of correct enunciation, whether it was Hindi or Urdu. He gave me another tip that I followed forever: that when you catch a beat, cross your voice in front of the mike to soften it: this will give the song a great sound quality. He was absolutely right. He also taught me how to tackle taans in filmy songs, which is entirely different from those taken in classical ragas. Naushad sahib was also very particular about pronunciation.

Anil da gave me tips on how to hold my breath and exhale without it being audible. He also guided me on how close or far to remain from the mike when singing particular parts of a song and how to throw my voice.

All these tips and lessons have been of immense help to me. What you hear in my voice today is what I learnt from all these teachers and a lot of my own hard work. My constant endeavour was how to incorporate all this in my singing so that I sounded fresh in each song I sang. For instance, when I sang '*Ram Ka Gungaan Kariye*' with Bhimsen Joshi, I copied a taan of Ustad Barkat Ali Khan to match Bhimsen Joshi's voice quality. I loved it when my seniors like Noorjahan or Zohrabai Ambalawali praised me or asked me to sing in a particular way. Do you know that even though my brother Hridaynath is younger than me, I include him in my list of gurus as well? I love it when people come and tell me how moved they are by my singing but at the same time I find it really strange that nobody has ever shown any interest in trying to find out from me what makes my singing special. I feel many singers today feel they know all there is to know and have no real need to learn more.

I am sure they are also given tips and advice by their music directors, just as we were in our time. However, I have no idea what they are taught and what they do when they stand in front of a mike to perform.

YM: You sang with some of our most famous voices. How did you learn to cope with various styles and pitches?

LM: Mukesh, Mohd Rafi, Hemant Kumar, Manna De and Kishore Kumar were all very accomplished singers. I can't immediately recall any special tip I was given by any of them but when we sang duets together, we always discussed how we would sing it together. The only one you could never be sure of was Kishore Kumar who was quite capable of completely turning a song on its head when recording. But that was Kishore da: he was a maverick to the core.

In those days, music directors gave precise instructions to singers. They would tell us when to step close to a mike or away from it, to match the changing pitch of a composition. And we faithfully followed their advice.

YM: Did you ever feel that if the orchestration of the background music was done differently it may have enhanced the quality of the song you were to sing?

LM: That area is not my concern; I am a disciplined singer and how a song is composed or what kind of orchestra it should ideally have is the music composer's responsibility and privilege. I never transgressed into someone else's turf unless my advice was sought. Mind you, if I felt that a particular violin was out of tune with the rest of the orchestra, I would point it out and draw the composer's attention to it. Naturally, when 40 violins are being played such a situation was bound to happen but even then the protocol was that the composer handled the re-tuning of the offending instrument.

You must remember that all the composers of that time were accomplished musicians and had a very sensitive ear. The composer and his assistant handled all these issues competently.

YM: There were some singers who had a great run as playback singers and then just faded away: Surinder Kaur and Rajkumari. Can you tell us something about them?

LM: Surinder Kaur had a deep voice, like many singers of that time. Do you know that Shashdhar Mukherji preferred her over me for his film *Shaheed*. He felt that her voice was better suited to match the voice of the heroine, Kamini Kaushal. Like me, Ghulam Haider, the music composer, was also a trifle disappointed because he had made me rehearse that song several times assuming that I would sing it in the film. However, such things happen and it is the director's or composer's right to choose whoever he thinks is best suited. I think that song was '*Badnaam Na Ho Jaye Muhabbat Ka Fasana*'. I did not really know her all that well at a personal level but she came across as a very decent and good human being. She was in the industry for a long time and I remember a record of her Punjabi folk songs, I can't recall the name now but it was very pleasant to hear.

Rajkumari was very popular and sang very well. I sang several songs with her. I remember a qawwali we sang together that became very popular. I once happened to see her in a TV interview when Anil Biswas requested her to sing something. She was quite elderly by then but sang so confidently that it was difficult to believe she had aged. I always found a special quality in her voice and perhaps this was the reason why even some of the songs composed with Shamshad Begum in mind were given to her. Just recall her '*Sun Bairi Balam Sach Bole Re*' (*Bawre Nain*) and '*Ghabra Ke Hum Sar Takrayaein To Kitna Achcha Ho*' (*Mahal*) that are rendered with great feeling. Think also of her thumri, '*Najariya Ki Mari*', from *Pakeezah* and you will know what I mean. In my opinion, she was a better singer than Shamshad Begum, Saraswati Rane or Surinder Kaur because she had the most haunting voice.

YM: What about Uma Devi?

LM: What a singer and what a large-hearted woman! She loved to make people laugh and was possibly the least complicated singer of her time. She and I sang for Kanu Roy (*Jaisi Karni Vaisi Bharani*) and one of our duets ('*Afsana Likh Rahi Hoon Dil-e Bekarar Ka*') with Naushad's music became very popular. I often wonder why she did not pursue her singing career more seriously. I think she took on comic roles on Naushad sahib's advice and went on to make a big name for herself as Tuntun. I am quite sure she would have been equally successful as a singer had she persevered in her playback singing because even though she recorded just a few songs, she is still remembered. Perhaps she would have been as popular as a singer as she later became as a comic artiste.

YM: What about Mubarak Begum and Sudha Malhotra?

LM: All I can say is that Mubarak Begum sang well but had a limited range. What little I knew of her as a person was from chance meetings at recordings. I liked her '*Mujh Ko Apne Gale Laga Le*' from *Humrahi* and '*Kabhi Tanhaiyon Main Yun Hamari Yaad Ayegi*'. She also sang a beautiful duet with Mohd Rafi in Kamal Amrohi's film *Dayra* ('*Devta Tum Ho Mera Sahara, Maine Thama Daman Tumhara*'). She is brilliant in that song.

Sudha Malhotra was not as talented as the others singers we have talked about. However, she sang all the songs she recorded very well. She and I have sung some songs together but working well together and an assessment of her as a singer are two different things. I prefer not to mix private opinion and professional relationships.

YM: There was another singer, Meena Kapur. What about her?

LM: She had a very delicate, thin voice but was very good at taking taans, etc. However, the fragile quality of her voice could not take her very far. For instance, as can be seen in 'Rasiya Re, Man Basiya Re' (*Pardesi*) that she sang for Nargis is a lovely rendering but doesn't really match Nargis' role in the film.

However, as you have just reminded me, there is a wonderful song we sang together for Anil Biswas, who loved to experiment with new styles and techniques. Or think of her 'Lagi Nahin Chhute Rama, Chahe Jiya Jaye' (*Sautela Bhai*) that we sang together. You can hear her competence and the sweetness of her voice. I am very fond of this duet and it is my all-time favourite song with her. I also love '*Ja Main Tose Nahin Boloon*', rendered in a classical style that I am very partial to. It also is a tribute to the genius of Anil Biswas.

YM: At a time when she was viewed as a serious contender for your position, what did you think of Suman Kalyanpur?

LM: I always felt she tried to imitate me so I never really considered her a serious threat. Look, when I came into this industry there were some really great composers and singers like Noorjahan, Zohrabai Ambalawali, Amirbai Karnataki, Parul Ghosh, Rajkumari and many others. I learnt so much from all of them and sang along with them as well. I want to tell you in all humility that I did not feel overwhelmed or threatened by these legendary people because I developed my own style. I was deeply influenced by Noorjahan but Ghulam Haider and Anil Biswas always told me to sing like Lata, not like Noorjahan. This is sadly what Suman Kalyanpur was not able to do. She never sang as Suman Kalyanpur but tried to copy me. It is true that she was often successful but she was always known as the poor man's Lata Mangeshkar. So although she was a good woman and a talented singer, she was soon forgotten because she only copied me, never tried to forge her own music identity.

I don't think it is fair to say that she was not given enough work because of me. At the time when she was around, I was at the peak of my career and singing for almost every lead actress. Nevertheless, Geeta Dutt and my sister Asha and Shamshad Begum continued to get assignments as well and were very popular too. I never dominated the industry so completely that other singers got pushed out because music composers decide whose voice is most suitable for a particular song. When they felt only I could sing a particular number, naturally they came to me. I can think of several films where Geeta Dutt and Asha, not I, have sung all the songs.

What I want to emphasize is that each one of us had our own special stamp: Asha was Asha, Shamshad Begum was Shamshad Begum and so on. Where Suman was concerned, her main claim to fame was that she sang like Lata Mangeshkar. Many composers felt that if the original Lata is available, then why should we settle for her imitator? This is really what explains her decline and fading away. In the world of art or music, no imitator can survive for too long. If I had continued to ape Noorjahan's style or Amirbai Karnataki's, I may never have touched the heights that I was able to by creating my own musical style. This is not to say that she has not sung well but, unfortunately, she did not pay sufficient attention to developing her own voice. Had she done so, I am sure she would have been very successful.

YM: And Meenu Purushottam?

LM: A good girl and she sang well. She and I sang 3–4 duets together and our '*Main Yaar Manana Nahin, Chahe Log Boliyan Bolain*' (*Daagh*) became a huge hit. She and I got along very well and still meet. I have seldom met a person as gregarious as her.

Another song I sang with her, a ghazal composed by Madan Mohan ('*Unse Nazrein Mili Aur Hijab Aa Gaya*') is another one I love. She and I shared a great synergy and I enjoyed her accompanying me. However, she did not take her career very seriously and left the film industry too soon.

YM: Kamal Barot?

LM: She is as good as a person as she was a singer. I liked her but the person she was always closer to was my sister Asha. They are still good friends. Interestingly, I introduced Kamal into the film industry after Kalyan ji asked me to assess her as a singer. I suggested that he use her to sing a duet with Mukesh that he had wanted me to sing. However, the song that made her really popular was our duet from *Parasmani*, '*Hansta Hua Noorani Chehra*'. That song created a storm and I received countless fan letters and requests for that song at my stage shows. Even today, people remember that song and we never imagined that it would be so successful. But that is how it works, who can predict which song will go on to become a hit and which will not? However, I must say that Kamal has sung it very well and worked really hard on it.

YM: Do you remember Arati Mukherji?

LM: Yes, but she did not attain the success that Meenu and Kamal did. I am not sure what happened but she stayed just for a very short while. Murphy Radios had once organized a talent contest, where Mahendra Kapoor and she had been chosen. He went on to become very popular but she disappeared.

YM: What did you think of Jagjit Kaur?

LM: She was very good and after she married Khayyam sahib, she sang some beautiful compositions for him. She sang

very rarely—just odd numbers really—but each one was a gem.
I loved her voice. Some of her memorable songs are: '*Dekh
Lo Aaj Humko Jee Bhar Ke*' (*Bazaar*) and '*Tum Apne Ranj-O-
Gham, Apni Pareshani Mujhe De Do*' (*Shagun*) and '*Kahe Ko
Byahi Bides*' (*Umrao Jan*).

YM: One last name: Sulakshana Pandit.

LM: She sang well but never got much of a chance in the
industry. Later, she became an actress and I sang for her as
a playback singer! She and her sister Vijeta were little girls
when I first got to know them and often came to our house.
Their brothers, Jatin–Lalit, became a well-known musical
duo. All four of them were very talented and had a great
desire to learn more.

YM: Are there other talented singers who you saw grow
into successful playback singers?

LM: Suresh Wadekar is one such singer. He joined the
industry at a very young age, when he was still learning and
developed into a very good artiste. He has a most pleasing and
sweet voice and has recorded many duets with me. He is as good
in his solo numbers as he is in duets and is a pleasure to listen to.

My sister Usha was very young when she came into the
industry. I myself had just entered this world. In 1955, I was
singing in *Azad* for C. Ramachandra which had a duet ('*Aplam
Chaplam Chaplai Re*') and she joined me. Frankly, I wasn't
sure she would be able to cope because she was so young. But,
slowly, she grew and became a popular singer herself, more
in Marathi films than in Hindi films and is still singing. Her
songs in a Marathi superhit film, *Pinjra*, became so popular
that everyone wants to hear them over and over again. Later
this film was remade in Hindi by V. Shantaram. Similarly, her
playback in *Jai Santoshi Ma* was very successful. So both Suresh

Wadkar and Usha, who I regarded as mere kids, grew into very successful artistes.

YM: Have you four sisters ever sung a song together?

LM: I don't think so, although Meena, Usha and I have sung together. I have sung with both Asha and Usha individually but never did all four of us sing one song together. Not just that, I don't recall any song that we sang even in my brother Hridaynath's composition. There was no special reason and this anomaly strikes me now because you have drawn my attention to it. (Laughs). Perhaps we were all too busy in our own worlds and music or perhaps it just never happened because we had such busy schedules. Each one of us has sung in combination with another sister, so let's leave out speculating what the reason could have been. Let me recall the songs with my sisters that I love to hear: '*Banno Ke Haat Bhare Mehndi*'; '*Duniya Main Hum Ayain Hain To Jeena Hi Padega*' and '*Dulhan Maike Chali*'.

Life is full of unfulfilled possibilities, so if I ever get another chance, I will try and arrange one song with all four of us singing together just for you.

YM: How many songs have you and Hridaynath sung together?

LM: I have sung one or two Marathi numbers with him but never any Hindi songs. In *Lekin*, he sang the opening of the number '*Rasoolullah*' in Raga Puriya Dhanashri (one of my father's re-worked compositions) although it was not released in the film's music disc. Later, to complete the situation, he added '*Ja Re Pathikuwa*' based on a variation of Raga Gujari-Todi. It is a beautiful composition where guru and shishya are shown singing together in the film.

I think *Lekin* had wonderful music and even though the film did not do well commercially, its music became very popular. I love to listen to its songs over and over again because they have such a soothing quality. The respect its music earned is doubtless due to my father's training and genes in all of us.

YM: The film truly had exquisite music and won you the National Award for it.

LM: After the success of *Madhumati, Mughal-e-Azam* and *Pakeezah*, I had always wanted to sing in a film where classical music occupied an important place. I am so glad I got an opportunity to do so in *Lekin*.

YM: Why do music directors invite classical music artistes to sing for them in a film? I am thinking of Kishori Amonkar, Shobha Gurtu and Parveen Sultana's contribution as I say this.

LM: No doubt they have felt that given a particular situation in a film, only a classical singer can do justice to their composition. Think of Parveen Sultana's '*Hamein Tumse Pyar Kitna*' in the film *Kudrat* which she sang for Aruna Irani in that film. In the film, Aruna is shown to be a trained classical musician and Parveen Sultana did a marvellous job of bringing that out. Similarly, Shobha Gurtu with her special Awadh style, reminded one immediately of Begum Akhtar. This is why her number in *Pakeezah* was so perfectly matched to the mood of the moment.

YM: Now for some fundamental questions regarding your faith. What is the place of religion in your life?

LM: In my opinion, those whom we regard as gods—Rama or Krishna—came to be worshipped as gods because of the work they did when they lived on earth. To me they are human beings who we worship because of their exemplary lives. This is the place they occupy in my life and religion to me means to place your faith in the pursuit of those qualities that you worship. My religion teaches me to love all my fellow human beings and spread peace. I feel strongly that anything that becomes a mere ritual and superstitious mumbo-jumbo should be rejected. My religion teaches me to place my faith in certain transcendent qualities of love and peace and inspires me to become a better human being.

YM: Are faith and belief different?

LM: Faith in my opinion is fundamental to belief. It is not easy to find one without the other. I think that faith is a measure of one's humanity and makes a person liberal and free. If you truly believe in something it will give you the courage to succeed. Here, I use faith in a secular sense and in the context of humanity and human relations. Connecting with one's inner and pure self is what strengthens faith.

YM: As you look around the world now, what saddens you?

LM: I feel sad that truth, morality and honesty are slowly receding in our world now. I feel that earlier people were more sincere, led simpler lives and had more love and compassion for their fellows. Please don't think I am being preachy when I say that it saddens me that all the values we were taught and lived by are no longer important to people. It is as if that world has vanished and the one that has taken its place is so different that I sometimes feel out of place in it. Violence, rioting, murders, rapes, terrorism—all these have slowly destroyed our faith in the essential nobility of human nature. I had never anticipated such a rapid and complete degeneration of values.

When I entered this industry, I was merely 14–15 years old. I moved about freely all over the city to go from one studio to another. I rode local trains and often returned home late in the night. The reason I never felt insecure was because we trusted people then. Many of those I worked with were very poor but we related at a human level, not on the basis of social or economic position. They brought food from their homes and generously shared their tiffin boxes. To me that world was full of love and trust. Slowly, over time, it has vanished and with it has gone our peace of mind.

YM: What brings you solace in moments of sadness?

LM: Just two things: music and my complete trust in God. Any kind of music that pleases the ear brings me joy. I love to listen to Pandit D.V. Paluskar, Bade Ghulam Ali Khan and Amir Khan sahib's music is so tranquil and soothing! They never fail to lift my mood. My faith in God is also a great source of strength.

YM: Have you ever lied in life?

LM: I try not to and only resort to lies when it helps someone. I don't believe in making excuses and if I am wrong, I admit it. After all, we are all human and do occasionally slip. As I said, if telling the truth can hurt and harm someone then it is better to lie to avoid pain. However, if it is not possible to tell the truth or lie, then silence is best.

YM: If you were to ask God one question, what would it be?

LM: (laughs). This is a difficult one to answer. Perhaps I would say why did you not make all men equal? Why did you send those who hate others enough to kill into this world? I would plead that He should only create those who are compassionate and tolerant and to make this world more equitable in terms of wealth distribution.

YM: Favourite songs?

Bhajan: *'Prabhu Tero Naam Jo Dhyaye Phal Paye'* (*Hum Dono*)
High-pitched song: *'Aji Roothkar Kahan Jaiyega'* (*Arzoo*)
Lullaby: *'Aja Re Aa, Nidiya Tu Aa'* (*Do beegha zameen*)
Raga based song: *'Manmohana Bare Jhoote'* (*Seema*)

Folk-based: '*Dhundo, Dhundo Re Sajana, Dhoodo Re Sajana More Kaan Ka Bala*' (*Ganga-Jamuna*)

Title song: '*Gumnaam Hai Koi, Badnaam Hai Koi*' (*Gumnaam*)

Off-beat: '*Raaton Ke Saye Ghane*' (*Annadata*)

Holi: '*Tan Rang Lo Ji Aaj Man Rang Lo*' (*Kohinoor*)

Mujra: '*Ja Main Tose Nahin Boloon*' (*Sautela bhai*)

Dance number: '*Pyar Kiya To Darna Kya*' (*Mughal-e-Azam*)

Chorus song: '*Ramiyya Vasta Vaiyya, Maine Dil Tujh Ko Diya*' (*Shri 420*)

Sad song: '*Ai Dil-E-Nadaan, Arzoo Kya Hai*' (*Razia Sultan*)

Qawwali: '*Kabhi Ai Haqeetat-E-Muntazar Nazar Aa Libas-E-Mizaj Main*' (*Dulhan ek raat ki*)

Mysterious song: '*Aayega Aanewala*' (*Mahal*)

Funniest: '*Woh Ek Nigah Kya Mili*' (in *Half ticket*, with Kishore Kumar)

Patriotic song: '*Ae Mere Watan Ke Logo*'

Cabaret number: '*Aa Jaane Jaan, Mera Yeh Husn Jawan*' (*Inteqam*)

For children: '*Ek, Do, Teen Char, Bahiya Bano Hoshiyar*' (*Sant Gyaneswar*)

YM: Which film do you consider the most complete in terms of its music?

LM: It is difficult to choose from the hundreds that I have sung for and while I love my work in *Madhumati*, *Mughal-e-Azam*, *Pakeezah* and *Lekin*, from the point of view of personal satisfaction derived, I would pick Salil Chaudhuri's songs in *Parakh*. I sang all the four songs in that film: '*Mila Hai Kisi Ka Jhumka*'; '*Mere Man Ke Diye*'; '*Yeh Bansi Kyoon Gaye*' and '*O Sajana, Barakha Bahar Ayi*'. I had sung the Bengali version of '*O Sajana*' earlier but I feel that there are few songs that match the perfect blending of folk, classical and western music that

Salil da achieved in composing these numbers. I would advise
you to hear these songs to see what I mean.

YM: Now choose a film that you did not sing for but still
love the music.

LM: I would choose R.D. Burman's *Teesri Manzil*. I
think the music he scored for it was fantastic. R.D. Burman
introduced a completely new idiom into Hindi film songs here.
I have to also praise Asha and Mohd Rafi's renderings of these
songs. They are great.

YM: Now to qawwalis, and those that were sung by others.
Which ones stand out for you?

LM: I remember a very old one sung by Noorjahan and
Zohrabai Amabalawali from a film made circa 1945: '*Anhain
Na Bhari, Shikve Na Kiye*'. It is brilliant. Then Roshan's
composition, '*Na To Karvan Ki Talaash Hai*' from *Barsaat
Ki Raat* is also beautiful. It was sung by a number of people,
Mohd Rafi, Manna De and Sudha Malhotra. In the fifties, a
Pakistani couple, Mubarak and Fateh Ali, came here and we
all went to hear them. They were so good that Roshan sahib
added another qawwali to the music of *Barsaat Ki Raat*: '*Yeh
Ishq, Ishq Hai, Ishq Ishq*'. This was a tune from their repertoire.
Outside films, I loved the qawwalis of Shankar–Shambhu.

YM: Didn't you ever want to try your hand at Shyama
Sangeet?

LM: I have never sung an authentic composition in this
style but I would have loved to do so if I were given the
opportunity. The thing is that those who were steeped in the
tradition of Bengali music styles (Anil Biswas, Salil Chaudhuri
and Burman Dada) are long gone. They were the true
connoisseurs of Shyama Sangeet and Rabindra Sangeet and
understood its depth and range. They have composed some

wonderful devotional numbers that are traditionally sung at Kali Puja. So if one of these composers were around, they may have chosen me to sing a number in the styles you mention. I am also hesitant about trying these on one's own because—as you know—there are very strict notations that protect them and cannot be trifled with. No artiste can try her own innovations while singing them. This is a matter of discipline and so, unless there is a composer who can guide a singer, it is not possible to attempt singing them. On a personal note, I am a great admirer of Gurudev Rabindranath Tagore's music and loved singers of that music (like Pankaj Mulick) and am aware of their contribution in popularizing this music style. But the question still remains: where are the composers who can try to bring this into film music?

YM: You have sung a stirring song, '*He Hindu Narsingha*'. What is the background of that story?

LM: This is a song written by Vir Savarkar, which he composed in honour of Shivaji as a peaen of praise. I have always loved it because I am a great admirer of Shivaji and the interesting anecdotes that Savarkar has included in it. I had recorded an entire album, *Shiva kalian raja* in Marathi which had songs on Shivaji by Samarth Guru Ramdas, Shivaji's guru, as well. The rest were mainly compositions by Savarkar and Kusumagraj. Another famous Marathi scholar and historian, Baba Sahib Purandari, gave the commentary that accompanies the songs in this album.

YM: Are there other spiritual compositions that are cherished memories?

LM: There are a few but the one that moves me most is Pandit Narendra Sharma's '*Satyam Shivam Sundaram*'. Every time I sing it I lose myself in its lyrics and beauty. I love the pride it evokes in me as an Indian and the concluding stanza, '*Ram Avadh main, Kashi main Shiv, Kanha Vridavan main, Daya karo Prabhu dekhoon inko har ghar ke angan main*', makes my hair stand on its end. There is a spiritual dimension in it that is very dear to me.

I have always considered music a way to reach God and ultimately lead to moksha and nirvana. Our religion actually has a tradition called Navdha Bhakti that considers music a way of worship.

YM: Can you recall an incident where you so lost yourself while singing that the world did not matter?

LM: There is one that comes to mind. During the sixties, when I was very busy, I used to leave home at 9 a.m. to reach the studios for a very busy day ahead. As I was leaving home one day, a few men approached me and said they were from the Income Tax department and wanted to check some details with me. I told them I had submitted all my accounts to their department and all I had apart from my earnings were the flat I live in and some cars. I gave them a list of my cars and asked whether I could leave for a recording in my car. They allowed me and said we have all the information we needed.

I reached the studio to record a song for Shankar–Jaikishan and spent a long time rehearsing. It was evening by the time we were able to finish and both of us were satisfied with the outcome. In fact, Shankar even said this was one of our best recordings. What I want to say is that all this while I had completely forgotten how the day began and how all the papers of my cars had been impounded by the IT people: all I was focussed on was the song I had to record that day.

YM: You have sung for a number of Urdu poets, renowned for their polished language and manners. What did you think of Ali Sardar Jafri sahib?

LM: I used to meet him regularly because he lived in the same city and often dropped in to see me. His edited version of Ghalib's *Diwan* is a brilliant book and I learnt much from it. When I recorded the Ghalib album for HMV, I used it as my basic source. He, his wife and sisters-in-law would often visit us. I am not aware of how many lyrics he wrote for films but all the great Urdu poets of that time – Jan Nisar Akhtar, Kaifi Azmi, Majrooh Sultanpuri, Shakeel Badauni – attended regular poetry sessions in his house.

YM: Have you sung Kaifi Azmi's lyrics?

LM: Yes, but not as many as I sang for Shakeel Badayuni, Sahir sahib and Majrooh Sultanpuri. I met Kaifi sahib only at recordings. I also had a slight acquaintance with his wife, the actress Shaukat Azmi. I loved his songs especially '*Kuchh Dil Ne Kaha*' (*Anupama*) and '*More Naina Bahain Neer*' (*Bawarchi*). I am amazed that a man who was such a pure Urdu poet could write such beautiful lyrics in Hindi as well.

YM: Majrooh sahib?

LM: Of all the poets, Majrooh sahib was the one I was closest to. I remember him today more as a family friend than poet. He was such a lovely human being, so kind-hearted and decent. He once told me he was reading the Bhagvad Gita to find out what it was in this book that made it so special to Hindus. I will never forget how, once when I was very ill, he would come every day to visit me and sit by my bedside to cheer me up. One day he said he was hungry and could he get a bite to eat? Of course, I replied, how can I let you go hungry? That was the kind of man he was: he spent the entire day to be with me when I was ill and needed some diversion. We talked for hours about shairi and because he was so knowledgeable it was a pleasure to listen to him hold forth on Persian and Urdu literature. We were family friends and my mother, sisters and brother would all go across to his house where his charming and hospitable wife would serve the most delectable food prepared by her. I learnt how to make *pasandas* and chicken curry from her.

YM: Shakeel Badauni?

LM: I have sung a number of his compositions under Naushad sahib's direction. There are too many to recall here but his non-filmy ghazal, '*Aankh Se Aankh Milata Hai Koi*' (music by *Mahavirji*) is delightful. When Mahavirji played it out on his harmonium for me, I loved it immediately and we recorded it with joy. I was delighted that I had been given a chance to sing such a fine poet's ghazal although all the ones he wrote for films were also wonderful compositions.

YM: You have sung a number of songs based on folk tunes from all over the country. Which are some of your favourite folk numbers?

LM: I love all of these but am partial to Rajasthani folk music. I adore the Muslim folk singers from there who are accompanied by little boys playing along with their wooden clappers and prancing around the singers. Their training and verve never ceases to amaze me. I once went to Rajasthan during the filmyng of *Lekin* and spent a few days. Every evening, these folk singers would arrive and regale us with their music. I will never forget that enchanted time.

Bengali folk music is also very soulful, especially their Bhatiyali amd Rabindra sangeet. I have sung some Assamese folk songs for Bhupen Hazarika and the way that Salil Chaudhuri used folk music in *Madhumati* is also unforgettable.

I am afraid I have little knowledge of the folk traditions of UP, especially Banaras, but Naushad sahib used a lot of folk music tunes from Awadh and they were a joy to sing. His music for *Ganga Jamuna* is steeped in the poorabiya ang and I love '*Daghabaz Teri Batiyan Na Manu Re*'. One of his most famous folk compositions ('*Chhod Babul Ka Ghar, Mohe Pee Ken Agar Ab Jana Pada*') sung by Shamshad Begum in *Babul* is unforgettable. Naushad sahib embellished these simple folk tunes with his own flourishes and brought them to life with beautifully orchestrated background music. He liked to compose his songs on a piano and I have heard him play several UP folk tunes on that piano. He'd then explain how a particular tune was a traditional bidai geet sung at the departure of a bride from her father's home amongst Awadh's Shia families. So he played with folk tunes but invested them with his own magical touches.

I totally agree with you that he used the Dadra in Raga Gara in *Mughal-e-Azam*'s '*Mohe Panghat Pe*', to take it to another level of delight.

YM: He also used the naat tradition of UP's devotional Muslim music and gave it his magical touches: '*Bekas Pe Karam Kijiye Sarkar Madina*' (*Mughal-e-Azam*). At the same time, he could also play with lilting folk tunes like '*Tumhare sang main bhi chalungi piya jaise patang sang dor*' (*Sohni Mahiwal*).

LM: Right. I have sung only three naat compositions in my entire career and all were under his direction. The first is the one you mention and the remaining two are '*Dil Ki Kashti Bhanwar Main Ayi*' (*Palki*) and '*Mera Bichra Yaar Mila De Sadka Rasool Ka*' (*Sohni Mahiwal*). Incidentally, all these three lyrics were composed by Shakeel Badayuni.

YM: Is there any other song that you consider special?

LM: I don't know whether you will agree but Jaidev made me sing a beautiful song in *Alap* ('*Kahe Manva Nache Hamar*'). I find the sweetness of this song is unmatched, perhaps because of its lyrics. I find the dialects of UP and Bihar, such as Awadhi and Bhojpuri very sweet on the ear. Chitragupta once composed the music for a film called *Ganga Maiya Tohe Piyari Chadhaibo* and its title song ('*Ganga maiya tohe piyari chadhaibo, saiyyan se kar de milanva hai Ram*') is an all-time favourite of mine. There is something so sweet and touching that it tugs at my heartstrings every time I hear it. I think of all the songs I sang in the folk style, this song is my favourite.

YM: Chitragupta did another film (*Bhauji*) with you and the tenderness and sweetness of those songs is unmatched. Do you remember '*O Chanda Mama, Are Aav, Pare Aav, Nadiya Kinare Aav*'?

LM: Of course I do! What a lovely composition! You know, I think all the Bhojpuri songs I sang are really sweet.

YM: Fakirs and travelling musicians (*Kabirpanthis*) sing Nirgun bhajans, and shabads and kirtans also fall into a similar tradition of devotional songs. How do you look at the tradition of folk and traditional genres in Indian devotional music?

LM: The first thing to remember is that when you sing devotional songs, whether one sings to a real god (*sagun*) or an abstract one (*nirgun*) they are all steeped in bhakti. These songs may not be classical in the orthodox sense because they have a definite bent towards the folk tradition of a particular region but this kind of music is nevertheless an accepted and deeply respected genre. I am less familiar with Sufi music but what I have heard of Abida Parveen and Nusrat Fateh Ali is very moving. Among the Nirgun singers, the one who I most admire is Kumar Gandharva. Not just for his voice but for his blending of classical ragas with the folk music of the Malwa region. This is a brilliant development in this style of singing. I think he almost erases the boundaries between classical and folk music and manages to create a genre where the sweetness and emotional content of the two streams merge seamlessly into each other. Since this blending is what I tried to achieve in my playback singing in films, it is especially appealing to me. He goes beyond the traditional way of bhajan singing in this country and yet does not break the boundaries of the classical training in which he is steeped. This, in my opinion, makes him the most amazing practitioner of devotional music.

YM: Another important classical singer in this genre is Pandit Bhimsen Joshi. How would you describe his style?

LM: You are right: one cannot speak of Kumar Gandharva without also recalling Pandit Bhinsen Joshi. Panditji sings Marathi Abhangs in the typical style of the Marathi Bhav Geet tradition. Yet, because his voice is trained in the Kirana style of classical music, he takes his version of Abhangs to another level altogether. Look beyond these two great artistes and behind their music you can see their gurus and individual gharanas. I am not really qualified to assess the work of these extraordinary artistes but this I know that if they did not have that spine of classical training behind them, their bhajan singing would have never been able to scale the heights it did. Mind you, they were gifted singers and so even as ordinary bhajan singers they would have drawn attention, but their training in classical music enhances the depth and reflective quality of their music. This is why Kabir in Kumar Gandharva's voice and Vitthala in Bhimsen Joshi's are above any other singer's version of the same bhajans.

YM: Just as the vibrancy, vivid colours and courage of Van Gogh's art marks a special place in the art world, would you say you are like him in this regard?

LM: I humbly accept this along with the hundreds of other compliments, awards and commendations I have received over the years. I can only claim that as a playback singer, I have always tried to understand the emotions, feelings and mood of every song and situation and tried to bring it out with all I have.

YM: Let's turn to semi-classical music now. Among thumri, dadra, tappa, chaiti and kajri, which is your favourite mode?

LM: Thumri, although all have their own place, thumri is my favourite genre. All the thumris sung by Ustad Bade Ghulam Ali Khan are marvellous and I find his 'Saiyan bina ghar suna' haunting. It travels straight to my heart each time I hear it. Other than that, I also love his renderings of 'Aye Na Balam' and 'Paiyan Parun Tore Shyam'. I also like dadras and kajris but thumris are in a class of their own. Naushad sahib was very fond of using thumris in his compositions and both Asha and I have sung quite a few for him. Thumris played a major part in his compositions and if you recall 'More Saiyan Ji Utarenge Paar' (Udan Khatola) and 'Aaj Mere Man Main Sakhi Bansuri Bajaye Koi' (Aan), you will know what I mean.

YM: Begum Akhtar used to love your song 'Maar Diya Jai Ki Chhod Diya Jai' (Mera Gaon Mera Des) and often spoke of it. Among her songs, which ones are your favourites?

LM: There is so much to love in her repertoire! I love the ghazals she has sung, such as 'Ai Mohabbat Tere Anjam Pe Rona Aaya'; 'Ulti Ho Gayin Sab Tadbeerain' and 'Woh Jo Hum Main Tum Main Karar Tha'; these are classics. And then her kajri 'Chha Rahi Kali Ghatain' and thumris like 'Dekhe Bina Nahin

*Cha*in'—the list is endless. She was a phenomenon and created magic with her voice for listeners.

YM: If it were possible to hear just one person from among the great singers from our past, such as Swami Haridas, Baiju Bawra, Tansen, Chaitanya Mahaprabhu, Mirabai and Amir Khusro, who would you invite?

LM: What an interesting idea! I bow before all these great names but if I were choose just one, it would definitely be Mian Tansen simply because ever since I was a little girl I was told that there has never been another singer like him in our country. So, in my eyes, if there is one artiste who reached the pinnacle of musical perfection, it is Tansen. I was enchanted by Saigal sahib's rendering of Tansen's character and his music in the film of that name and always wondered how Tansen himself would have taken a particular taan or tackeld a certain alap. Why would I not want to hear the real man himself?

YM: What in your life do you regard as moments of disappointment?

LM: I can only speak of this in the context of music. Often, when I am unable to perform as I wanted to or am unable to bring out exactly what I want in my voice, I feel dejected. This can happen when I am not feeling well or you are distracted and somehow lose focus. I have had spells when this has happened and in my early days, I suffered from trouble with my sinuses. However, I was busiest in those days and could not afford to take time off and this gave me the courage to sing no matter how unwell I may have felt later in life.

YM: What is the most moving moment in your life?

LM: During the course of a stage performance, when the audience applauds spontaneously touches me deeply.

YM: Which songs do you like to hear when alone?

LM: I like listening to my Meera bhajans from 'Chala vahi des'. I sang them with great feeling and they touch me deeply.

YM: When you hear someone sing off-key or unrhythmically, what do you feel?

LM: (laughs) I can tolerate unrhythmic songs but if a person sings off-key I cannot bear it. I feel such singing is an insult to God. I am deeply pained and often get angry.

YM: If you had to give an exam, who would you choose as your examiner?

LM: When I stand in front of a mike whether at a private recording or in a concert, I consider that an exam and when people like it, I consider myself successful. Each time I sing, I pass a test if you ask me.

YM: What is the greatest truth for an artiste?

LM: Devotion to one's art and the ability to sacrifice everything at its altar. One should not merely chase fame and money: such a person is not fit to be called a great artiste.

YM: While singing duets with someone who you have had a disagreement with, has it affected your performance?

LM: No, never. I just do not like to carry on disagreements even after they have been resolved. I try and take our relationship to the place it was before and did not ever allow personal feelings dictate my performance.

YM: Is it difficult to switch from one mood to another when recording a duet?

LM: Yes, this was occasionally a problem. We would be laughing and joking about something before a recording and then suddenly one had to sing a serious song. In this respect, the person who troubled me the most was Kishore Kumar. He was a born clown and could keep one in splits with his antics – jumping, all over the place. No matter how hard I tried to keep the serious mood alive, he would find ways of distracting me with funny faces or gestures. Once in a while, I had to request him or his friends to restrain him. Where he was concerned, however, he could switch effortlessly from all that clowning and give a most serious performance without losing a beat. I am sure our listeners never found out but there were occasions when I had to hold my sides before recording a sad song because Kishore da was holding forth.

YM: You have sung certain songs that I would like to explore in greater detail. Let's start with Sahir Ludhianvi's '*Aurat Ne Janam Diya Mardon Ko*' from *Sadhana*, where you have captured the depth of the song brilliantly. How do you do it?

LM: Do you know that I was never really very happy about singing that song. I found its words very disturbing and it affected my state of mind. Mind you, it articulates a deep truth but somehow I never warmed to it. However, I sang it as I was directed to but could never get myself to see that film because of that song.

YM: There is another song, by Shailendra ji ('*Mitti Se Khelte Ho Kyun Bar-Bar*') which Shankar–Jaikishan composed for *Patita*.

LM: This is a lovely composition and I like it very much. Sahir has written almost like a Nirgun poet and it has a deep metaphysical mood that attracts one. Shankar–Jaikishan's music has done its lyrics full justice and I rate it as one of their best songs.

'*Mitti se khelte ho baar baar kis liye*
tute huye khilono se pyar kis liye

banake zidganiya bigaadne se kya mila
meri ummid ka jaha ujaadne se kya mila
aayi thi do dino ki ye bahaar kis liye
mitti se khelte ho baar baar kis liye'

YM: There is a beautiful song in Zia Sarhadi's film, *Hum Log* (1951), composed by Roshan sahib ('*Chali Jachali Ja Chhod Ke Duniya, Ghamon Ki Duniya, Aahon Ki Duniya*'). Can you tell us something about it?

LM: All I remember is that when I first heard it, it really appealed to me even though it was a disturbing composition, set as a very sad song. Roshan saab had attempted a completely different kind of style here. However, it became very popular and critics wrote reams about it. However, there is another song from the same film that I sang with Durrani sahib and I like very much: '*Gaye chala ja, gaye chala ja, ik din tera bhi zamana ayega*'.

YM: *Seema* (1955) had a beautiful song by Hasrat Jaipuri ('*Suno Choti Si Gudiya Ki Lambi Kahani*'), set to music by Shankar–Jaikishan. Are there any special memories about it you'd like to share with us?

LM: (Thrilled). For me the most memorable fact about this song was that Ustad Ali Akbar Khan agreed to play his sarod for it. When I stood near the mike to sing, he came very close to me to play alongside, so I remember every bit of its recording for this reason. The words of this song are also very beautiful and I really enjoyed recording it. I can never forget the utter concentration of Ali Akbar bhai as he played his sarod and believe that if that song has a special appeal it must be because of his brilliant sarod.

YM: In this category of songs, your number from *Hum Dono*, '*Allah Tero Naam*', is a perennial favourite.

LM: You are right, this has become a bhajan for the whole country and what makes it special is how beautifully it incorporates one of Gandhi ji's favourite bhajans: *'Raghupati Raghav Raja Ram'*. Sahir Ludhianvi is at his best here, I think. Perhaps you may know that at the time this was to be recorded I had serious differences with Jaidev and had stopped singing for him. Both Vijay and Dev Anand went to him and told him, 'We would like this song to be sung only by Lata.' So they came to me and persuaded me to let bygones be bygones and if I still felt strongly about singing for Jaidev, they would consider changing him as their music director for this film. I was very upset, for I felt that I would hate to be known as someone who insisted that they change such a good music director, so I agreed. Initially there was some awkwardness between us but after the song was recorded (many rehearsals later), there was a thaw and Jaidev asked me to sing another song in this film, *'Prabhu Tero Naam Jo Dhyaye Phal Paye'*. After this, I sang for him in countless films.

Today, *'Allah Tero Naam'* is considered a milestone in my career and wherever I went for a stage show, this was the one song that I was always requested to sing. And each time the audience would break into delighted applause as soon as I sang the opening lines. Sahir sahib has written such moving lyrics here that if one pauses to hear them, tears well up in one's eyes. This song speaks of bringing people closer to each other, a sentiment I endorse completely.

YM: Sahir sahib and Roshan sahib have also created a lovely song in *Chitralekha* (*'Sansar Se Bhage Phirte Ho'*). Any memories with that song?

LM: This is also a lovely song and I want to emphasize that, in my opinion, Roshanlal was a very accomplished composer. This was mainly due to the fact that he had a deep understanding of classical music and used it brilliantly in his compositions. This is why I consider *Chitralekha* as a film with wonderful songs. The philosophical tone of this song comes as much from Roshanlal's music as from its lyrics. This song is also a perennial favourite with my fans the world over and, along with '*Ae Ree, Jane Na Doongi*' (also from this film), it is always requested at my stage shows.

In *Arti*, I sang '*Kabhi Na Kabhi, Kahin Na Kahin To Milegi, Baharon Ki Manzil Rahi*' for Roshanlal but this time the lyrics were penned by Majrooh Sultanpuri. Roshalal made me sing it at a very high pitch and the song became very popular in its time. You will notice that in all these songs there is a strong social message that underpins the lyrics. I am very partial to songs that have this dimension and when all of us – the lyricist, the music composer and I – are able to successfully bring out this dimension, they make the song a classic. I have been so fortunate that some of the finest lyrics and compositions came my way and that I was able to do them justice.

In this context, I'd like to speak of a special song I sang for Naushad sahib in *Mother India*: '*Duniya Main Hum Aye Hain To Jeena Hi Parega*'. It is a song that plumbs such deep recesses of human existence that it never fails to move me. How true it is that we are all doomed to live this life, no matter how full of pain and despair. And yet, we carry on, even when death seems a better option. The message of this song seems to be that we have to live our lives with courage and fortitude. Just like Nargis, fighting to stay alive because of her children, we must carry on. Even as I sang this song, I felt its deep pain and am still moved by its message. Another song from the same film, '*O Mere Lal Aaja*' takes the plight of women a notch higher.

It shows how women can fight like tigresses to protect their children and when Naushad sahib gave it to me and Meena and Usha to sing, it seemed like such a sad song. Today, I feel it inspires a woman to continue her struggle.

YM: Were there any incidents when you were put into trouble because of some problem with recording?

LM: I have spoken of how singing at a pitch higher than my normal one could prove irritating. So I can think of two occasions when I had some problems. During the filming of Shammi Kapoor's *Junglee*, Mohd Rafi had sung his part of the song '*Ehsaan Tera Hoga Mujh Par*' when the director decided to also give a few lines to Saira Bano in the scene. So they shot the scene on her with Rafi's voice and asked me to record her part by watching her on the screen and synchronizing my lip movement with hers. It was an odd request but I agreed to do it. Now because it was recorded originally only for a male actor and in Rafi sahib's pitch, it was very difficult for me to match that pitch and scale my voice to that level. Then, when I saw Saira Bano's lip movements, it became even more difficult to reach that pitch while keeping my voice soft to match her voice quality.

Similarly, in the film, *Woh Kaun Thi*, Sadhana's song '*Naina Barse Rimjhim, Rimjhim*', Madan Mohan had recorded the song in his voice for the filming. Once again, I had to do a blind recording and match our lip movements. Thankfully, this time the scene was shot so that Sadhana was shown from a distance and doing these acrobatics with my voice were not as painful as they were in the earlier incident. There was also the difficulty of matching the pitch of a male voice that added to the difficulty. In some other songs, too, which have male and female versions of the same song this used to be hard to do.

Songs she likes.

1. 'O Sajana, Barkha Bahar Ayi' (Parakh; Salil Chaudhuri)
2. 'Bekas Pe Karam Kijiye Sarkar-E-Madina' (Mughal-e-Azam; Naushad)
3. 'Lag Ja Gale Ki Phir Kabhi Yeh Haseen Raat Ho Na Ho' (Woh kaun thi; Madan Mohan)
4. 'Main Piya Teri Tu Mane Ya Na Mane' (Basant Bahar; Shankar-Jaikishan)
5. 'Woh Chup Rahein To Mere Dil Ke Daag Jalte Hain' (Jahanara; Madan Mohan)
6. 'Rula Ke Gaya Sapna Mera' (Jewel Thief; S.D. Burman)
7. 'Kuch Dil Ne Kaha' (Anupama; Hemant Kumar)
8. 'Piya To Se Naina Lage Re' (Guide; S.D. Burman)
9. 'Nainon Main Badra Chhaye' (Mera Saya; Madan Mohan)
10. 'Dil Ka Diya Jala Ke Gaya' (Akashdeep; Chitragupt)
11. 'Rasm-E-Ulfat Ko Nibhayain' (Dil ki rahain; Madan Mohan)
12. 'Kahe Manva Nache Hamara' (Alap; Jaidev)
13. 'Chalte-chalte Yun Hi Koi Mil Gaya Tha' (Pakeezah; Ghulam Mohammad)
14. 'Bara Natkhat Hai Yeh Kishan Kanhaiya' (Amar Prem; R.D. Burman)
15. 'Tujh Se Naraz Nahin Zindahi Hairan Hoon' (Masoom; R.D. Burman)
16. 'Suniyo Ji Araz Mhari' (Lekin; Hridaynath Mangeshkar)

YM: Did you ever meet Ustad Allauddin Khan sahib?

LM: I did not meet him but I have heard him play the sarod. This was in 1946 or 47 and had recently entered this world. He had come to Bombay to the Deoghar Music School and was playing there. I wasn't really even aware of what a

great artiste he was and what a rich tradition he had created
in baaj playing. I remember that he said his namaz there on
the stage before he began his recital and what little I can
remember of it, the sound of his sarod was very sweet. It was
only later that I got to know that Pandit Ravi Shankar, Ali
Akbar Khan, Annapoorna ji, and Pandit Nikhil Banerji were
all his disciples. I consider it a rare privilege that I was able
to hear him live. I believe he also had a fearful temper and I
heard tales of this from Roshanlal ji who also spent some time
learning from him.

YM: Any memories associated with Kamaladevi
Chattopadhyay?

LM: I met her just once or twice, although I used to often
meet her husband, Harindranath Chattopadhyay, here in
Bombay because he was also an actor. I don't know whether
you know that she had also acted in a few films and played a
small role in *Tansen*, which had Saigal and Khorsheed as the
lead actors.

I think I met her in 1965 when I had gone to Calcutta for a
music conference. She had come there and listened to everyone
who sang. I remember I ended my performance with '*Ai Mere
Watan Ke Logo*' and she started to cry in the middle of the song.
Later she came to the Green Room and met me very lovingly.
'You sang this song with such feeling that my eyes welled up,'
she told me. 'Such songs move one deeply and I wish more
artistes sang songs such as this one to inspire people. You must
always include such songs in your repertoire at stage shows
because the whole nation follows them and their message can
change lives . . .I am a fan of your voice and when I heard
you today I felt that it was something so pure and so moving.'
Then she embraced me and called me over for tea but I could

not accept her invitation because I had to return to Bombay straightaway. I remember her as a commanding personality and a very dignified lady. It was such a pleasure to have met her. I had heard of the work she had done to promote art and theatre and worked tirelessly to help artistes in need. Where are such people to be found today? She was herself such a great person yet when she met a fellow artiste, she gave such respect that it became easy to relate to her. Meeting her was certainly a memorable experience.

YM: That you made Pandit Nehru cry with your rendering of 'Ai Mere Watan Ke Logo' is now the stuff of legend. Tell us what happened.

LM: More than a legend, this is an integral part of my life now. I consider it an honour that I was able to sing a deeply moving patriotic song before the country's prime minister. In 1962, as you know, after our humiliation at the hands of the Chinese, the whole nation was plunged into despondency. All Indians were shocked at the betrayal of the Chinese. The poet Pradip ji wrote a long poem that was set to music by C. Ramachandra. He requested me to sing it at the 1963 Republic Day celebrations in Delhi. Although I was busy with the preparations for my sister's wedding at that time, I could not refuse him. I remember taking a tape recorder along with me on the flight to rehearse it.

As I was singing that song before a large audience, I noticed that a whole lot of people from the Bombay film industry— among them Dilip Kumar and Raj Kapoor—were seated in the audience as well. After I finished singing, I went behind the stage and Mehboob Khan came looking for me. 'Lata, Pandit ji is asking for you,' he told me. I went with him and found Pandit ji sitting there with Indira Gandhi and some other political leaders. Mehboob Khan introduced me to Pandit ji who said, 'Beta, you made me cry today. I am going home now so you also come along and we can chat over tea.' We all accompanied him to Teen Murti, his official residence, and I went and sat quietly in a corner. Indira Gandhi came to me and said, 'Please wait here because I want you to meet two people who are your ardent followers. They will be thrilled to meet you.' A little later, she returned with her two sons and said, 'These are my sons Rajeev and Sanjay: they listen to your songs all the time and are great fans.' I met them both warmly and after some tea and small talk, we left Teen Murti.

YM: What was your relationship with Pandit ji and Indira Gandhi like?

LM: I did not have the chance to meet Pandit ji too often but whenever we did, he always greeted me with a great deal of affection and warmth. Sometime in early 1964, I had to go to Brabourne Stadium to sing at a charity concert. I sang *Aji Rooth Kar Ab Kahan Jayiyega* from *Arzoo*, when I was told that Pandit ji had come and wanted to hear *Ai Mere Watan Ke Logo* from me. I sang it. Pandit ji was quite unwell by then and was not going to stay long. I was told he wanted me to meet him before he left. So I went to his car and he took both my hands in his and said, 'Beta, I had come here today only to hear you sing that song. I am so happy that you sang it for me.' His sister Vijaylakshmi Pandit was also in the car and after a few minutes, he bade me a loving goodbye and left. That was my last meeting with him. I carry an abiding picture of his charming face and warmth and consider it such an honour that I was able to meet him personally because I deeply regret not meeting Gandhi ji and the other great freedom fighters of that generation.

Indira Gandhi was also very warm whenever I had a chance to meet her. Even after she became the prime minister, she gave artistes great respect and never let them feel intimidated by her presence. She rose above her political status and came across as a very warm and caring person in her personal dealings with people. She took an enormous pride in Indian culture and, like her father, gave all artistes the respect they deserved. I still remember her with warmth and respect.

YM: Which political leader do you admire most?

LM: At a personal level, I have a great deal of respect and love for Indira Gandhi. I also bow to the memory of Pandit Nehru and consider Lokmanya Bal Gangadhar Tilak a great political leader. Apart from active political leaders, there are some whose patriotism has impressed me and Veer Savarkar is one such personality that I can think of. We had a warm family connection and my father used several of his works in his plays. I am deeply influenced by his writings, although I am not political in any sense nor have I ever been close to any political party or leader.

I don't really understand politics nor do I wish to. Whatever I know of it makes me believe that art and politics are two opposing streams. One is full of deception and the other is premised on truth. This is exactly what separates the two, I think. A successful politician has to often use lies and subterfuge whereas art takes you towards truth and nothing else. There is no place in it for lies or subterfuge. Such a path has no place for a politician.

Among the arts, I consider music the purest form of expression because it uses neither make-up nor costume to attract attention. A singer has to surrender herself to her music and consider it as pure as her God. The moment you strike a pure note, you are transported to the presence of divinity: this is why music is considered a form of worship. This is also why I think it is seen as the highest form of artistic expression. I always imagine that when Lord Krishna gave the lesson of the Gita to Arjuna in the Mahabharata, he must have sung or chanted the slokas. This is why we call it the eternal song.

YM: Among the political leaders, who has given you the most love and respect?

LM: Indira Gandhi, Atal Behari Vajpayee and Lal Krishna Advani. Once when Indira ji was our prime minister I had gone to London in connection with some programme and they were going to honour me there as well. In the speech I gave after receiving the honour, I said that for me the highest honour has been that I was born in India and that I am very proud of being an Indian. This was widely reported in the press at that time. When I returned to India, I found a very sweet letter from Indira ji waiting for me. She had written that she was delighted with what I said in London and that I had said so to an audience abroad. I consider her letter an important one in the pile of cherished letters from famous people and fans that I have received over the years. Another very affectionate and loving person is Atal ji. I once joked to him that if we reverse the spelling of his first name (Atal), it will read as Lata. He guffawed in response. I find Advani ji a very humble and polite person and he always greets me with warmth and love. So these are the three political leaders from whom I have received special respect and love. All three come across as very humble, intelligent and strong people. I respect them all deeply.

YM: Have you ever put your music directors to trouble because of a personal pique, especially when it is an important recording and you asked for a postponement?

LM: Never. I have never down let any producer or music director because of a personal difference. It is a different matter that often when I am not well enough, I have asked for a postponement. If that was not possible, I used to say then they should look for another singer who could meet the deadline. Once Madan Mohan said that the producer was in a hurry and the duet I was to sing with Mohd Rafi could not be postponed. So I requested him to take on someone else and that duet ('*Humsafar Saath Apna Chhod Chale*') was recorded with Asha instead. Something similar happened when I was recording for *Dulhan Ek Raat Ki* where Asha and I had to sing a qawwali together but she was not free. So I sang it alone.

YM: There was some problem with a Filmfare award regarding Shankar–Jaikishan, wasn't there?

LM: Yes, but it was a difference over a principle, not a fight. In those days, there was a convention that the lyricist and singer were never given an award for a song. In 1956, Shankar–Jaikishan were given the Filmfare award for their music in the film *Chori-Chori* and Jaikishan asked me to sing '*Rasik Balma*' on stage because that was the song for which they had been awarded. I told him that since I had not been given the award as the singer but they had been awarded for its music, they should play the music rather than have me sing it. We had a serious disagreement over this episode. A little later, J.C. Jain, the editor of *Times of India* rang me up saying that I should sing the song as it would bring good publicity for their award ceremony and I told repeated what I had said to Jaikishan. Jain retorted that even in Hollywood, singers are never awarded an Oscar. So I informed him that Hollywood films rarely had songs and that the Oscar was therefore given for the background score. This is not true of our films, which often become silver jubilee hits because of their songs, I said. Since they do not consider lyricists or playback singers important enough to award, I do not wish to be part of their ceremony. If you do not give us the honour we deserve, why should I accept their invitation to perform at their award ceremony, I asked. He replied that they would consider my feelings seriously and think about instituting awards for lyricists and playback singers as well.

This is how, in 1958, I was awarded the first Filmfare trophy for my song 'Aa Ja Re Pardesi' (Madhumati) and Shailendra was awarded the Filmfare trophy for his lyrics in Yahudi ('Yeh Mera Deewanapan Hai').

YM: What happened between you and S.D. Burman that you did not sing for him for several years?

LM: I had sung for Nargis under his direction for the film, Miss India. After the recording, he said I should have sung the song with more tenderness because it needed to match the situation of the film. A few days later, he said we should record the song again. I told him I had no problem except that I was busy then and would do it after a few days. Three or four days later, he sent someone to me to firm up the dates for recording. I learnt later that instead of reporting to Dada that I needed more time, this person went and told him that I was not ready to record it again. Naturally, Burman dada was very upset and angry and felt that I was avoiding recording for him. So he declared that he would not record with me in future. So I also retorted that he should not worry because I too will never record for him again.

So this is how a simple misunderstanding flared into a full-blown war between us. For many years after this episode, he and I did not work together.

Then, around 1960 or so, when his son R.D. Burman (Pancham) became a music director, he came to me with an offer

to sing for his first film, *Chote Nawab*. Since I had no problem
with Pancham, I happily agreed to sing for him. He, along with
Bimal Roy, then intervened to sort out the differences between
his father and me and I started singing for Dada once again.

YM: Which was the first song you sang for him after this
thaw?

LM: '*Mora Gora Ang Lai Le, Mohe Shyam Rang Dai De*' in
Bandini.

YM: What are your views on the royalty issue?

LM: This became such a huge controversy that I had to
speak up. You see, I have always viewed this as a fight for a
principle. When I first raised it I was worried about what would
happen to us in future. In those days, we were all earning well
and did not see that one day when we were unable to generate
sufficient incomes. What would happen then?

This is why I proposed that that all record companies
ought to keep aside an amount to be paid to us as royalty but
this ballooned into a big controversy. Rafi sahib was one of my
staunchest opposers and felt that if we have already been paid
for our work, why should we expect any further payment? My
stand was that record companies play our songs for a long time
and earn fortunes out of our hard work, so why not pay back
what we deserve instead of allowing some singers to spend their
last days in dire poverty? Mukesh, Kishore Kumar, Manna De
and Talat Mehmood stood by my side: only Asha and Rafi
sahib did not think this was a legitimate demand. This created
a misunderstanding between us and the result was that I did
not sing with him for many years. Between 1963 and 1967, we
did not sing together at all.

YM: How did relations between the two of you normalize
and when did you resume singing with him?

LM: Burman Dada was largely responsible because he intervened to resolve the issue. I remember so well that in 1967, during the course of a S.D. Burman Night in Bombay's Shanmukhnanda Hall, we came together once again. Rafi Sahib and I sang 'Dil Pukare Aa Re Aa Re' from the film Jewel Thief. Nargis ji announced the song from the stage and also that from now on, Mohd Rafi and I would sing together once again.

YM: O.P. Nayyar started his career with Dalsukh Pancholi's film Aasman (1952). As far as I know, you were supposed to sing the song 'Mori Nidiya Churaye Gayo' for him. What happened that, after everything was decided, the relationship ended abruptly and you never sang for him ever again?

LM: There was no special reason for this. In those days, I used to sometimes suffer from a sinus attack. After we had agreed and a recording date was set, I suffered a bad attack of sinusitis and felt that I may not be able to do justice to the song. So I called him and apologized for postponing the date and asked can we do another day. I don't know what happened after that but he cancelled the recording and told me I was not required to sing for him. I felt that there is no need for me to pursue this matter if, as a music director, he would make no allowances for a sick artiste and looked only to his convenience.

However, I will also say that I never really warmed to his style of music and always believed that it did not suit my temperament or preference. He was also aware of this and openly said that only Geeta Dutt and Asha could sing his kind of songs. Majrooh sahib tried very hard to bring us together but neither he nor I were willing to budge. That is how I never sang for him.

YM: How unfortunate! Rajkumari ji once said in an interview that she does not know why he gave 'Mori Nidiya

Churaye Gayo' to her when that song was actually composed with Lata in mind. This means that everyone in the industry was aware of this episode.

LM: She was right: that song was meant for me. Perhaps he told people this, but I can't say this with any certainty because till date I haven't heard that song.

YM: How many offers were made to you to compose music for films?

LM: Not many because I was not inclined that way. In the days when I was really busy, I couldn't spare the time. Hrishikesh Mukerjee asked me to do the music for *Anand* but I refused saying I could only handle one career at a time. Years ago, V. Shantaram had also asked whether I would score the music for one of his films but at that time, song recording was a very tedious affair and it took weeks, sometimes months, before a song was finally done. Often, compositions were cancelled and the whole process was re-started. How on earth would I found the time to take on such an onerous responsibility?

YM: I have heard that M.V. Raman once published an advertisement in Baburao Patel's well-known film magazine *Film India* where he claimed that a film called *Jhuki Jhuki Aankhein* would have music by you. Is this true?

LM: I have also heard this but as far as I know, Raman sahib never published any such advertisement. And if there indeed was such an ad, he did not take my permission to publish it. Raman sahib always preferred to take C. Ramachandra as his music director in his films and there was no question of his asking me to do so. So why would he publish such an ad?

I had wanted to make a Marathi film on the subject of music, which would also later be made into a Hindi film. I had wanted to do so and had asked Roshanlal sahib to score the music for the project with Nalini Jaiwant and Om Prakash as the lead stars. The film was to be called *Bhairavi* but somehow the gentleman who was writing the script in Marathi did not impress us and so we eventually dropped the whole idea, although the music for it was being prepared. I remember Roshan sahib had persuaded Ali Akbar Khan sahib to give the music for one song, which would be filmed a duet. I think the song was based on raga Kalawati and later Roshan sahib used it for a song in *Chitralekha*. That song ('*Kahe Tarsaye Jiyara, Yauvan Ritu Sajan Ja Ke Na Aye*'), sung by Asha and Usha, was actually a part of the music of that aborted venture.

YM: How many temples have you sung in?

LM: Not many but there are some 3 or 4. When I was given the Asthan-Vidwan honour at Tirupati Balaji, I sang for the Lord. Apart from that, I sang a composition in Bhoopali at the Minakshi temple but I don't recall the words now. Once during a puja I had organized in Kolhapur's Mahalaxmi temple, the people there persuaded me to sing for the Devi. I sang a Marathi song I remember. When I went to Vaishno Devi, the temple priest told me that all singers who come to worship there have to sing so I should also sing something. The other pilgrims also joined in so I sang Mirabai's bhajan, '*Karman Ki Gati Nyari Santo*', as an offering. These are some occasions I recall.

YM: Have you ever felt like singing on the banks of the Ganga?

LM: Not really, although I enjoyed my trips to Haridwar and Rishikesh and lost myself in admiring the majesty and beauty of the river. Haridwar is beautiful but when I was standing on the banks of the Ganga, I forgot all my songs. I could think of nothing but the beauty of the moment.

YM: Is there any place in India where you have spontaneously wanted to sing?

LM: When I went to Ajanta and Ellora I was deeply moved by the paintings I saw. There are also some musical pillars there that send out pure notes when you hit them, so I did sing there out of sheer joy.

Similarly, when Hridaynath, Meena, Usha and I went to see the Taj Mahal, the sight of the monument in moonlight and the echoing chambers were so wonderful that Hridaynath and I wondered how they would sound if we sang. So we sang raga Yaman with open throats, matching each other's taans. Suddenly, a man appeared from the main gate and said sternly that music is forbidden here, who is singing? So we immediately shut up and went out rather sheepishly. (Laughs).

YM: Have you ever had an opportunity to sing the *kritis* of the great South Indian musicians, such as Thyagaraj, Muttuswami Dikshitkar and Syam Shastri?

LM: Sadly, no. there was a time when I really wanted to sing some of Thyagaraj's kritis because whenever I heard them, I was drawn to their innate purity. Somehow I was never able to find someone who would guide me to locate those original works and correct my pronunciation. So I was never able to fulfil that desire.

YM: What do you think of M.S. Subbulakshmi's music?

LM: I love it, especially her devotional songs. D.V. Paluskar among male singers and M.S. Subbulakshmi among female voices are my favourite devotional music artistes. I am also a great admirer of her classical music. Her work in the film Meera is outstanding. There is a transcendent, other-worldly quality about her singing that is unique, I think.

I met her once and mustered up the courage to tell her, 'I love your bhajans and when I hear your rendering of the Vishnusahastranam, I feel as if I have been purified and have just come out of a temple.' She thanked me and said, 'Lata ji, I also listen to your film songs and have also heard your Meera bhajans. I want to know how you are able to invest such feeling and sweetness into a song in just three or four minutes.' I was thrilled with her praise.

YM: There are some beautiful legends about music in ancient times. For instance it is said that that Tansen could light lamps with his voice and that his daughters' chanting brought down rain. Do you believe these myths and legends?

LM: Perhaps when Swami Haridas and Tansen lived, they were able to strike such pure notes that such miracles could occur but how can one believe them to be true when I have never experienced such a miracle? However, I do believe that music has the power to make the impossible happen and all of us have experienced something that leads us to believe in its power. I remember going into a trance when I heard my father sing something very beautiful but let me tell you of one incident that I will never forget. Once at a concert where Pandit Ravi Shankar and Ustad Ali Akbar Khan were playing, we were all mesmerised by the music we were hearing. After about an hour or so, suddenly a string on Ali Akbar's sarod snapped and the spell was broken. Later, when I met him in the Green Room, I told him, 'You were playing so beautifully! I wish the string of your instrument had not broken the spell you cast over us today.'

His answer remains with me till today. 'Lata bahen,' he replied, 'When you manage to play pure and perfect notes, even the string of your instrument breaks in ecstasy.' This convinces me that if even a lifeless string can respond so to music, it is entirely possible that when Tansen sang he moved the world around him and that lamps spontaneously lit up or clouds burst into rain.

YM: What would you say can be done to improve one's voice?

LM: Look, I firmly believe that a good singing voice is a divine gift. You can't really create a singing voice. However, if you are blessed with a tuneful ear and good voice, then hard work is all that I recommend to develop it. Learn from a guru and practise every day as he directs you to. Do all you can to develop the voice you have been blessed with and it will take you ahead in your career.

What often happens now, I fear, is that a young girl who enters the film world wants to sing like a Lata or an Asha and all male singers want to sing like Kishore Kumar or Mohd Rafi. What they don't realize is that a copy lasts only for the duration of that song. What they should aim for, I feel, is to develop their own personal style so that it becomes a unique signature. So whereas a copy of another singer's voice will only last for 3–4 minutes, a new voice will attract a new audience. If you limit yourself to merely aping someone else, how will you ever progress? I say this to all aspirants who enter this industry. While I am flattered by the admiration for my voice (or for any other singer), pause and reflect on what attracts you to his or her style. Pay attention to the way they pronounce their words, the modulation they bring into their voice to suit sentiments, and so on. Learn to be patient and be open to learning.

Let me tell you my own experiences. When I first started to sing, I used to listen to all of Noorjahan's records very carefully. I realized that while others said '*Mohabbat*', she used to pronounce the word as '*Muhabbat*'. I also started to pronounce it her way and realized that soon the other singers also followed this pronunciation! So even as small a detail as making that little change can help develop a unique style. I learnt so much from others, apart from correct Urdu diction, and this is what the singers of today do not realize. Just being able to copy competently or win a talent competition does not make a great singer. What is essential is a complete surrender, single-minded devotion and sacrifice—all for one's art. If you can do that, believe me you will go far beyond a Kishore Kumar or a Lata Mangeshkar.

YM: By this logic, you have read Noorjahan's style like a book.

LM: Not just her, my father's classical training has played a very important role in shaping my musical career. So while it is true that I used to faithfully follow Noorjahan's style of singing, I paid equal attention to how she said, 'Uff' or 'Hai' to bring in an emotional quality into a song. All this I owe her.

YM: Which are her songs that you most admire?

LM: (Laughs). I find all her songs wonderful! She managed to make even mundane compositions sound different. I love her songs from *Jugnu, Anmol Ghadi*, and *Bari Ma*. '*Javan Hai Muhabbat, Hasin Hai Zamana*' from *Anmol Ghadi*, '*Kis Tarah Bhulega Dil Unka Khayal Aya Hua* (*Village Girl*); '*Aandhiyan Gham Ki Yun Chalin*' and '*Bulbulo Mat Ro Yahan*' (*Zeenat*); '*Aaj Ki Raat, Saz-e-Dil Purdard Na Chhed*' (*Jugnu*) are some of my favourites. I still feel a thrill when I hear them and wonder how she managed to invest such magic in them when technology and recording machines were still so raw. My most favourite song by her has to be '*Diya Jalakar Aap Bujhaya, Tere Kaam Nirale*'

(*Bari Ma*). Her way of enunciating the lyrics and her timing is flawless. In *Mirza Sahiban*, she has sung a sahiban, a Punjabi folk song, which I find unforgettable even after all these years. Among her non-film songs, '*Gul Khile Chand Raat*'; '*Mujhse Pehli Si Muhabbat Mere Mehboob Na Maang*' are unmatched. Then there is a song she sang for a Pakistani film, '*Bachpan Ki Yaadgaron*', *that I can't forget. I can't recall the name of the film but that song still haunts me.*

YM: Suppose it had been possible to ask her to sing one of your songs, which one would you have chosen?

LM: '*Ai Dil-e-Nadaan*'. I love the tenderness that Khayyam sahib's music has given the lyrics. I would certainly like Noorjahan ji to sing that song for me. And here I must tell you that once when we both happened to be in London, I went to visit her. At the end of that visit, she came to the door to see me off and said, 'Beta, sing *Ai Dil-e-Nadaan* for me once before you leave.' Quickly, before the lift arrived, I sang a snatch for her and she was delighted. 'That was just wonderful,' she told me. 'May Allah give you a long, long life.'

YM: Apart from K.L. Saigal and Noorjahan, which one your contemporary singers do you like the most?

LM: This is very difficult to answer because they were all brilliant in their own way and choosing one name would imply that the others weren't as good. As I see it, we all stood at the same level and all of them were great singers. I love Mukesh Bhaiyya, Rafi saab, Kishore da, Manna De, Hemant Kumar, Talat Mehmood as much as I admire Geeta Dutt, Asha Bhonsle and Usha Mangeshkar. This is a list of my most favourite and admired singers, I can't choose any one.

Even in the generation that preceded me apart from Saigal saab and Noorjahan ji, there were some equally great singers:

Amirbai Karnataki, Kanan Devi, Parul Ghosh, Rajkumari and
Zohrabai Amabalawali. Each was better than the other: how
can I dare to exclude even one name from among them?

YM: In the fifties, you sang a number of Marathi songs
under the music director, Vasant Prabhu. In the neginning of
that era, you sang a Meera bhajan, '*Maiyya Mori, Main Nahin
Makhan Khayo*', *that brings out a very special aspect of your
singing. How do you remember Vasant Prabhu?*

LM: You have brought up a name and a song that takes
me back to virtually to the beginning of my singing career.
One day, Vasant Prabhu came to my house and showed me
this bhajan from a book of Meerabai's Padavali (collection
of poems) and requested that I sing it for him. That is how
this song came to be recorded, although I had already sung
several Marathi bhajans, Bhava-geet and film songs for him.
There is one song written by P. Sawalaram, '*Ganga Jamuna
Dolyat Ubhya Ka*', went on to become hugely popular. This
song is sung by a mother as she bids farewell to her daughter at
her wedding and where she blesses her daughter as she leaves
one home for another. The mother hopes that her daughter
finds happiness in her new home. I must tell you that in the
fifties, this song was played at almost every Marathi wedding
and people wept copiously whenever they heard it. I was told
by many people that whenever a girl was getting married, the
family would gift her a record of this song. What I want to
say is that Vasant Prabhu had made it so moving that there
was a time it was played in every Marathi home. I also sang
another Sawalram composition with great feeling; '*Alinguni
Aangekara*'. *Vasant Prabhu also made me sing some poems by Bha
Ra Tambe which are very close to my heart. I consider Vasant
Prabhu a musician who could plumb the deepest layers of a poem.*

In those days, whenever I sang a Marathi song composed by him or Hridaynath Mangeshkar, they became super hits.

YM: You have also sung *Ave Maria*: what was that experience like?

LM: That song brings back wonderful memories! You see, there was a very talented musician in Goa called Anthony Gonzalves. He was Pyarelal's (of Laxmikant-Pyarelal) mentor and guru and taught him how to arrange the orchestra accompanying playback singing. This is probably why Laxmikant-Pyarelal had such a strong grip on music orchestration. He made Manna De and me sing two compositions in the Goan language that were based on western symphonies and since Salil Chaudhuri had already introduced me to western symphonic and choir music, I had little difficulty in performing them to his satisfaction. In fact I really enjoyed the challenge to sing in another musical tradition. I don't think these were ever released commercially and we dedicated them to the Church after performing them on stage for a show. Do you remember a song from *Amar, Akbar Anthony* that has the lines, '*My name is Anthony Gonzalves*'? It was sung for Amitabh Bachchan by Kishore Kumar in the film but it was actually Pyarelal's homage to his guru, he told me later.

YM: Perhaps the first garba song you ever sang was '*Kanha Bajaye Bansuri Aur Gwale Bajayen Manjeere*' for C. Ramachandra in *Nastik* (1954). What do you say of this tradition of folk songs?

LM: I love the composition of this song and I remember correctly, this was the first time I did a playback number for Nalini Jaiwant. The music director may well have been C Ramachandra but it was based on the lyricist, Pandit Pradipji's memory of this popular Gujarati folk song. Pradip ji was a

Gujarati and knew a lot about the folk music of that region so both collaborated to compose this lovely song. Pradip ji often sang the lyrics he wrote for the music composer to get the feeling behind its words. Bharat Vyas also did this. However, Salil Chaudhuri resisted this intrusion into his territory and they often exchanged angry words over such suggestions. Anil da was like Naushad sahib in this respect and I remember how once, when I was recording 'Uthaye Ja Unpar Sitam' (Andaz) for Naushad sahib, Mehboob Khan asked him to repeat a particular line twice. Naushad sahib said nothing but his face darkened with anger. Such episodes often took place. You see, in those days, music composers spent a very long time to compose the music and had a typical style that they regarded as their own signature.

YM: Salil Chaudhuri composed a beautiful lullaby for Awaaz ('Jhunjhuna-Jhunjhuna, Jhume Gagan Jhume Pawan'), which is very different from the other lullabies you have sung, Why?

LM: You are right, it is different. You see, Salil da was a master in composing lullabies and each one he created was better than the last. I first sang a lullaby for him in Do Bigha Zameen ('Aaja Re Aa, Nidiya Tu Aa'), which is among my favourite songs. It was picturized on Meena Kumari and sung very, very softly and tenderly. There are one or two more that he composed that are also very tender: 'Neend Pari Lori Gaye, Ma Jhulaye Paalna' (Chardeewari) and 'Chale Thumak-Thumak Tare, Meethe Sapnon Ke Dware' (Ek Gaon Ki Kahani). These are all Salil da's compositions and so delicate and sweet that they haunt one.

YM: Burman dada composed a song based on a classical raga for you in Munimji ('Ghayal Hiraniya Main Ban-Ban Doloon'). Do you have anything to say about it?

LM: I have sung so many beautiful compositions that it is difficult to remember each one individually. Burman Dada, Naushad saab, Roshanlal, Madan Mohan and Khayyam have created hundreds of such beautiful numbers. This particular song was picturized on Nalini Jaiwant, who was herself an accomplished singer. When the producer of the film told her that Lata will sing this for you as a playback singer, she was delighted and did not hesitate for a minute to give her permission. I was so touched by her generosity and will always remember her as a great actress and a noble soul.

YM: You have often said that you were never comfortable singing mujra songs and rarely agreed to sing one. Why?

LM: It is not as if I have taken a vow to never sing such songs and if I feel it is appropriate to the situation in a film, I have no issues. For instance, in *Devdas* and *Pakeezah*, I never felt the mujra numbers were forced because they an organic strand of the film's narrative. Just think of '*Ab Aage Teri Marzi*' and '*Thare Rahiyo O Banke Yaar*' and you will see what I mean. Similarly, in *Mamta*, '*Chahe To Mora Jiya Le Le Sanwariya*' *is also a mujra kind of* song but so meaningful. As long as its words are not vulgar, such a song in itself is not repugnant to me. That is why I choose these sings carefully before I agree to sing them.

YM: Which mujra songs do you consider as different?

LM: there must be several but the ones that I can think of now are: '*Sanam tu bewafa ke naam se mashoor ho jaye*' (*Khilona*) and '*Salam-e-ishq*' (*Muqaddar ka Sikandar*) I feel cannot be placed alongside those from *Devdas*, *Mamata*, *Sadhana*, or *Pakeezah*.

YM: Let us now talk of literature. What kind of literature attracts you?

LM: I read a lot and have a very eclectic taste in books. The closest to my heart is Saratchandra. I've re-read *Sarawatichandra* and *Devdas* many, many times, but I consider *Vipradas* his best work. I am a great admirer of Pemchand's works. I have also read almost all of the classic Marathi works and love the bhajans and abhangs there. *Jyaneshwari* is a favourite work although its language is hard to follow because it is very terse. However, I love it and have sung many verses from it. In Hindi, I like bhakti literature, especially Mirabai, Surdas, Kabir and Tulsidas. I love the poetry of Ghalib, Mir, Zauq and Daagh and often go back to them for pleasure.

I consider some works of our famous film writers important: Sahir Ludhianvi and Majrooh Sultanpuri wrote exquisite poetry I think. Apart from these two, I also like the work of Shakeel Badauni and Hasrat Jaipuri. What attracts me to such writers is the fact that they were equally proficient in writing in Hindi and Urdu. Shailendra is one such person and Sahir saab and Majrooh Sultanpuri, despite being Urdu poets, were also sensitive writers of Hindi. Nowadays, I find Gulzar saab such a person. His work from the early days to now has been consistently good.

I want to remember Pandit Narendra Sharma here, because he was like a father figure in my life. He, too, considered me his daughter and we shared a special bond. I have sung countless filmy and non-filmy songs by him and consider his song, 'Tum Asha Vishwas Hamare Rama' (*Subah*), a morning hymn, outstanding. Then there is his unforgettable '*Satyam, Shivam, Sundaram*', the title song of that film. When Raj Kapoor was making this film, he said, 'Panditji, I am making a film called *Satyam, Shivam, Sundaram*, where I want a song that can bring

all these three words together'. That is when Pandit ji composed
the song and I sang it. Till today, I rank it as one of my best.

You'll be glad to know that I have read a lot of Hindi poetry
as well: I still love Jaishankar Prasad's 'Kamayani' and 'Aansu'
and Maithilisharan Gupt's Bharat Bharati', which I bought in
1959 and love. There was a time when I could recite several lines
from these works and I think that the beauty Maithilisharan
Gupt created as seen from a woman's perspective in 'Saket', is
unmatched. I have read very little of Nagar ji's works but have
heard high praise of his novels.

YM: Have you met any Hindi writers?

LM: Apart from the ones associated with the film industry,
I used to hear of them from Pandit Narendra Sharma. He
would often speak of Maithilisharan Gupt, Sumitranandan
Pant and Amritlal Nagar and I loved listening to his anecdotes
and stories about them. I once met Ramdhari Singh 'Dinkar' at
Padma Sachdev's home and Harivanshrai Bachchan saab once
or twice at Pandit Narendra Sharma's home. They were great
friends. I think I also met Dharamvir Bharati once or twice.
I always enjoyed such encounters.

YM: Have you ever read any foreign poet, especially in
translation?

LM: No, never: partly because I was so busy and also
because I never found a companion who would guide me
towards such works. I have not read Pushkin, but heard his
poems being recited because Shailendra ji used to read Pushkin
during recordings or rehearsals and would often read out
something touching and explain its finer nuances to me. He was
a communist but never tried to dump his political preferences
on me. If I ever heard any non-Indian poetry, it must surely
have been something Shailendra ji recited to me.

YM: What do you think of Kabir?

LM: Unlike his popular image of being a fakir, I think Kabir articulated deep truths in a quiet way. I love his *'Dinanath Ab Tumhari Baari'*, a song that I have sung. Just see what deep implications are contained in a weaver telling God, it is your turn now. Personally, I believe he was a remarkable philosopher as well.

Favourite Ghulam Mohammad song: *'Bedard tere dard ko seene se laga ke'* (*Padmini*)

Husnlal–Bhagatram: *'Woh paas bhi rahkar paas nahin, hum door bhi rahkar door nahin'* (*Afsana*)

Anil Biswas: *'Tumhare bulane ko jee chahta hai'* (*Ladli*)

Naushad: *'Bekas pe karam keejiye'* (*Mughal-e-Azam*)

C Ramachandra: *'Yeh zindagi usi ki hai, jo kisi ka ho gaya'* (*Anarkali*)

Sajjad Husain: *'Ai dilruba nazrein mila'* (*Rustom Sohrab*)

Shyam Sundar: *'Sajan ki galiyan chhod chale'* (*Bazaar*)

Madan Mohan's ghazal: *'Rasm-e-ulfat ko nibhain to nibhain kaise'* (*Dil ki rahain*)

Madan Mohan film song: *'Lag ja gale ki phir kabhi yeh haseen raat ho na ho'* (*Woh kaun thi*)

S.D. Burman: *'Rula ke gaya sapna mera'* (*Jewel Thief*)

Roshan: *'Duniya kare sawal to hum kya jawab dain'* (*Bahu Begum*)

Khayyam: *Apne aap raaton main chilmanain sarakti hain'* (*Shankar Husain*)

Shankar–Jaikishan: *Main piya teri tu mane ya na mane'* (*Basant Bahar*)

Vasant Desai: *'Ae malik tere bande hum'* (*Do aankhain barah haat*)

Hemant Kumar: *'Kuch dil ne kaha, kuch bhi nahin'* (*Anupama*)

Ghulam Mohammad: '*Chalte-chalte yun hi koi mil gaya tha*' (*Pakeezah*)

S.N. Tripathi: '*Aa ja, aaja bhanwar suna dagar*' (*Rani Roopmati*)

Pandit Ravi Shankar: '*jane kaise sapnon main kho gaiyin ankhiyan*' (*Anuradha*)

Dattaram: '*Luti zindagi aur gham muskuraye*' (*Parvarish*)

Jaidev: '*Yeh dil aur unke nighahon ke saye*' (*Prem Parbat*)

Chitragupt: '*Dil ka diya jala ke gaya*' (*Akashdeep*)

N Datta: '*Main tumhi se poochti hoon mujhe tum se pyar kyun hai*' (*Black Cat/Coat?*)

Sudhir Phadke: '*Jyoti kalash chhalke*' (*Bhabhi ki chooriyan*)

Usha Khanna: '*Ek sunehri sham thi, bahki-bahki zindagi raah main*' (*Aao pyar karein*)

Ravi: '*Woh dil kahan se laoon, teri yaad job hula de*' (*Bharosa*)

Kalyan ji–Anandji: '*Kankariya maar ke jagaya*' (*Himalay ki god main*)

Laxmikant–Pyarelal: '*Jivan ki dor tumhi sang bandhi*' (*Sati Savitri*)

R.D. Burman: '*Tujhse naraz nahin hai zindagi*' (*Masoom*)

Rajesh Roshan: '*Yeh raatain nayi purani, aate-jaate kahti hain koi kahani*' (*Julie*)

Bhappi Lahiri: '*Tumhain kaise keh doon main dil ki baat*' (*Angan ki kali*)

Shiv–Hari: '*Yeh kahan aa gaye hum*' (*Silsila*)

Ravindra Jain: '*Chithiye dard firak baliye, le ja-le ja sanesa sone yaar da*' (*Hina*)

Bhupen Hazarika: '*Dil hoom-hoom ghabaraye*' (*Rudali*)

Ram–Lakshman: '*Dil diwana bin sajna ke mane na*' (*Maine pyar kiya*)

Jatin–Lalit: '*Mere khwabon main jo aye*' (*Dilwale dulahniya le jayenge*)

Vishal Bharadwaj: '*Bhej kahar piya ji bula lo*' (*Machis*)

A.R. Rahman: '*So gaye hain, kho gaye hain dil ke afsane*' (*Zubeida*)

Favourite abhang: *Tukaram's* '*Runjhunu- runjhunu re bhramara*' (*Hridaynath*)

Non-filmy ghazal: *Mirza Ghalib's* '*Hazaron khwaishain aisi*' (*Hridaynath*)

Non-filmy bhajan: *Meerabai's* '*Mai ri kaise jiyun ri*' (*Hridaynath*)

Other languages:

'*O mor mayna go*' (Bengali non-filmy song; Salil Chaudhuri); '*Latpat-latpat tujh chalan*' (Marathi film Amar Bhupali; Vasant Desai); '*Mehndi te vaavi manve aine rang gayo Gujarat re*' (Gujarati film *Mehndi rang lagya*; Avinash Vyas); '*Rassi ute tangiya dupatta mera dolda*' (Punjabi film *Madari*; Allarakha); '*Pala sepiyan dogariya*' (Dogri, non-filmy song; Pritam Singh); '*Bhagvad Geeta ka navan adhyaye*' (Sanskrit, non-filmy; Hridaynath); '*Jona kore rati, ankhon mi re mati*' (Assamese film *Era batar sur*; Bhupen Hazarika) and '*He Ganga maiya tohe piyari chadhaibo*' (Bhojpuri film Ganga maiya tohe piyari chadhibo; Chitragupt).

YM: Pick one song from among your repertoire that you consider the best.

LM: (Thinks deeply) No, I can't do this. Let this go.

YM: Among Mukesh's songs, which are the ones you like the most?

LM: There are so many songs that I like: there was something about his voice, a ceratin quality of gravity and control that made his work very special. Listen to his '*Kisi ki muskurahaton*

pe hon nisar' from *Anari*, '*Sajanuwas bairi ho gaye hamaar*' from
Teesri Kasam, or '*Jane kahan gaye woh din*' from *Mera Naam
Joker* and you realise that he gave sadness a new dimension. I
don't think any other singer could handle songs of this genre
with greater sensitivity. Take another set of examples: '*Aansoo
bhari hain yeh jeewan ki rahen*' (*Parvarish*); '*Bhooli hui yadon
mujhe itna na satao*' (*Sanjog*); '*Yeh mera deewanapan hai ya
muhabbat ka salook*' (*Yahudi*), to name just a few. Just see the
pain he captures here. Some of his songs make you sit back
and ponder at the meaning of life and reflect on the serene
acceptance of suffering. The title song of Raat aur Din, '*Koi
jab tumhara hriday tor de*' (*Poorab aur paschim*) and '*Kahin door
jab din dhal jaye*' (*Anand*) are some of my personal favourites.
Later, when he sang the Ramcharitmanas, I think he reached a
new height. His voice has such a soothing quality that it lingers
in your mind: I don't think anyone else could have done a
better interpretation of the essence of the epic.

YM: And how do you rate the songs of Mohd Rafi?

LM: Rafi saab was an incredibly talented singer, tuneful
and emotionally perfect. His gentlemanliness was reflected in
his singing style. Of the many soulful singers in this industry,
he was among the best. The only area that he could not shine
in was perhaps the dance numbers and except for '*Madhuban
main Radhika nache re*' (*Kohinoor for Naushad*), he was not as
effective as Manna De. I love all his songs from *Hum Dono*, *Tere
ghar ke samne* and *Guide*. Also the ones he sang for Naushad
saab '*Koi sagar dil ko behlata nahin*' (*Admi*) and '*Hai kali-kali
ke lab par tere husn ka fasana*' for Khayyam (*Lala Rukh*); '*Aise
to na dekho ki humko nasha ho jaye*' (*Teen deviyan*) for Burman
dada and for Roshan saab in *Chitralekha* ('*Man re tu kahe na
dhir dhare*'). He sang some wonderful numbers for Madan

bhaiyya as well, of which I love '*Ek hasin sham ko dil mera kho gaya*' (*Dulhan ek raat ki*).

I did not always like the fun-filled songs he sang for Shammi Kapoor under R.D. Burman and Shankar-Jaikishan's direction. I prefer the sober ones he sang for Shammi ji, such as '*Is rang badalti duniya main*' (*Rajkumar*) and '*Tumne mujhe dekha*' (*Teesri manzil*). I also love those that he sings at a very high pitch composed by Shankar–Jaikishan, such as '*O mere sha-e-khuban*' (*Love in Tokyo*). And how beautifully he has sung Sahir sahib's lyrics in *Pyasa*, especially '*Jinhain naaz hai Hind pe woh kahan hain*'! There are simply hundreds of songs to choose from where he is concerned! I admired him deeply and am so glad that most of his famous duets were sung with me as partner.

YM: Tell us about your favourite Talat Mehmood songs.

LM: Despite his beautiful voice and perfect delivery, he was unfortunately never able to reach the same heights as Rafi saab, Kishore da or Mukesh bhaiyya. I love many of his songs: '*Seene main sulagte hain armaan*' and '*Nain mile nain huye banware*' (*Tarana*), both duets sung with me. Also '*Muhabbat tark ki maine, gareban see liya maine*' (*Doraha*) under Anil Biswas is also a favourite of mine. Majrooh Sultanpuri wrote the lovely '*Ae dil mujhe aisi jagah le chal jahan koi nahin ho*' (*Arzoo*) that Talat Mehmood and Anil Biswas did full justice to. His unforgettable duet with Suraiyya '*Rahi matwale*' (*Waris*) was also composed by Anil Biswas. Others that I also love are; '*Sham-e-gham ki kasam*' (*Footpath*), '*Phir wahi sham, wahi gham*' (*Noorjahan*), '*Jalte hain jiske liye*' (*Sujata*) and '*Jayen to jayen kahan*' (*Taxi driver*). Such songs can never age.

YM: And what about the evergreen Kishore Kumar?

LM: Again, there are too many to remember but all the ones he sang for S.D. and R.D. Burman alone can fill pages. All his songs from *Amar Prem* (R.D. Burman) or *Padosan* and *Pyar ka mausam* are superb. One delightful number is '*Raat kali ek khwaab main ayi*' (*Buddha mil gaya*) and if you hear '*Yeh sham mastani*' *and* '*Tum bin jaoon kahan*' (*Kati patang*), you are struck at the synergy he shared with R.D. Burman. The same is true of the songs he sang for Burman dada: films such as *Jewel Thief, Teen Deviyan, Prem Pujari* are simply brilliant. He could bring alive both romantic and sad numbers alive with his special voice. '*Koi laute de mere beete hue din*' (*Door gagan ki chhanv main*), '*Jiwan ke safar main rahi*' (*Munimji*), '*Koi humdum na raha*' (*Jhumroo*) and '*Woh sham bhi kuch ajeeb thi*' (*Khamoshi*) are a few examples of this quality. A duet he sang with Asha (Bhonsle) in *Chalti ka naam gari* is a favourite of mine '*Main sitaron ka tarana . . .panch rupaiya barah aana*'. Only Kishore da could get away with the antics he has performed here.

Later, this same playfulness could be heard in some of the songs he sang for Amitabh Bachchan. '*Khaike paan banaras wala*' (*Don*) may sound like a simple fun number but it is actually quite difficult to sing. Listen carefully to the long sequences he has sung without taking a breath in this song and you will understand what I mean. He was both a clown and a very sober artiste.

YM: What about Manna De who was trained in classical music and had a wonderful voice?

LM: You are right, he had a deep knowledge of classical music and used it to bring a special quality to his singing. There was also a deeply soothing quality in his voice. Think of '*Laga chunari main daag*' (*Dil hi to hai*), '*Sur na soojhe*' (*Basant bahar*), '*Phulgaindwa na maro*' (*Dooj ka chand*), '*Kaun aya mere man ke dware*' (*Dekh Kabira roya*) and '*Tu pyar ka sagar hai*' (*Do aankhain barah haat*) and you'll agree that these are immortal songs. He handled comedy so well, especially for the songs he sang for Mehmood. '*Ek chatur naar*', which he sang with Kishore da in *Padosan*, is still so popular and perhaps the best of its kind.

His first hit, '*Upar gagan vishal, niche gahra patal*' (*Mashal*) is a sober number but as tuneful as the perky '*Dil ka haal sune dilwala*' (*Shree 420*) and '*Chalat musafir moh liyo re*' (*Teesri kasam*). All the duets that Shankar-Jaikishan composed for us are very dear to me. He gave everything he had to his songs.

YM: Which are the songs of Hemant Kumar that you like most?

LM: Hemant da was as great a composer as he was a singer, blessed as he was with a deep, sage-like voice. I have sung several duets with him, many of him songs composed by him. I love his '*Yeh nain dare-dare*' (*Kohra*), '*Zara nazron se keh do ji*' (*Bees saal bad*); '*Ya dil ki suno duniya walo*' (*Anupama*) and '*Tum pukar lo*' (*Khamoshi*). His '*Zindagi pyar ki do-char ghari hoti hai*' (*Anarkali*) under C. Ramachandra's direction is another delightful song by him. Among other favourite songs by him are '*Teri duniya main rehne se to behtar hai ki mar jayen*' (*House No 44*) and '*Rulakar chal diye*' (*Badshah*).

YM: Among the songs sung by Ashaji, which are the ones you like most?

LM: Most songs have been mentioned before and are those she sang along with others. They are all delightful so I will speak of those that are not as popular but beautifully rendered by her. '*Radha Ke Pyare Krishna Kanhai*' (from *Amar* for Naushad saab); '*Maang Main Bhar Le Rang Sakhi Ri*' (from

Mujhe Jeene Do for Jaidev); 'O Panchchi Pyare, Saanjh Sakare'
(in *Bandini* for Burman Dada); 'Tora Man Darpan Kahlaye'
(in *Kajal* for Ravi); 'Hai Gajab Kahin Tara Toota' (*in Teesri
Kasam* for Shankar–Jaikishan); 'Ambar Ki Ek Paak Surahi' (in
Kadambari, composed by Ustad Vilayat Khan). I consider all
the songs she has sung in *Umrao Jan* for Khayyam her best
performance.

YM: Which of her songs makes you envious and wish that
you could have sung it?

LM: She has sung so many that are outstanding performances
and I can hear them over and over again without tiring. For
instance, 'Yeh Hai Reshmi Zulfon Ka Andhera' (*Mere Sanam*);
'Nigahain Milane Ko Ji Chahta Hai' (*Dil Hi To Hai*); 'Aaiye
Meherban' (*Howrah Bridge*); 'Dil Cheez Kya Hai' (*Umrao Jan*)
are just stunning. There is another I must mention here; 'Aaj
Aja Main Hoon Pyar Tera' that she sang with Rafi saab in *Teesri
Manzil* (composed by R.D. Burman). I have no hesitation in
admitting that I could have never succeeded in bringing the
verve and vivacity she has effortlessly put into this song.

YM: What was it like to sing with her?

LM: To tell you the truth, I loved singing duets with her and
Geeta Dutt. I regarded them as joyous occasions. Of the many
songs Asha and I have sung together, the ones closest to my
heart are 'Yeh Barkha Bahar, Sautaniya Ke Dwar' (*Mayurpankh*)
and 'Hai gajab kahin tara toota' (*Teesri kasam*), a song I still
love to hear. Shankar-Jaikishan had told us both to sing it in
our own individual styles and take whatever liberties we wished
with the alap and its melodies. So we both put whatever we
could into that song and this is perhaps what made it special.
C Ramachandra's 'O Chand Jahan Woh Hain Jayen' is another
spectacular composition. If you hear it, you get the feeling that

two girls are singing it in different moods and I love both its presentation and composition. Similarly, Madan Bhaiyya's composition from *Jahanara*, '*Jab-Jab Tumhain Bhulaya Tum Aur Yaad Aye*', and Naushad saab's '*Jaaneman Ek Nazar Dekh Le*' (*Mere Mehboob*) *are two of our outstanding songs, I think.*

In *Jis Desh Main Ganga Behti Hai*, Raj kapoor made us sing a song ('*Kya Hua, Are Yeh Kya Hua*') which always made us laugh because we both disliked it. Despite that, we gave it our best but you can make out that our hearts were not in this song. The same happened with our song in *Miss Mary* ('*Sakhi Ri, Sun Bole Papiha Us Paar*'), which I thought was a very ordinary composition, although it became very popular and is considered among our best performances together. Later, Laxmikant–Pyarelal's '*Chhap Tilak Sab Chhini Re, Mose Neha Lagaiye Ke*' (*Main Tulsi Tere Angan Ki*) is one I love. This song was a modification of Amir Khusro's famous work, slighty reworked for the film. I love it and consider it one of our best songs. It was slightly longer than other songs and gives Laxmikant-Pyarelal new ground to break. Shashi Kapoor's *Utsav*, similarly developed '*Man Kyoon Bahka Re Aadhi Raat Ko*' in a new fashion. I place this as the best among our songs together.

You may be surprised to learn that none of us ever practised a song at home: that was reserved for our rehearsals in recording studios. At home we only practised classical ragas and compositions. This was also Asha's way and I have never felt any sense of competition with her. I feel all such tales were manufactured by the media, so it is best to keep silent about this aspect of our relationship. Both of us are joined together in the world of music and that is a very strong bond. I take great pride in declaring her as a star in this industry and in the joy we have provided our listeners.

Where Geeta Dutt is concerned, we got along so well that it was a joy to sing together. I never felt she was different from any of my sisters. She was always cheerful and slightly harried, and I remember her warmly as a very dear friend. There are one or two songs with her where I feel you can hear this sense we shared as if we were singing at a joyous function: '*Ta Thaiyya Kar Ke Aana, More Jadugar More Saiyyan*' (*Panchayat*) and '*Bechain Dil Khoyi Si Nazar, Tanhaiyon Main Sham-o-Sahar*' (*Yahudi*).

YM: What about the songs you have sung with Usha Mangeshkar?

LM: (laughs). When I came to this industry, I was completely new and unsure of my reception. So when C. Ramachandra told me that Usha would accompany me in two songs in *Azad*, I was taken aback and wondered how she would ever manage to sing for such an important composer. I was just 22–23 then and Usha must have been 16–17 when we sang '*Aplam Chaplam*' *and* '*O Baliye Chal Chaliye*' together. '*Aplam Chaplam*' went on to become a huge success and later I was to sing many songs with Usha, most of them composed by Chitragupta ji, although we also sang several songs for Laxmi-Pyare as well. My personal favourite is GS Kohli's '*Tumko Piya Dil Diya Kitne Naaz Se*' (*Shikari*). Usha and I have also recorded quite a few albums of bhajans and mantras. I have to say that I get the same pleasure in singing with her that I got when I carried her in my arms as a child. (Laughs).

YM: The world is as enamoured of Lata's vice as she is of the Egyptian Um Kulsum's voice. What is so special about her?

LM: There was a time when I was crazy about her full-throated voice: she sang the kind of songs I had never heard another singer perform. Apart from her, I was also very fond of the Lebanese

Fairooz, whose voice was deep and strong. Do you know that Shankar-Jaikishan's song 'Ghar Aya Mera Pardesi' in Awara is based on Kulsum's 'Ala Balad, Al Mehboob'? She had sung this in 1936 for a famous Egyptian film, Vidid. When I was told this, I scoured as many of her songs as I could to hear her voice. So this Awara number became special for me and it gave me such pleasure to sing one of 'her' songs. I must tell you here that there was a famous Egyptian music composer called Abdul Wahab whose music was adapted by many of our music composers for Hindi films. Even Naushad saab's 'Mera Salam Leja, Dil Ka Paigham Leja' (Udankhatola) was based on one of his famous compositions.

During my travels abroad, I became aware of how popular our film music was in many countries. Interestingly, many fans there listen to familiar tunes from their countries and think we are singing them in our language!

YM: Are they any absent friends you miss?

LM: There are so many whose death is difficult to accept and I grieve for them even after all these years. I had two woman friends whose deaths were a deadly blow. I am speaking of 1946, when I had a friend, Nirmala Shirodkar, who was a close confidante. Her death really shook me and I wasn't able to even speak about it to anyone. The other friend was a psychiatrist, Nalini Mhatre. She lived in Canada and I think she went there in 1968. We often visited each other, I went to her in her home in Kingston in Canada and she came to our house in Bombay. We used to exchange confidences with each other and share our problems. I sometimes made a tape and sent it to hear: what I want to say is that we were really close. She died a few years ago of cancer and I was absolutely devastated.

Apart from these two friends, I was also very close to my mother and miss her terribly. Even now, whenever I speak of her, I am filled with sadness. She was a wonderful homemaker. When my father died, she must have been about 45 years old and took on the task of re aring the five of us without ever making us feel it was a burden. She never made any demands on us or complained. Her whole focus was in keeping us together and happy. She died in 1995 and Nalini followed a year later. So the two people I was closest to after my father left this world died within a short time of each other. I was just 13 years old when I lost my father and spent the rest of my life looking after the family. When he was around, I had such a carefree life. After him my whole life revolved around my family and music, music, music . . .

I cannot forget my mother's last few days. She was in hospital and all of us tried to make her as comfortable as we could. Whenever she opened her eyes, Hridaynath would hand a paper where he had written down 'How are you? How are you feeling?' or something like that. Then he handed her a pen to write down the answers to these questions. One day, she wrote, 'Let me go to my husband, don't stop me now.' I was deeply moved by this and realised that we were actually prolonging her agony by keeping her alive.

YM: Which artiste do you miss the most?

LM: I miss all the ones we have lost. Mukesh Bhaiyya died in front of me during a performance. He had a massive heart attack and just collapsed on the stage. For a long time after that, I could not get over it and ran a high fever for many days. I was in such pain that I cannot describe the feeling. I grieve the death of all the singers we have lost. Kishore da's death was also a big blow and I remember that about a month before his death in September, he met me and asked me to visit him. 'I have to tell you something,' he said. When I went across, he began to cry and told me, 'I may make people laugh but my own life has been full of sorrow. I have so many problems that I don't know where to begin.' He did not elaborate those problems but perhaps they were so private and related to his personal life that he could not speak of them. He was such a clown that he could make you laugh until tears ran down your face. What a terrific mimic he was! How sad that he himself was such an unhappy person. Geeta Dutt's death was also such a mystery and I heard of it from Salil da when he rang up to say I should immediately rush across because Geeta had passed away. What made her take her own life will always puzzle me.

Then there was another wonderful lady, Madan Mohan's wife Sheela bhabhi, who I miss terribly. She was such a loving person and because we lived on the same road, we were in and out of each others' homes. Sometimes, when I visited them, Madan Bhaiyya would call out from the kitchen to say he was cooking mutton and I should not leave without eating some. He knew I liked to eat the delicious mutton he made at home. Sheela bhabhi often gave me gifts, a perfume or something she knew I liked. We could chat for hours and not tire of each others' company. Our birthdays were close to each other's: mine on Septemeber 28 and hers was September 26 and we celebrated it together. All this came to an end with her death: she died of blood cancer. I think it was the same year as Nargis ji's death.

So there are some with whom I shared such a deep relationship that their absence hurts me terribly. Even their memories bring pain now when I remember them and my blood pressure rises. This happened when I lost Kishore da, R.D. Burman and Mai, so my doctor told me to avoid seeing dead bodies. Now tell me, is this possible? And this pain comes from within, not from seeing a dead body.

There are some whose death hurts for other reasons: in Jaikishan's case, it was that he died too young and also that towards the end he and Shankar had drifted apart and were not getting much work either. He was such a talented man that I feel he died an unfulfilled life. When Madan Mohan died, it was like losing a family member and I just did not feel like singing for some time. He was like an older brother and no one has filled that absence in my life.

I was also very shaken by the deaths of Roshan saab, R.D. Burman and Chitragupt. Hemant da was also such a generous man and so loving. When he'd drop in to our home, he would shout from the door as he entered, 'Lata! Coffee!' And when I brought him a cup, he stirred in 5-6 spoons of sugar, despite my warning him that it will raise his sugar levels.

The loss of all these wonderful people made my world emptier and, however hard I try, I cannot forget their wonderful faces and personalities. Apart from the personal loss, it was also the sad awareness that a wonderful era of music was coming to an end with their going away. We were fellow travellers on a journey that had now ended.

YM: So many of our gods are shown as lovers of music or dance. Which one do you venerate the most amongst them?

LM: Look, I worship every god who is a lover of music because my entire life has been dedicated to music. It is my calling and my religion and wherever I find music, whether in a place or being, I am drawn to it. As for our gods, what can be a better indication of their love than that they all are associated with some musical instrument or the other? One holds a damru, a veena, another a mridang or a flute. So I bow to all of them.

YM: You have sung many songs in praise of Krishna, so which of his literary worshippers do you like the most?

LM: I think the deepest levels of veneration are to be found in Surdas and Mirabai's poetry. One saw him as a comrade, the other as a lover. I am drawn to both their works, although as a woman I empathise more with Mirabai. A long time ago, when Maharana Bhagwat Singh of Udaipur was alive, I happened to meet him several times in his palace. He would also visit me whenever he could on visits to Bombay. After him, his son Maharana Arvind Singh kept up this very intimate personal relationship. Once, when Pandit Narendra Sharma, Hridaynath, Usha and I and a few other friends happened to be in Udaipur on some work, we went to meet Bhagwat Singh ji. He was delighted and said, 'Lata ji, you are such a great devotee of Krishna and you know how I love to hear you sing Mirabai bhajans. I will take you today to worship at the shrine that she used to worship.' As you know, Mirabai was married to a Maharana of Udaipur. So he took me to the royal temple which had a beautiful Krishna statue and told me, 'This is the Krishna that Mirabai carried in her arms and worshipped.' I cannot describe what I felt when I heard that and to see the Krishna that Mirabai has so evocatively portrayed in her verses. Tears fell from my eyes as I thanked the maharana for this rare privilege. I have never spoken of this to anyone till now.

YM: The classical Geet Govind by Jaidev is also replete with the love of Radha–Krishna. Did you ever think of singing it?

LM: Of course, it was among the Sanskrit books in my collection of great poetry. There was a time when Hridaynath and I seriously considered doing it but somehow we could never find the time to sit down and work out the details. I wish now that I had attempted it: I feel it would have been a great achievement.

YM: Which deity do you prefer to worship?

LM: From childhood itself, I was strongly attracted to Krishna and whenever I wrote down the lyrics of a song I was to sing, I always wrote 'Sri Krishna' on top of the page. I read all I could by Surdas and Meerabai and loved to read about his childhood antics.

However, when I was preparing the album '*Ram ratan dhan payo*', Pandit Narendraji said to me, 'Always remember that Rama is the only One who can grant you anything you want. He is the One who stands at the end of life to take you across.' This touched me deeply and after recording the album I felt drawn to Rama-worship. I have not been able to find a comparable deity. Narendraji had once told me, 'Wait and see! This album will become your most popular work.' And he was right, as always. Till today, I receive fan mail about it and it has outsold every other album I have ever done. I consider this a vindication of my bhakti (laughs).

YM: Among the poets who wrote in chaste Hindi, who do you rate as the best?

LM: I think I would name Neeraj ji, because there is no doubt that he wrote a kind of Hindi not often heard in film songs. On one hand, there were writers like Kedar Sharma and Pandit Narendra Sharma but their Hindi was more classical and so intimidated certain producers, although I did not think so. Neeraj ji was fortunate in that despite his lyrics being written in chaste Hindi, they were accessible to the common listener as well and it was like a breath of fresh air. I respect him very deeply and my duet with Rafi saab in *Nai Umar Ki Nayi Fasal* ('*Karavan Guzar Gaya Ghubar Dekhte Rahe*') is my favourite Neeraj composition.

Among the others he wrote, '*Rangeela Re*' (*Prem Pujari*), '*Jaise Radha Ne Mala Japi Shyam Ki*' (*Tere Mere Sapne*); '*Megha*

Chhaye Addhi Raat Bairan Bhai Re Nidiya' (*Anupama*) are some others I am very fond of. His songs shine with a different light among the works of other lyricists. Although he wrote very rarely for films, each one of his lyrics is memorable for this reason.

Apart from him, Rajendra Krishen, Pandit Bharat Ram, Prem Dhawan, Indivar, Gulshan Bawra and Yogesh also wrote some memorable songs in Hindi.

YM: What is your opinion about Gulzar sahib both as a director and a lyricist?

LM: He has always been a favourite lyricist and all the films he has made have been very successful and different from the usual run of Hindi films. The first song by him that I sang was one from *Bandini* ('*Mora Gora Ang Lai Le*') for Burman dada. What is a special quality of his songs is that he never writes in the current language of popular slang. This is why it gives me a great sense of satisfaction to sing his compositions. He has a very modern sensibility but never bows to the merely fashionable or popular. There are very few like him in this industry.

When he made made *Lekin* for Hridaynath Productions, he kept in mind the classical touch to the music of the film and wrote accordingly. I love two of these songs for their lyrics in this film, '*Main Ek Sadi Se Baithi Hoon*' (sung by me) and '*Surmai Sham Is Tarah, Aye*' (sung by Suresh Wadekar). I like almost all his songs and can only remember a few just now: '*Tere Bina Zindagi Se Koi Shikwa To Nahin*' (*Aandhi*), '*Beeti Na Bitaye Raina*' (*Parichay*), '*Aapki Aankhon Main Kuchh Mahke Hue Raaz Hain*' (*Ghar*), '*Na, Jiya Lage Na*' (*Anand*), '*Tujhse Naraz Nahin Zindagi Hairan Hoon*' (*Masoom*). Among his later songs, there is one from *Maya Memsahib* that I love: '*Is Dil Main Baskar Dekho To, Yeh Shahar Bahut Purana Hai*'.

He has done wonders with those lyrics. I think he and R.D. Burman made a great team.

YM: What did you think of Anand Bakshi?

LM: Like Pradip ji and Bharat Vyas, Anand Bakshi also had a deep understanding of music and often sang out his lyrics for the music director. I sang '*Bagon Main Bahar Ayi, Hoton Pe Pukar Ayi*' (*Mom Ki Gudiya*) for him in the 70s. At one time he was so popular that every other film had his songs, like Laxmikant-Pyarelal's music. Since he was at the top for so long, many of his songs went on to become big hits.

On a personal level, he was a pleasant man, full of jokes and laughter. I rate his '*Kuch* To Log Kahenge, Logon Ka Kaam Hai Kehna' (*Amar Prem*), sung by Kishore da, as his best. My own song from the same film, '*Bara Natkhat Hai Re Krishna Kanhaiya, Kya Kare Yashoda Maiyya*' is also a lovely composition. There is a freshness in his lyrics, like his '*Mujhe Kuch Kehna Hai*' from the super hit *Bobby*. I really enjoyed singing all the songs in that film. His partnership with Laxmikant-Pyarelal became as successful as Shailendra's with Shankar-Jaikishan and Shakeel Badauni's with Naushad saab.

YM: Who would you say was a lyricist with whom you never had to raise the issue of vulgar lyrics?

LM: Majrooh Sulatanpuri saab. Both he and his pen never transgressed the boundaries of decency.

YM: Who were the later writers who followed this line?

LM: Gulzar saab and Javed Akhtar. There can be no two views on the fact that both write beautiful poetry, free of any innuendos and vulgarity. This makes every song they write worth listening.

YM: In Hrishikesh Mukherji's film, *Musafir*, Salil Chaudhuri persuaded Dilip Kumar to sing a duet with you. Can you share that experience?

LM: Oh, that was a hilarious episode. Yusuf Bhai (Dilip Kumar) was quite nervous and scared and wondered how he would be able to perform with me. He sat down to sing after asking me all kinds of questions about how he should handle this or that aspect. When he was ready, he shut his eyes unaware that Salil Chaudhuri was sitting opposite him. So he was completely oblivious that Salil da was signalling that the next section was something I had to sing, or where he had to stop and start again.

(Laughs as she recounts this). Now, as you know, no one can talk when a recording is underway. I remember how loudly he sang the opening lines and Salil da signalled that I should now take over and modulate the pitch. So this is how we recorded the song. After he opened his eyes, he found us all laughing but he was unable to join in. Dilip Kumar is a very serious man and does not like levity. I have still not been able to fathom how he allowed himself to be persuaded to sing and still cannot believe that he actually came to a recording studio. I am sure Hrishi da and Salil da must have really worked on him.

YM: You have sung some really sweet songs for S.N. Tripathi. What about his work attracted you?

LM: Like Vasant Desai, Tripathi ji was also essentially a classical musician, and this quality is visible in his compositions. He mostly scored music for religious, mythological and historical films, which lend themselves very naturally to a classical musical style. Some of his best known films are *Rani Roopmati*, *Sangeet Samrat Tansen*, *Lal Qila* and *Kavi Kalidas*. You will find his signature in all these films. personally, I love all the songs he scored for *Rani Roopmati*. Two lovely examples are 'Aa ja bhanwar soona dagar' and 'Jiqan ki beena ka taar *bole*. Similarly, *Lal qila* and *Jai Chittor* have some exquisite compositions.

There was a time when his number for Rafi saab, *'Zara samne to aaja chhaliye'* (*Janam-janam ke phere*) became a super-hit and every lane reverberated with it. It was on every hit-list chart on radio. And his songs in Sangeet Samrat Tansen, particularly Mukesh bhaiyya's *'Jhoomti chali hawa yaad aa gaya koi'*, are among my favourites. He was an outstanding composer in my opinion.

YM: Your musical journey is really interesting because you have sung so many wonderful songs for R.D. Burman whereas it is well-known that his kind of music really suited Asha Bhonsle's voice better.

LM: R.D. Burman always created a different kind of music for me, in fact every music director made a special effort for me while composing songs that I had to sing. They would tell me, we have created this song specially for you and if you refuse, it will not be able to get the same quality from someone else. This is not just true of Pancham but of Burman dada, Roshan saab, S–K, Madan Mohan, Jaidev and Laxmi–Pyare. Burman dada had heard a Hindi compliment that literally translates you have added four moons to this' (*tumne char chand laga diye*). So every time he was pleased with me he would tell me in his heavy Bengali accent, 'Lata, you have added four moons to my song.'

Sometimes, when they were pleased with my rendering of their songs, they would say, 'You have made this song better than we had hoped it would be.'

YM: Roshan saab's last song was *'Mahlon Ka Raja Mile'* for *Anokhi Raat*. Tell me something about that song.

LM: This is a very sad story to recall. Roshan saab passed away before the song was recorded and what made it even worse was that he kept asking that we record it and for one reason or another I was unable to give him the time. That is why his death really shook me and to this day I regret that we could not record it before his death. However, I was so close to his family that when we did I was almost numb with grief. His wife, Iraji, supervised the recording and wept all through it. Naturally, all of us were deeply affected . . . and virtually every musician was in tears as well. As you know, the song itself is very moving and I sang it with such a heavy heart because right in front of me was a portrait of Roshan saab with a garland draped over it. So in a sense, this was our collective tribute to his memory but it was an incredibly sad occasion. Added to all of this were the lyrics by Indivar that are written as a farewell to a beloved daughter.

YM: It seems to me that Jaya Bachchan's role in *Abhiman* was moulded keeping you in mind. From the way she holds herself in front of the mike and her manner of draping her sari—all this brings you instantly to mind. True?

LM: Yes, it is true that Jaya copied my mannerisms when she performed this role. At first I found it awkward to sing when she would arrive at the recording studio and sit directly in front of me and watch me intently as I sang. I did not know then why she was doing so, later I realised that Hrishida had instructed her to observe me closely and replicate my mannerisms as I sang. It was only when I saw the film after it was released that it all became clear to me. So you are absolutely right in saying that she really copied me well and brought out every detail of my persona, especially in the songs '*Piya Bina Baje Bansiya*' and '*Ab To Hai Tumse Har Khushi Meri*'. She stands in front of the mike exactly as I do, so I really appreciated her work in the film. In any case, she is a brilliant actress and understands the nuances of her role better than most.

YM: The film industry beieves that you helped Laxmikant-Pyarelal to reach where they did as composers. Is it true that you made the careers of some composers in this industry?

LM: (Laughs). I don't subscribe to this theory at all. Look, it is only individual talent and luck that get a person success and fame. However, it is true that some are fortunate in getting some lucky breaks early in their careers and the credit often goes to the artiste that made it possible. I knew Laxmikant-Pyarelal from before because when Hriday set up Surel Bal Kala Kendra in the 1960s, Meena and Usha went there to perform. The Kendra was a nursery for young singers who gave stage performances in and around Bombay and the Maharasthra region. I first met Laxmikant at K.L. Saigal's brother, Mahendra Saigal's home. He was just 10-12 years old and Mahendra ji told me to help some of the young artistes. He pointed out that Laxmikant was a gifted mandolin player. In the same way, I met Pyarelal with his father Pandit Ramprasad Sharma and he was a very good trumpet and violin player. He was also a good musician and they both joined Hriday's Surel Bal Kala Kendra. That is when I saw them perform together. So I had known them almost from their boyhood. Later, when they became music composers, I gave them the same encouragement that I always gave other promising young artistes.

Since they worked with Hriday, they often came to our home. In their early days, I would mention to Shankar-Jaikishan, Ghulam Haider, Madan Mohan and Naushad that they were gifted musicians. They also became assistants to Kalyan ji-Anandji. Perhaps you may not know that Laxmikant played the mandolin in Hemant Kumar's '*Jadugar saiyyan chhod mori bayyan*' (*Nagin*) and also for '*Koi aya dharkan kehti hai*' (*Lajwanti*). Similarly, Pyarelal played the violin in countless songs. I remember Madan Bhaiyya's song '*Main uske dar se utha tha*' (*Haqeeqat*), where Pyarelal played the violin beautifully. If they had not been so talented, no amount of promoting by anyone would have got them the success they deserved. Certainly, I would not have promoted or recommended them to any music composer. Incidentally, at the time when they were at their peak, I sang many songs for S.D. Burman, Chitraguptji, Kalyan ji-Anandji, R.D. Burman and Bhappi Lahiri as well.

YM: What is the utility of a dummy track in music recordings?

LM: Suppose a singer is not free to record a particular song but the film's producer pressures the composer to give the song that is needed at that point. In such a situation, the composer records the song in another voice and gives it so that the film's shooting schedule is not held up. Later, when the 'real' singer is ready, it can be recorded and replaced because her name has been announced in the film's publicity material.

YM: Do you carry some special instrument to provide the drone?

LM: When I sing, a violinist is placed next to me, so that he can provide the drone and keep the scale from wavering. If you listen carefully to some of my old songs, you can clearly hear the faint sound of the background violin. Sometimes, this accompaniment is provided by an organ or a sarangi. This not unlike the tanpura that always accompanies a classical music performer. It is just to make sure that the singer stays in tune at all times.

YM: Are the accompanying orchestra players given slips with notations written on them?

LM: I haven't seen this because mostly they are given verbal instructions by the composer that they memorize. Some players of western instruments such as violin, cello or saxophone like to make their own notes but as far as the Indian instrumentalists are concerned (sarangi, sitar, tabla or ghatam), they memorise the instructions.

YM: Which part of you is present in the songs you song?

LM: All of me is present in every song I have sung: I forget who I am outside that moment when I sing . . . (Smiles).

YM: How did you convey your lack of enthusiasm for certain songs to their composers?

LM: Among the thousands I have sung in my lifetime, there were bound to be some I never really cared for. But I always kept my feelings to myself, and just sang them as I was asked to. The only person I expressed my opinion to was my brother Hridaynath and told him that even though I did not care much for a particular composition, I would sing it for him. After all, one can say this only to one's own brother.

YM: Since you have always spoken openly of your great admiration for Noorjahan, let me ask you about some other Pakistani singers: Mallika Pukhraj, Iqbal Bano, Fareeda Khanum, Munni Begum and Tahira Sayyid.

LM: These are all distinguished names but I have heard little of their work. I have met just Farida Khanum and she was a marvellous performer. Her voice is a little deep but her style and training are impeccable. We sometimes speak with each other on the phone and if she was in Delhi she would come over to Bombay to meet me. Once she even stayed for some 2-3 days in our house. I enjoyed these encounters because we shared so much. I love her ghazals '*Mere Hamnafaz, Mere Hamnava, Mujhe Dost Ban Ke Dagha Na De*' and '*Aaj Jane Ki Zid Na Karo*'. *She has such perfect mastery over her voice and the emotion of the lyric. I consider her a very fine* artiste.

I have heard only a fleeting acquaintance with Mallika Pukhraj's work, although I have sung one of her famous songs, '*Abhi To Main Jawan Hoon*', in a film, which was composed by Husnlal–Bhagatram. But truthfully, I did not like all I heard of her music. I feel her songs lack life. I haven't heard her daughter Tahira Sayyid nor Munni Begum. These singers performed over Pakistan radio and I enjoyed the way they incorporated classical music into ghazals. They are also accomplished tappa and dadra singers.

Apart from Noorjahan, the other ghazal singers from Pakistan I enjoy listening to are Mehndi Hasan saab, Ghulam Ali and Farida Khanum. Among their classical music artistes, I like Nazakat Ali-Salamat Ali, and Roshara Begum. I also like Abida Parveen and her naat qawwalis and sufi music is beautiful. I love the way she immerses herself in her songs and reminds me of the abandon with which fakirs sing. Among folk singers, I think Reshma is without parallel. I am sure there must be many other singers from Pakistan who are also very talented and accomplished that I have not heard.

YM: Weren't you invited to perform in Pakistan?

LM: Several times but I was scared of accepting their invitations. I have such a huge number of fans there that I thought they may decide to keep me back and prevent me from ever coming back! (Laughs loudly). They still complain that I never went across and still beg me to come but the tension between our two countries was always a problem.

YM: Indira Gandhi often took famous Indian personages from cinema, literature and music on her foreign trips. Were you ever part of such a delegation?

LM: No, never. Perhaps I was not considered worthy because no Indian Prime Minister has ever invited me for such foreign visits. Raj Kapoor, Nargis, Dev saab, Begum Akhtar – all these great artistes have been taken by our Prime Minsters but somehow I was never one of that group. However, I did accompany Sunil Dutt's Ajanta Arts' on their visits to entertain our troops and I have really enjoyed those experiences, because I was happy to do my humble bit for our brave jawans.

YM: Some 15 years ago, during a conversation with some friends in New York, I was told that of all the Indian performers who came to Broadway, Pandit Ravi Shankar and your concerts were always a sell-out event. People even bought tickets in black to attend them . . .

LM: (Enjoys this). This is a divine gift, what else can I say? It is true that audiences in London and America love me and whenever I sing 'Bekas Pe Karam Keejiye' from Mughal-e-Azam, they go delirious. In London, too, all my songs from Mughal-e-Azam, Pakeezah and Anarkali are huge hits and they beg me to sing a Punjabi Heer. Then, of course, there is the perennial demand for 'Ai Mere Watan Ke Logon'; I can never leave the stage without singing that number! Mind you, there were no wolf whistles and loud cheers: they heard me in such a disciplined way. This is what I love about my audience in London. And at the end of a concert, the applause goes on and on. I got a standing ovation each and every time I sang there. Things may be different now: I haven't given a stage performance either here or abroad for so long that I no longer know whether that decency still exists.

YM: Tell us about the film parties you have enjoyed.

LM: I have never really been a party goer but there were always some special invitations I never refused, such as Raj Kapoor's birthday and Holi parties. He gave lavish parties on these occasions and ordered food from every part of the country for his guests, in addition to delicious continental food. I relish the memory of those wonderful parties. Majrooh sahib was another person whose home I often visited for a meal. His wife was such a great cook that even a simple dal-chawal made by her had an unforgettable taste. The warmth and love in that house is a savoured memory. Another loving host was Naushad saab and Madan Bhaiyya was just 5-6 buildings away from where I live. I often walked over or called them over for a shared meal.

Once, after we had finished recording a song ('*Teri Aankhon Ke Siva Duniya Main Rakha Kya Hai*'), Madan Bhaiyya went over to where the song's writer, Majrooh saab, was standing and punched him playfully. 'What is all this?' Majrooh saab asked in mock anger. And Madan Bhaiyya said, 'You have written such a great song and Lata has sung it so brilliantly that you both have to come over to my house now and I will cook a mutton curry for you.' We all burst out laughing. Whenever Madan Bhaiyya was pleased with a recording, he would display his appreciation by cooking for those who had helped in crafting its success.

Similarly, Chitrguptji hosted me so many times after a successful recording and the evening would become a happy session with many of us sharing our delight. Prem Dhawan often joined us on such occasions. These were all large-hearted, generous people who shared their table with all their friends.

YM: Did you ever have a prophetic dream?

LM: Years ago, when I had just entered this industry, I used to get a recurrent dreamt that I am at a Shiv temple made of black stone. I go and sit at the steps behind it and the sea is spread before me. It was a deserted spot and although I knew it had to be a shiv temple, there was no idol I could see. Just the open doors and windows, a large courtyard and the limitless ocean before me – this is all I could see. I felt this was a strange dream and asked my mother what it could possibly mean. She said it meant I would get great fame and success in the future.

YM: What do you like most about this country?

LM: I love this land and am proud I was born here. This is the land of saints and sages and is blessed by the gods. I believe that every Indian is also a blessed soul . . .and each one of us, rich or poor, has a natural inclination towards spirituality. We Indians are truly blessed.

YM: To be a successful artiste what is most important?

LM: The spirit of sacrifice is important but passion would perhaps be more apt. However, unless this passion is also backed by hard work and God's grace, an artiste may not be able to achieve true success. Divine benediction is a rare gift, I feel.

YM: You are a very good photographer, so when did your interest in this begin?

LM: Photography is my hobby, nothing more. I started taking pictures in 1946 or so after I bought my first camera, a Rolliflex for 1200 rupees. I was taught the fundamentals of photography by Madhavrao Shinde, a widely respected film editor who later also directed a few Marathi films. He taught me how to load a roll of film, which camera to buy, and how to adjust the lens according to the light and so on.

I began to really enjoy taking photographs and often went out to catch interesting situations. However, I had to abandon this after people began to gather round because they recognised me. It was so distracting that I quit going outdoors. I concentrated on taking family pictures and have taken hundreds of photos of the children in my family. Photography was also my way of relaxing after a gruelling day at work. I used to often indulge in my hobby when I went broad. However, I don't particularly like digital photography because I liked taking technical decisions myself when shooting a picture.

YM: According to you, which music director had the most imitators?

LM: I think it must be R.D. Burman. He died so young and till today people try and ape his style. Do you know that his tunes are even plagiarised by the advertising world?

YM: Which talented music director never made it to the heights that say S.D. Burman, Naushad and all reached?

LM: Although this is largely a matter of chance and fate, I think Chitragupt was a music director who made some beautiful compositions and broke fresh ground but never got the fame his contemporaries like Shankar-Jaikishan and Laxmikant-Pyarelal received.

YM: Which western musician do you admire?

LM: I love Nat King Cole, the Beatles, Barbara Streisand and Harry Belafonte. As I told you earlier, I was also crazy about the Egyptian singer Um Kulsum at one time. I have heard Harry Belafonte live and still get goosepimples when I think of that experience. Western classical music gives you far more scope to innovate and try out new things. I love Mozart for this reason. I have heard very little of Elvis Presley but enjoyed what

I have heard of him. Among the classical musicians Beethoven, Chopin, Tchaikovsky are wonderful to hear.

YM: If you had ever been given an opportunity to sing with a western singer, whom would you choose?

LM: Do you know I once wanted very badly to sing with Nat King Cole. I would have loved to cut a disc with him.

YM: If you had been given a chance to sing as a playback artiste for Marilyn Monroe, Ingrid Berman, Elizabeth Taylor, Audrey Hepburn, Julia Roberts, Natalie Portman—whom would you choose?

LM: These are all important names but if I had my way I would definitely choose Ingrid Bergman. I adore her acting and feel my voice would match her perfectly. The song I would sing would be unique, not like what I have sung for Hindi films. It would be a sad song but composed in the wesetern style. (Laughs).

List of favourite songs of contemporaries.

- Noorjahan: '*Diya Jalakar Aap Bujhaya*' (*Bari ma*; K Datta)
- Kanan Devi: '*Ai Chand Chhup Na Jana*' (*Jawab*; Kamaldas Gupta)
- Suraiyya: '*Socha Kya Tha, Kya Ho Gaya*' (*Anmol ghari*; Naushad)
- Amirbai Karnataki: '*Dheere-Dheere Aa Re Badal, Dheere-Dheere Aa*' (*Kismet*; Anil Biswas)
- Zohrabai Ambalawali: '*Ankhiyan Mila Ke Jiya Bharma Ke, Chale Nahin Jana*' (*Rattan*; Naushad)
- Parul Ghosh: '*Main Unki Ban Jaoon Re*' (*Humari Baat*; Anil Biswas)
- Rajkumari: '*Sun Bairi Balam Sach Bol Re*' (*Bawre nain*; Roshan)

- Saraswati Rane: *'Bina Madhur-Madhur Kachu Bol'* (*Ramrajya*; Shankarrao Vyas)
- Shamshad Begum: *'Nainon Ke Baan Ki Reet Anokhi'* (*Khazanchi*; Ghulam Haider)
- Geeta Dutt: *'Waqt Ne Kiya Kya Haseen Sitam'* (*Kagaz ke phool*; S.D. Burman)
- Asha Bhonsle: *'Nigahain Milano Ko Jee Chata Hai'* (*Dil hi to hai*; Roshan)
- Usha Mangeshkar: *'Mungara-Mungara Main Gur Ki Dali'* (*Inkar*; Rajesh Roshan)

YM: Have you ever felt a touch of arrogance about your talent?

LM: I am so grateful to God that I remained untouched by any kind of pride or arrogance. I have never considered myself a great singer and that is what perhaps kept me grounded all through my life. I believe I am an ordinary woman and no different from thousands of other working women. Let me tell you a story from my childhood. I had once won a dilruba as a prize in a singing contest (the one we have spoken about earlier). One day, I was sitting in front of my father as he played on the dilruba (my father could play all musical instruments very well) and he was totally immersed in his music. Then, we noticed a small mouse that would dart and in and out of the room. I think that must have disturbed Baba, because he picked up the bow of the dilruba and threw it at that pesky mouse. The mouse ran away but the bow broke and I began to cry. 'I won that dilruba as a prize, 'I wailed. 'Baba, how could you break it?'

My father replied, 'You are crying over a broken bow, beta? You have no idea what your future holds and how many awards you will receive one day. As long as your talent remains with you, rest assured nothing else matters. So why weep over a broken dilruba that was just a prize?'

Even though I was just a child, something in that struck home and understood the worthlessness of a mere award. Baba was absolutely right: when God has awarded me this voice, why did any other prize matter? After that day, I never shed tears over any disappointment in my career, nor did I yearn for any award. When I was awarded the Padma Bhushan in 1969, I went straight to my mother on my return from Delhi and told her, 'Look what I got as a result of your blessings, Mai! A Padma Bhushan!' And my mother asked in an offhand way, 'What is this Padma Bhushan?'

'It is among the highest awards given to an artiste by the government,' I told her. 'Every artiste yearns to be given one.'

'Oh!' she replied calmly. 'Then I am happy for you.'

I was immediately reminded of my father and decided that, like him, she also set little store by such awards. These are the values that I was brought up on, so I have always looked at my art with respect and confidence but remained as free of any arrogance as far as possible. I am grateful for whatever has come my way but I have no special pride in myself as a result.

YM: When did you develop this indifference towards awards?

LM: Look, I must make clear that I am not indifferent to awards per se but that I was always taught to concentrate on refining my art rather than chase awards. I acknowledge that it is because of the blessings of my parents and gurus that I have received so many awards and such love in my lifetime. Mind you, I have fought for awards not for myself but to make the process of giving awards more equitable and fair. You know of my tussle with the Filmfare Awards people. It was only after I protested at the unfairness of not awarding a trophy to playback singers and lyricists that they began to award them after 1958. I did not fight for myself but for all of us who worked so hard. Later, I also humbly requested that I should not be considered for any more Filmfare trophies because I had won so many and felt that other, newer, singers should be given a chance as well. So I have fought for a principle on the matter of awards, not for promoting myself. Otherwise, the contributions of such great artistes as Mukesh, Mohd Rafi, Kishore Kumar, Asha, Shailendra, Hasrat Jaipuri, Shakeel Badayuni, Gulzar would have gone unrewarded. It was not about my getting an award but about getting these great people the respect and recognition they so richly deserved.

I also strongly believe that one must respect the expectations of the public. This is why when people began to openly say that I should be awarded the Bharat Ratna and I actually did receive it, I realized that it was also fulfilling what millions of my fans have so earnestly wished for me. How happy this must have made them! I accepted it with great pride and immense gratitude on behalf of all of them.

YM: What did you feel when you learnt you had been awarded the Bharat Ratna?

LM: I was in London and out somewhere when it was announced. I heard the phone ringing in the house the moment I stepped out of the car. My first thought was that it must be from Bombay and was scared that something bad had happened. I picked up the phone with trepidation and it was my niece Rachna, delirious with joy as she told me that the Government of India was going to award me a Bharat Ratna. Naturally, I was delighted and when I sat down after that news my initial thoughts were that if my parents and gurus could have known this, how proud it would have

made them that I had achieved this for music! Whenever
I am given an award for my music, my first thought always
goes to my father. When he used to tell me as a child that I
would win many awards, I thought it was only to encourage
me to work hard.

As the news spread, God knows how many friends and fans
called me up and the phone would not stop ringing till late
in the night. So while I bow my head to the Giver who has
showered so much on me, I also know that in the end it will
be my work and not these awards that people will remember.

I was awarded the Bharat Ratna in 2001 but for me the
most memorable award was the one I received in 1981, when
I was decorated with the title of the 'Asthan Sangeet Vidwan
Saralu' by the Tirupati Temple Trust. This prestigious title is
conferred on a musician for two years and the ceremony is held
within the temple precincts. It is like receiving a divine gift
from the Lord Himself. My whole family—mother, sisters—
accompanied me and watched me as I sang a bhajan and raga
before the deity. The priest then picked up a shawl from the
pile draped over the feet of Lord Venkatesh and placed it on
my shoulders. It was as if the Lord had personally blessed
me. Later, in 2006, I recorded an album in honour of Lord
Venkatesh and dedicated it to the Temple Trust. I was then
given the title of 'Asthan Sangeet Vidwan Saralu' permanently,
a very rare honour indeed.

YM: After receiving all these honours and awards, do you
feel fulfilled in your quest?

LM: Fulfilment does not come from receiving awards and
degrees, it comes from within. What helps in achieveing it is
one's dedication and confidence in one's abilities. Before me,
the artistes who were awarded the Bharat Ratna were Pandit

Ravi Shankar and M.S. Subbulakshmi and I was thrilled when they were so honoured. I respect both very deeply and feel that they richly deserved the honour. I myself received it with Ustad Bismillah Khan and this doubled my joy. Recently, when Pandit Bhimsen Joshi was given it I felt a trifle sad that he received it so late in life: he should have got it long before they gave it to me. However, all the artistes who have been awarded the Bharat Ratna had reached such a pinnacle that after that point, there remained no other award that could justly honour their achievement. They had truly fulfilled their purpose in life in every way.

On the question of awards and fulfilment I will share something with you that I have never shared with anyone before this. You know that after my father's death, our family went through great financial tribulations and my mother was compelled to sell off all her jewellery. One by one, she quietly pawned off everything till all that was left was her nose-ring. Meanwhile, I was running from place to place to earn what I could to keep the family going: but I was also determined to once again drape my mother with all the jewellery she wore when my father was alive and we were prosperous. I remember how her wrists used to be covered in the traditional Maharashtrian gold ornaments called gote and patli and that a mohanmala used to hang from her neck. I was ultimately able to replace my mother's lost jewels and felt such a sense of fulfilment when I draped the mohanmala round her neck because it completed a promise I had made to myself. I don't think I will ever forget the expression on my mother's face as I did so.

She said nothing to me but went into her room and wept as she realized that from now on, I would be able to give the family all that they had lost after my father's death. Never again in my life have I experienced the joy I did that day when my mother looked at me with such tenderness. I tell you no award could ever match the deep sense of fulfilment I felt that day. (Looks pensive and sad).

YM: The Bengal Film Journalists' Association Award is a highly coveted award. Between 1964 and 1985, you received it 12 times, when some of your most famous films (such as *Woh kaun thi* and *Saraswatichandra*) were chosen. What do you have to say about this?

LM: (Laughs). Tell me, who doesn't like to receive awards? Of course I am thrilled with the fact that they considered me worthy of such an honour because they are reputed to be great connoisseurs of art. So what more can I say?

In 1964, when I received this award for *Woh kaun thi*, I was gratified because the music for it had been scored by Madan Bhaiyya. I want to share the fact that I was certain he would win the Filmfare Award that year for his music in this film and was deeply disappointed when that did not happen. I even went over to his house to tell him so. He told me then, 'Lata, if you think that I should have been given that trophy and are upset about it, then I think I have received my prize. What can be a greater award for me than that you appreciate the fact that my music deserved it?' That is why when I was given the award for this film by the Bengal Film Journalists' Association, it became special for me.

YM: You were also once given a state award by the UP government. Do you remember that?

LM: Oh I remember it very well, even though this happened quite a while ago. Mulayam Singh ji was the chief minister at the time and I think the award they gave me was either called

'Awadh Gaurav' or 'Shan-e-Awadh'. I went to Lucknow to receive it and have some special memories of the occasion. You see, either because the commercial flight timings did not suit us or because we had very little time to spare, the chief minister arranged a special plane to ferry us across. It was a small aircraft with seating for just 8–10 people and Naushad Saab and two or three members of my family were travelling with me. Naushad saab had told me that if I was going to his hometown, he had to come along. Now as we neared Lucknow, the plane started to wobble rather alarmingly and Naushad saab was terrified and said to me, 'Lata ji, this *udankhatola* is not going to make it, I think. May Allah land us safely in Lucknow: I am really scared.'

Believe me, I was not scared at all and tried my best to calm him down by saying, 'You are not alone, we will land safely. And if this is how it is destined that we will die, so be it! There is nothing that you or I can do to change what will happen.' But he was beyond comfort and when we alighted, he was so relieved. We spent the day sightseeing the city even though it was blisteringly hot. I loved whatever little of the city I was able to see. I remember when we were touring the markets, I could hear my voice blaring from almost every shop. The ceremony was also very beautiful and everyone was so warm and welcoming. We all ended the trip with a dinner at the chief minister's residence.

YM: Have you ever felt bored while recording a song?

LM: (Laughs loudly). Occasionally, yes. There were some songs that I did not like but I sang them nevertheless. One of these is '*Bindiya Chamkegi, Churiyan Kharkengi*' (*Do Raaste*). I was very bored with it but the challenge I set myself was to not let this seep into the recording. So I had to work extra hard on the songs I did not like!

YM: In your opinion what qualities should a song have?

LM: First and foremost, it should be original and pure. If it is based on a certain idea or emotion, that should be brought out clearly. Whether it is a film song or not, each song must be an original composition.

YM: What is the reason behind the fact that you always read the lyrics from a sheet of paper while recording?

LM: You see I like to write the lyrics in my own hand because it is easiest to read. Occasionally some words are not clear to me if they are written by another hand and I like to pronounce words clearly as I sing them. It is also important that you can see the break-up of the words in front of you to decide where to take a breath and where to pause. Occasionally, a word jumps out at you and it is difficult to sing it until you have ingested it properly. This is why I prefer to read my own notes and writing. I must tell you that Shailendra ji used to always give me the lyrics he had written down and I never had any trouble reading his handwriting because it was such a clear and beautiful script. In fact I sang 'Ai Mere Watan Ke Logo' from a paper he had written the lyrics for me.

YM: Which instrumentalist would you have liked to learn from?

LM: If I had ever got the chance to, I would have loved to learn sitar from Pandit Ravi Shankar and Ustad Vilayat Khan and the flute from Pandit Pannalal Ghosh.

YM: Among your contemporaries, who was an accomplished classical artiste?

LM: This is difficult for me to say because I only know that Manna De had learnt classical music. I don't know much about Rafi saab but he rendered classical compositions very well and worked hard to bring that purity in his songs. I think Zohrabai Ambalawali was also a trained classical singer. I know that Kishore da had never learnt classical music but the man I consider my idol, K.L. Saigal, made me aware of how classical music could also be used in filmy music. I think nearly all the singers in this industry have taken some form of music lessons at some time in their lives.

YM: How many tanpuras do you possess and when did you buy a harmonium for yourself?

LM: I must have some 5–6 tanpuras of which the two I really cherish belonged to my father. Some years ago, Hridaynath commissioned two six-stringed tanpuras from Miraj. They have a wonderful tone when properly tuned. I don't sing with a harmonium so I never bought one. However, once while on a trip to Calcutta I was presented a harmonium by the famous Das Brothers Company. I gave it to my brother Hriday because he composes and sings with one.

YM: Are you fond of jewellery?

LM: Not much but I love diamonds and like to wear diamond tops, rings and bangles. The first diamond ring I bought was in 1948 and I designed myself. It was a small cluster of diamonds surrounding my initials (LM) set in rubies. I wore it for many years and still have it. It then cost me about 700 rupees. I also like emerald studded rings and used to often wear an emerald ring that belonged to my father. Unfortunately, it was stolen.

If I ever wear earrings or bangles, they are usually set with diamonds. I don't much care for gold bangles although I do wear gold anklets. In the early years I used to wear silver anklets and had to persuade Mai for years to allow to me wear gold on my feet. She believed that only royal ladies wore gold on their feet.

Once Pandit Narendra Sharma saw silver bangles on my wrists
and became very angry. 'Beta, no one from your family should
ever wear silver ornaments. Go take these off immediately and
wear something of gold. Gold will be lucky for you. We do not
consider silver jewellery auspicious'. After this, I never wore silver
ornaments ever again. Once while recording, Raj Kapoor saw
my gold anklets and told me angrily, 'Lata, gold should never be
worn beneath one's waist. Only royalty are allowed the privilege
of doing so. Gold is the symbol of prosperity and you wear it
on your feet? Why?' So I told him Pandit Narendra Sharma had
forbidden me to wear silver and will not take these gold anklets
off. I always wear these gold anklets and often design them myself.

Apart from these, I don't like to wear too much else.
Occasionally, I may wear a string of rudraksh beads or an ivory
piece that belonged to my father but that is it.

YM: What about toilettries?

LM: I have always had a soft spot for perfumes and love
to wear one. I also love gifting perfumes to my close friends
and family members. I like Paris and always ask friends going
abroad to get me a bottle. I once smelt a lovely perfume on
Noorjahan ji and asked her what she was wearing. She told me
it was called White Linen, a perfume she always wore. Then
she got one and gifted it to me. I was thrilled. I have worn so
many perfumes that I've forgotten most names by now.

I like putting some powder on my face and kajal in my eyes
and use my finger to apply kajal, just as my mother applied it
on me when I was little. (Laughs). I don't like the way some
women put on kajal nowadays, smearing it above and below the
eyes. I never liked wearing lipstick and my father thoroughly
dispproved of anyone who wore lipstick. When I acted in a few
films, I was forced to wear it but have never worn any since

then. I put powder on my face because it hides the fatigue lines. However, when I hear of the hundreds of things that are now used as make-up, I am appalled.

YM: What oil do you apply to soothe a headache?

LM: I don't see its relevance in a book on me but if you must know I use Parachute Hair Oil.

YM: Why do you only wear white saris?

LM: No special reason and I like bright-coloured saris on others but when it comes to me, I prefer white, off-white or light colours at most: baby pink, light blue, etc. I cannot see myself in bright red and orange: I feel someone has just sprayed Holi colours on me if I do. It is just a matter of personal choice: I love coloured borders on white saris. This has now become my stamp and badge of identity.

Let me narrate an interesting story here. Once, many years ago, I had to go for a recording and it was raining cats and dogs outside. I wondered what to wear and picked a printed orange chiffon sari. When I reached the studio, the recordist asked me, 'What is this Lata bai? You are in a coloured sari today?' I explained that I was afraid I would get wet and crepe and chiffon dries faster than a cotton sari that clings when you get wet and he replied, 'This just doesn't go with your image. You must wear what you always do. We like you best then, not in these coloured clothes.' I realized then that even those who know me understand that white is what suits my temperament the most.

I almost always wear cotton saris and am partial to certain weaves, such as Chanderis and Chikan work saris. I have always liked Bengali and Maharashtrian saris, especially those from Kolhapur. Among silk saris, I prefer Kanjeevarams to Banarasi saris because the latter are often too dressy. Nowadays I like prefer soft and light saris and find the ones that are heavy and that irritate my skin not too pleasant.

YM: In photographs of your early days, you are seen with a pallu draped over your head. Why?

LM: In Kolhapur, which was Shivaji's territory, women always wore saris with their heads covered. Even those who worked in the fields did not let their *pallu* drop from their heads. I once asked my father what this denoted and he replied that a head draped with a pallu was considered the mark of womanly modesty. Even the women of the royal houses did not break this rule. So, rather than see it as a sign of orthodoxy, it should be regarded as a mark of modesty. I liked this description and started covering my head after this. Later, when this began to interfere with the recordings, I stopped doing so.

YM: You are also said to be very fond of cars. Among the ones you bought, which ones were your favourite?

LM: In the fifties, I bought a Hillman that cost me 8000 rupees, which was a lot of money in those days. However, Mai had saved this out of the money I gave her and so I bought it. For a long time, I loved that car and felt so proud that I could now afford such an expensive car. Later, I sold it and bought a blue Chevrolet and this remained a great favourite for a long time. Then I bought an old Buick from the character actor Rehman and after that a Mercedes.

(Laughs). So I bought and sold cars for a long time. The Mercedes I now use was lovingly gifted to me by Yash Chopra saab after I recorded my songs for his film *Veer-Zara*. This was perhaps because I had refused to accept any money from him since I considered him a younger brother.

You know I find it really odd that in the early days I sweated over earning enough and now I have so much that money has ceased to have any meaning for me. All that I value is the legacy of my music and consider the love and honour I have received for my work my most prized possession.

YM: So tell us what you feel when your fans give you such adoration. How do you feel?

LM: You know when my fans call me a Saraswati, I feel very embarrassed and wonder why they compare me to a Goddess. I feel like telling them to rather consider me the recipient of Sarawati's blessings rather than the goddess herself. The fact that we film singers have become what we have is really due to divine grace. I thank God for this every day but don't like at all to be considered some kind of divine being.

I realize that in the eyes of some diehard fans, I may appear above ordinary mortals but—as I said—it really embarrasses me deeply. I just know how to react such praise. Let me just say that I am not unaware or unappreciative of such selfless love and adoration. If my music has given them such joy and satisfaction, then that is what I value above all. I view them as part of a huge family and perhaps this is why I have never felt alone in all my life

YM: If you could change one ill in this world, what would it be?

LM: This is a very difficult question to answer: I can only undertake to change myself. Who am I to change the world?

YM: If apocalypse stares us in the face, what would you save?

LM: If this were to happen, then nothing that I or anyone can do will save anything. Who can change the laws of Nature? If possible, I would naturally choose my family and loved ones.

YM: What makes you angry?

LM: If someone says an unkind or untrue word about me—slander and malicious rumours make me angry. However, I get over this soon enough by telling myself that this is the way of the world and no one is above such false accusations. So why waste my time over such trifles?

YM: What makes you sad?

LM: Partings always sadden me: but then who has not lost a loved one? I miss Pandit Narendra Sharma who was like my surrogate father as much as I miss my own father. He has written somewhere, 'When will we meet those whom we are parting from today?'

And this is exactly what I ask myself this every time I have lost a dear one: When will we ever meet again?

YM: Who are your intimate friends in this industry?

LM: I think I can be proud of how widely and deeply I have received love in this industry. I have had good relations with almost all the people I have worked with over the years. Naturally, there are some who have been closer than others and among the actresses, I would name Nargis ji, Meena Kumari ji, Madhubala, Nalini Jaiwant, Geeta Bali, Saira Bano, Tanuja and Helen as special friends. Among the later ones Hema Malini, Jaya Bachchan, Rekha, Madhuri Dixit and Juhi Chawla are very dear and close. Dilip Kumar among the actors and Dev Anand, Raj Kapoor, Shammi Kapoor, Sunil Dutt and Mehmood are some names. Also Dharmendra, Jitendra, Randhir Kapoor and Rishi Kapoor are close to me. I have shared a close relationship with Krishna Bhabhi (Raj Kapoor's wife) and Neela Bhabhi (Shammi Kapoor's wife). I love Krishna Bhabhi for her loving and dignified personality that has remained the same for the 50 years that I have known her. I was also very fond of the South Indian singer P. Susheela and Shivaji Ganeshan, both of whom were my close friends.

Naushad, Salil Chaudhuri, Mohd Rafi, Sajjad Husain saab, Hemant Kumar, S.D. Burman, R.D. Burman, Madan Mohan,

Khayyam, Chitragupt, Shankar–Jaikishan, Sudhir Phadke, Laxmikant–Pyarelal, Sriniwas Khale, Jatin–Lalit, and Abu Malik were really dear friends. In the same way, lyricists Majrooh Sultanpuri, Gulzar and Javed Akhtar are almost like family. Apart from these, among other people from the industry I have deep affection is Bhalaji Pendharkar and his family who were like my own family. Pandit Narendra Sharma was a surrogate parent, and, of course, Master Vinayak, Mehboob Khan, Madhav Shinde, Dinkar Patil, Hrishikesh Mukherji, Yash Chopra treated me as their own. One person who has always given me great respect and affection is Amitabh Bachchan.

There are so many others but let me name just a few more: Suresh Wadekar, Alka Yagnik, Kavita Krishnamurthy, Udit Narayan and Sonu Nigam. Madan Mohan ji's son, Sanjiv Kohli, is also a dear friend.

YM: You have had a very close association with Dilip Kumar. Can you share some memories?

LM: I have so many memories of this very special relationship and some are really moving. There is no doubt that of all the actors at present, he is the one who I am closest to. After all, we go back a long, long way. He has known me from the time I was a struggling newcomer to the industry and when I used to commute in the local trains, he was already a successful star. There is one occasion that I recall with love because it made me see that he looked at me as a protective older brother. He is such a gentleman and so compassionate that I fear there are not many that I can compare with him.

One evening, after a dinner at Kalyan ji's house, I picked a paan from a plate on the table and offered him one. He face clouded over with disapproval and he turned to tell me a little sternly, 'Lata, this is not done. Girls from good families do not offer paans to men. Now promise me that from now on, you will never offer a paan or supari to any man. I consider you my younger sister and have the right to ask this of you.'

Believe me, I was not offended at all: rather, I was thrilled that I have a brother like him in this industry who looks out for me. Only someone like him could have got away with ticking me off like that in a roomful of guests. Again, in 1974, I was in London to give my first public performance at the Royal Albert Hall and he was the compere for the programme. Being a fastidious man, he asked me for a list of the songs and the order in which I was planning to sing them. He noticed '*Inhi Logon Ne Le Lina Dupatta Mera*' from *Pakeezah* and frowned. I was a little taken aback at this because I intended to inaugurate the evening with that number.

He asked me, 'Why do you want to include this song when its lyrics are a little racy?' and I said that it was very popular those days and I feel the audience here will love it. He wasn't convinced with my reason but said nothing. However, his disapproval raised some doubts in my mind and I wondered if it was appropriate to make it the first song. But I loved that he cared enough for my reputation to warn me about this aspect of the song.

I was also very close to his older sister Sakina Apa and since we lived close to each other, I often visited her. There is a side to Yusuf bhai that is not readily visible to most people who think he is very reserved and remote. The truth is he is honest to his core, and has a warm and generous heart. I consider him an exceptional man and cherish this bond we have.

YM: Who do you consider your all-time favourite actor?

LM: I consider Mehmood a terrific actor and a brilliant comedian. I don't think anyone can take his place as a comedian. What a man he was and what a personality he had!

Just think of his work in *Padosan*, *Ziddi*, *Love in Tokyo*, *Pyar Kiye Ja* and *Gumnaam*. I just loved his films and always felt that he dominated every film he acted in. The only other actor who came close was Kishore da.

YM: Of all the actresses you saw in this industry, which one do you consider the most beautiful?

LM: They were all beautiful but personally, I liked Nargis the most. Even off the screen she was a beautiful person: her style, diction—everything had grace and beauty I think. All those who knew her thought so as well.

YM: If you had sung for an actor, who would it be?

LM: Dilip Kumar.

YM: What do you seek in a film?

LM: Not much but that they should have some social message and are worth watching with your entire family. A good story and high thoughts is all I ask.

YM: Give me a list of your favourite cricketers.

LM: Gary Sobers and Rohan Kanhai from the West Indies, Richie Benaud, Ray Lindwall, Alan Davidson and Neil Harvey from Australia, Sanat Jayasuriya and Alsith Malinga from Sri Lanka, Imran Khan and Wasim Akram from Pakistan. Amongst the Indians, Mushtaq Ali, Vinod Mankad, Vijay Merchant, Nawab Mansur Ali Khan Pataudi, Vijay Manjrekar, Sunil Gavaskar and Sachin Tendulkar are those who I admire. From the present players, Mahendra Singh Dhoni, Virat Kohli, Harbhajan Singh and Shikhar Dhawan are my favourite players, although I haven't met any of them personally. And of course Australia's legendary player Don Bradman is in a category all by himself.

I consider Sachin my son and he calls me 'ma' as well. Sachin and his whole family give me great respect and love.

Vijay Hazare has been a family friend and I have also been very close to Vinod Mankad, Bishan Singh Bedi, Sunil Gavaskar and Kapil Dev.

YM: Among politicians who are you close to?

LM: I have very few political friends but N.K.P. Salve, Atal Behari Vajpayee, Lal Krishna Advani, Sharad Pawar and Balasaheb Thackrey are close personal friends. I also think of the Prime Minister, Narendrabhai Modi, as a personal friend.

YM: Apart from cinema, cricket and politics, who are some of your other friends?

LM: They come from different worlds but have been friends. I count among them Udaipur's Maharana Bhagwant Singh and his son Arvind Singh ji and their families, Rajsingh Dungarpur and his family, Maharaja Vijay Singh Patwardhan and his family (including his actress daughter Bhagyashree) of Sangli. R.P. Goenka and Sushila Goenka, Pandit Jasraj, B.K. Birla, Dr R.P. Kapoor, Prof. Shanta Shelke, Amin Sayani, Anil Mohile, Padma Sachdev and her husband Surinder Singh ji, Harish Bhimani, Mohan Wagh, Prof. Ram Siwalkar, Vachaspati Shankar Abhayankar, Shankar Vaid, Sajjan Dewra, Rashesh Shah, Subhash Bhoj, Dr Rajeev Sharma, Babasaheb Purandari and his son Prasad, Pankaj Khimji, Mr and Mrs Raj Gopal Dhoot—are all dear friends.

YM: Classical singers you like?

LM: I love both Hindustani classical music and Carnatic music and can't name a huge list here but the my most favourite players are Ustad Bismillah Khan, Pandit Ravi Shankar, Ustad Ali Akbar Khan, Vilayat Khan, Ustad Allarakha, Pandit Pannalal Ghosh, Ustad Abdul Halim Jafar, Pandit Kishan Maharaj, Pandit Shivkumar Sharma, Pandit Hariprasad Chaurasia and

Ustad Zakir Husain. Among the vocalists Kesarbai Kerkar (the first among Hindustani classical singers), Ustad Bare Ghulam Ali Khan, Pandit D.V. Paluskar, Ustad Barkat Ali Khan, Ustad Amir Khan, Ustad Salamat Ali khan, Dagar bandhu, Gangubai Hangal, Pandit Kumar Gandharva, Pandit Bhimsen Joshi and Pandit Jasraj. Among the semi-classical singers: Siddheshwari Devi, Begum Akhtar, Shobha Gurtu and Girija Devi and of the Carnatic artistes, M. Balmurali Krishna (who I rate the best Carnatic music singer), Rajratnam Pillai and M.S. Subbulakshmi. I also love folk singers like the Langas and Manganayars, Alla Jilai bai and Asa Singh Mastana. Apart from all these, I consider the Kabir bhajans and Malwa compositions of Kumar Gandharva divine.

YM: How do you rate Kavita Krishnamurthy, Alka Yagnik and Shreya Goshal?

LM: All three are my favourite contemporary singers in the film industry. They have a solid grounding in music and take great pains over their work. I feel that they are the only ones who have preserved the sweetness of film music. I am very fond of Alka Yagnik and her '*Pardesi, Pardesi Jana Nahin*' (*Raja Hindustani*) '*Tum Aye To Aya Mujhe Yaad Gali Main Aaj Chand Nikla*' (*Zakhm*) and '*Tujhe Yaad Na Meri Aayi Kisi Se Ab Kya Kehna*' (*Kuch Kuch Hota Hai*) and her duet with Sonu Nigam '*Suraj Hua Madham*' (*Kabhi Khushi Kabhi Gham*) are beautifully rendered. Similarly, Kavita's '*Pyar Hua Chupke Se*' (*1942: A Love Story*) and '*Mar Dala*' (*Devdas*) really make me happy when I hear them. Her title song for *Hum Dil Deke Chuke Sanam* and '*Nimbooda*' are so well done. Shreya Ghoshal is another promising voice and her '*Bairi Piya Bara Bedardi*' (*Devdas*) is lovely. I find hers one of the most pleasing voices to emerge recently.

YM: Among Pakistani artistes, who are the ones you like the most?

LM: I have always been an admirer of Mehndi Hasan and Ghulam Ali and think that Nazakat-Salamat Ali are great singers. I also love Fareeda Khanum's semi-classical music. Among the Sufi singers, I like Abida Parween the most. Apart from these, I also love their qawwali singers, such as Mubarak and Fateh Ali and Ustad Nusrat Fteh Ali Khan. Roshanara Begum, who went from India to Pakistan, and Reshma who also migrated from India, are first-rate singers. However, if I had to choose just one Pakistani singer, I would choose Noorjahan.

YM: Among living eminent people, who would you like to meet?

LM: I have been fortunate to meet so many eminent people in my life but I would love to meet His Holiness the Dalai Lama once. I want to speak with him . . .and ask how he can live a peaceful life in these turbulent times. How does he interact with ordinary men and women? What is it about him that he enraptures everyone who comes in contact with him? I would dearly love a chance to meet him. Let's see when this wish will come true!

YM: Which place do you regret not having visited? Would you still like to go there if given a chance to?

LM: Jwalaji in Himachal Pradesh, which is one of the Devi's *shaktipeeths*. I want to visit it at least once in my lifetime.

YM: Living in Bombay, what do you yearn for?

LM: You may laugh when you hear this but the gulab jamuns of Indore and the yoghurt you get there. I really miss those. (Laughs).

YM: Did you ever want to write your autobiography?

LM: Years ago, I used to keep a diary. Then one day I decided there was no point in it and after that I have never even read what I had written there. I believe that one must be totally honest when writing an autobiography and if you do so, you are bound to hurt many people. Perhaps it may record some embarrassing facts about your life as well. This is why I feel that one should keep one's secrets to oneself: why share them with those who don't know you? Why hurt other people?

YM: I am going to ask that so many must have asked you at some point or another. Why did you never marry?

LM: (laughs) My answer is the same I have always given to those who have asked this question before you. I believe that a human being has no control over three things: birth, marriage and death. No one knows the answer to any of these mysteries. Did I ask to be born in Pandit Dinanath Mangeshkar's family? Similarly, I had no idea who I would marry and when. One also hears of broken marriages and those that survive have God's blessing, I think. I personally believe that I was not destined to marry . . . and this is no big deal. Who knows if I would have achieved all that I did if I had married? No one in this world gets all that is desired.

YM: What do you regret not having recorded?

LM: I wanted to record all the 18 chapters of the Gita but the problem was that in those days each chapter had to be recorded in 40 minutes. As you know, there are some chapters that have over 50 slokas and it was difficult to fit them in this time frame. Now it is possible to do so because we have CDs. However, because this technology was not available then I was able to record just a few chapters.

YM: Everyone who knows you knows how you love jalebis. What are some other sweets you like?

LM: I like caramel custard and Christmas plum cake. I used to freely indulge my sweet tooth earlier but now health restrictions have reduced my sweet intake . . . However, now that you have reminded me, I have a sudden craving for one! (Laughs).

YM: Which is your favourite Indian city?

LM: Bombay because it is full of so many happy memories. I have spent the longest part of my life here and so cannot find any other place to match its delights.

YM: Which part of the day is the one you like most?

LM: Without a doubt, dawn and daybreak. This is when light enters our lives and 'sada' is performed. Raga Bhoopali is sung. Earlier, I used to find evening and dusk depressing and sad although I don't feel the same any more. However, I can say that I am not an evening person.

YM: What is it that you are unable to do despite a strong desire to do so?

LM: There are many times when I feel like going out to eat at a small dhaba or just walk on a street. However, I have to think carefully whether it is safe or advisable to do so. I think what God gives you with one hand, He takes away with another. There is nothing I can do about this. (Laughs).

YM: What is your favourite line from a poem?

LM: 'Durdin main ansoo bankar aaj utarne aayi', from Jaishankar Prasad's Ansoo.

YM: In how many languages have you sung?

LM: (Laughs as she recounts). Almost 36 languages, I think. I have sung in almost every other Indian language and also in Dutch, Russian, Fijian, Swahili and English.

YM: Are you on Twitter?

LM: Yes, I like to occasionally write on my Twitter account, like sending birthday greetings to someone I like. If I like the work of some new music director, I definitely send him a message to congratulate. However, I don't like frivolous and foolish messages. I feel no one should misuse this medium for writing rubbish.

YM: When you sing a composition that your father had also sung, do you remember his version?

LM: Truthfully, I never forget anything my father sang. Even when I am singing a composition by another person, I am conscious of his presence. I first bow to him before I record anything and the reason that I never go off tune or miss a beat is because the ragas he taught me constantly echo in my mind.

YM: Do you ask for moksha as you sing?

LM: Moksha is a beautiful concept; I often pray that I am never reborn.

YM: And if you were given a choice between moksha and music?

LM: Then I would choose music. I feel my music alone will ultimately release me from this unending cycle of birth and death.

YM: Have you ever sensed the presence of God when you are alone?

LM: I am always surrounded by music, which I consider my God.

YM: Didi, you have entered the hearts and homes of so many people. Your voice is what many begin their day with. I think you are immortal and believe that such a person will not be born for many, many years . . .

LM: God has given me so much that I really have no desires left. I am content and feel that if people like you think my voice is immortal, what more can I ask for? My voice may be immortal but my body is not and one day, sooner or later, I will pass on. I have no fear of death and am reminded of a

Marathi saying, '*Gaav gela vahun, naav gela rahun.*' (A village gets washed away but a name stays forever). What delights me the most is that I have been able to take my father's work forward and done my best to honour his memory.

My final wish as I thank God for all He has blessed me with are: when my time comes, let me go in peace. I would like to be spared of suffering nor do I wish to inflict pain on my loved ones . . .

Acknowledgements

There is a host of people, many of them distinguished musicians or musicologists, who I need to thank for helping me craft this book. Foremost among them are Pandit Hariprasad Chaurasia, Sonal Mansingh, Girija Devi, Usha Mangeshkar, Adinath Mangeshkar, Khayyam Sa'ab, Muzaffar Ali, Pandit Satyasheel Deshpande, Sunil Sethi, Sharad Dutt, Prasoon Joshi, Shantanu Moitra, Sooraj Barjatya, Aneesh Pradhan, Atul Tiwari, Biswanath Chatterji, Prerna Shrimali, Malini Awasthi, Liladhar Mandloyi, Mahmud Mirza, Chaya Ganguli, Ira Bhaskar, Sanjay Dube, Atul Chaurasia, Uday Bhawalkar, Amarnath Sharma, Kushal Gopalka, Sunanda Sharma, Madhu V. Joshi, Partha Chatterji, Himanshu Vajpeyi, Nidhish Tyagi, Rajesh Priyadarshi, Aradhana Pradhan, Sandeep Bhutoria, Rajeev Srivastav, Om Nishchal, Prabhat Ranjan, Anant Vijay, Manisha Kulshreshta, Richa Anirudh, Vandana Rag, Deepak Mashal, Anu Singh Chaudhuri, Mohan Bane, Mahesh Rathore and Pankaj Rag.

I owe a special thanks to Gulzar Sa'ab, who told me some wonderful anecdotes about Lata ji and guided me in my quest. In the same breath, I must remember Shubha Mudgal, whose insights into Lata ji's music introduced me to the grammar of film music, a genre that deserves attention. She read this manuscript and made very valuable suggestions. Next come my writer friend, Narendra Saini and someone I consider a younger brother—Rohit Sharma. Their comments and sharp insights were a huge help. Namita Gokhale has been a friend and advisor throughout. I sometimes feel that she became a fellow traveller as well.

Time now to remember an absent friend, Vijay Mohan Singh. Only I know how many times I would call him in Wardha to clear countless doubts and queries. I will always regret that he passed away before this book was published.

Next come all those enthusiastic music lovers who helped me in locating Lata ji's songs from personal collections, when I could not source them from old record companies or YouTube. My friend and writer–editor, Gyanranjan ji in Nagpur, put me in touch with a phenomenal scholar, the late Hansmukh Dalwadi and his son Jignesh Dalwadi, who generously gave me access to their astounding personal collection of Lata ji's songs. Others who located half-forgotten songs were Sanjay Pandya and Om Prakash Pandya from Indore. Another generous friend was Praveen Kaushal of the *Sa re ga ma* (HMV) team who helped me with the record covers of Lata ji's LPs. In the same way, Gauri Yadavdakar of Times Music and Yunus Khan of Vividh Bharati filled in several gaps. Ajit Singh Bisen and Aditya Pratap Singh enthusiastically joined my web search for some tough quests.

Most of the photographs in the book came from Lata ji's own collection. Mohan Bane was another generous collector who gave me access to his collection while Mangeshji helped me with some from Gautam Rajadhyaksha's archive. Some illustrations are from my own collection.

I wish to thank Manish Pushkale, an artist and friend, for providing me with the idea that ultimately formed the title and cover of this book.

Finally, my deep gratitude to my publisher Arun Maheshwari and his daughter, Aditi Maheshwari Goyal, whose trust in me has given me the courage to put all this together. I would also like to thank Meru Gokhale, Chirag Thakkar and Aparna Abhijit from Penguin Random House India for their contribution to the project.

I thank them all.

Yatindra Mishra

मनिषभाईस
शुभआशशो।

लता मंगेशकर

4.9.2016

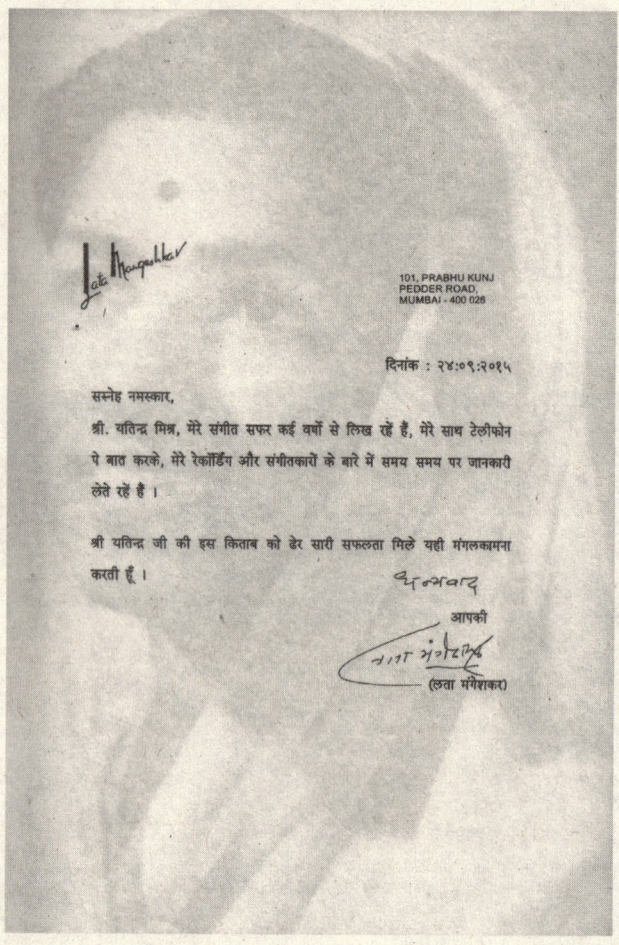

Within the letter image:

Lata Mangeshkar

101, PRABHU KUNJ
PEDDER ROAD,
MUMBAI - 400 026

दिनांक : २४:०९:२०१५

सस्नेह नमस्कार,

श्री. यतिन्द्र मिश्र, मेरे संगीत सफर कई वर्षों से लिख रहें हैं, मेरे साथ टेलीफोन पे बात करके, मेरे रेकॉर्डिंग और संगीतकारों के बारे में समय समय पर जानकारी लेते रहें हैं ।

श्री यतिन्द्र जी की इस किताब को ढेर सारी सफलता मिले यही मंगलकामना करती हूँ ।

शुभकामना

आपकी

(लता मंगेशकर)

Greetings and love,

Shri Yatindra Mishra has been tracking my musical journey for several years. We have had several phone conversations about various recordings and my memories of the music directors associated with them.
I sincerely hope Shri Mishra's work brings him great success and send my blessings to him.

With thanks,
Lata Mangeshkar
Thank you!

Scan QR code to access the
Penguin Random House India website